The Changing United Nations

The Changing United Nations:
Options for the United States

Proceedings of
The Academy of
Political Science

Volume 32
Number 4

Edited by David A. Kay

New York, 1977

Copyright © 1977 by The Academy of Political Science

Library of Congress Catalog Card Number 77-089037

Cover design by Gordon Miller

Printed by Capital City Press, Montpelier, Vermont

Contents

ECONOMICS AND THE UNITED NATIONS

ARMS CONTROL AND INTERNATIONAL PEACE

Preface

Although the United Nations continues to have a major interest in the maintenance of peace, the limitation of arms, and the protection of human rights, it has changed significantly since it was founded in 1945. However, the major change that will have the greatest effect on the United States is the formation of a common front on economic policy by the developing countries.

The purpose of this volume is to describe and evaluate UN activities in all of these areas with special attention to the challenge of the third world. The United States must carefully weigh its options for dealing with the problems posed by the changing UN. To describe the nature of these options is a major goal of this study.

The authors of these essays are affiliated with various universities, research organizations, and government agencies. The views that they express, however, are their own and do not necessarily reflect the positions of the institutions with which they are associated nor those of the Academy.

The Academy wishes to express its appreciation to David A. Kay, who organized the project and edited the volume, and to William Farr, Gordon Miller, and Frederick Wegener for their editorial assistance. The Academy is indebted to Harvey Picker, dean of the School of International Affairs, Columbia University, and Aaron W. Warner, dean of Continuing Education and Special Programs, Columbia University, for chairing the sessions of the conference held at Columbia University. A distinguished group of knowledgeable persons participated in panels at the conference. Among them were Roberta Cohen, James Mittelman, John P. Entelis, Giulio Pontecorvo, and Carlyle E. Maw. The Academy wishes to thank the participants in the conference and the contributors to this volume.

ROBERT H. CONNERY
President of the Academy

Contributors

DAVID A. BALDWIN is John Sloan Dickey Third Century Professor of Government, Dartmouth College.

ABRAHAM BARGMAN is Professor of Political Science, Brooklyn College of the City University of New York.

BETH BLOOMFIELD is Policy Analyst, National Security and International Affairs Division, Congressional Budget Office.

GUY F. ERB is Senior Fellow, Overseas Development Council.

C. CLYDE FERGUSON, JR., Professor of Law, Harvard University, was formerly United States Representative to the UN Economic and Social Council.

SEYMOUR MAXWELL FINGER is Professor of Political Science, the Graduate Center of the City University of New York, and Director, Ralph Bunche Institute on the United Nations.

DANA D. FISCHER is Assistant Professor of Political Science and International Affairs, George Washington University.

DAVID P. FORSYTHE is Professor of Political Science, The University of Nebraska—Lincoln.

ROBERT W. GREGG is Professor of Political Science, American University.

ALFRED O. HERO, JR., is Director and Secretary, World Peace Foundation.

JOHN W. HOLMES is Research Director, Canadian Institute of International Affairs, and Professor of International Relations, the University of Toronto and York University.

HAROLD K. JACOBSON is Professor of Political Science, Center for Political Studies, Institute for Social Research, The University of Michigan.

DAVID A. KAY is Director, International Organizations Research Project of the American Society of International Law.

EDWARD C. LUCK is Deputy Director of Policy Studies, United Nations Association of the USA.

GENE M. LYONS is Professor of Government, Dartmouth College; formerly he was Director, Department of Social Sciences, UN Educational, Scientific, and Cultural Organization.

DONALD W. MCNEMAR is Associate Professor of Government, Dartmouth College.

IVOR RICHARD is Permanent Representative of the United Kingdom of Great Britain and Northern Ireland to the United Nations.

SEYMOUR J. RUBIN is Professor of Law, American University, and Executive Vice President, American Society of International Law. He was the United States Representative to the UN Commission on Transnational Corporations.

JOHN TEMPLE SWING is Vice President and Secretary, Council on Foreign Relations. A member of the National Security Council Advisory Committee on the Law of the Sea, he is also a United States delegate to the Third United Nations Conference on the Law of the Sea.

SIDNEY WEINTRAUB is Dean Rusk Professor of Public Affairs, The University of Texas at Austin.

Initialisms and Acronyms

ACDA	U.S. Arms Control and Disarmament Agency
ACP	African, Pacific, and Caribbean countries
CCD	Conference of the Committee on Disarmament
CIEC	Conference on International Economic Co-operation
ECOSOC	Economic and Social Council
FAO	Food and Agriculture Organization
G-77	Group of 77 developing countries
GATT	General Agreement on Tariffs and Trade
IAEA	International Atomic Energy Agency
IBRD	International Bank for Reconstruction and Development (World Bank)
ICJ	International Court of Justice
IFAD	International Fund for Agricultural Development
ILO	International Labor Organization
IMF	International Monetary Fund
LDCs	Less developed countries
NATO	North Atlantic Treaty Organization
NGOs	Nongovernmental organizations
NIEO	New International Economic Order
NPT	Non-Proliferation Treaty
OAS	Organization of American States

OECD	Organization for Economic Cooperation and Development
OPEC	Organization of Petroleum Exporting Countries
SALT	Strategic Arms Limitation Talks
SDR	Special drawing rights
SSOD	Special Session on Disarmament (General Assembly)
TNCs	Transnational corporations
UNCTAD	UN Conference on Trade and Development
UNDP	UN Development Program
UNESCO	UN Educational, Scientific, and Cultural Organization
UNDOF	UN Disengagement Observer Force
UNEF	UN Emergency Force
UNIDO	UN Industrial Development Organization
USSR	Union of Soviet Socialist Republics
WHO	World Health Organization

Diplomacy in an Interdependent World*

IVOR RICHARD

To a certain extent I am a diplomat by accident. I was in the House of Commons for ten years until my constituency was redistricted out of existence, so that when the 1974 general election was called in Britain I had no one to represent. The incoming Labor government then asked me whether I would like to come to New York as the British ambassador to the United Nations. I must say that I did not know a great deal about the UN. I had followed it as best I could in a general way, but I had no direct experience of it, so I naturally did what all aspiring ambassadors are supposed to do: I took advice from those who were supposed to know better. I went to see a former British ambassador to the UN, who will be nameless here, and I said, "Well, tell me what it's like." And he said, "Don't worry too much about it. You'll find it a bit like the Church of England. It revolves around you above your head just below the stratosphere, doing 'good' in a generalized sort of way. You can't be certain about precisely what it does, who it does it to, how it does it, or indeed sometimes even why it does it. But if it ceased to exist, the world would surely be a more sinful place."

It was therefore with that ringing diplomatic endorsement that I came to New York in March of 1974. I can only say that through my experience I have found the UN infinitely more worthwhile than I expected it to be before I came. I have also found it, and this may surprise some people, rather more efficient in its operation than I had expected it to be before I arrived. One of the problems that the UN has, certainly in my country and also here in the United States, is that expectations in the institution were pitched unreasonably high in

* An address delivered at a conference sponsored by the Academy of Political Science and the Program of Continuing Education, Columbia University, in New York City on June 13, 1977.

1945. If one reads some of the discussions that took place immediately prior to the signing of the charter, it is quite clear that the founding fathers of the institution—or the founding countries of the institution, if you prefer—really believed that by creating this new institution of international cooperation the world would enter into a new era, that peace, concord, and amity would prevail, and indeed, as one sees in the preamble to the charter, that we would be able to save succeeding generations from the scourge of war. Of course, things have not happened in quite that way. They rarely do. The UN, whatever else it can do, will not abolish sin. It can make international sinning rather more difficult, however, and it will make the sinner more accountable. But it has not yet succeeded in changing the hearts and minds either of the people who lead countries or of the people who make them up.

The last thirty years have been years of immense change. In 1945, fifty-one countries signed the charter. There were forty-nine real countries, not counting the Ukraine and Byelorussia. Nevertheless, there were fifty-one signatories to the charter. We now have 148, many of which have come into existence in the last thirty years and no less than thirty-five of which are ex-colonies of Great Britain (thirty-six if we include the United States). It is hardly surprising, therefore, that the ground rules for trying to create an international order now look rather different than they did in 1945.

If the UN has changed, it is because the world has changed. But if the UN has not accomplished everything that the founding fathers thought it would, it is because we, the nations of the world, are not yet prepared to give to any international institution the degree of sovereignty that is necessary for it to operate properly. After all, the UN has no executive authority. It cannot take independent action. The only power that it has is the power that the nations of the world—yours and mine and everybody else's—are prepared to cede to it. While one is prepared to cede a certain amount on issues that directly touch the perceived national interests of the major powers, I am afraid that none of those powers has been prepared to accept the degree of international oversight that would be necessary if the UN were in fact to work as it was perhaps originally intended.

I would argue, however, that in the last thirty years there have been three massive achievements to the credit of the UN. First of all, I think it has hastened a process of decolonization, which was going to take place anyway. It probably made it slightly more orderly than it would have been otherwise, and it certainly produced a situation in which the birth of new nations took place in a relatively short period. The first British colony in Africa to become wholly independent of Britain was Ghana in 1959. If one thinks, therefore, that in a period of some eighteen or twenty years we have had this enormous creation of so many different countries, I must say that in the spectrum of human history and human experience, it really is a very short period indeed.

Secondly, the UN helped limit the cold war to the battleground of rhetoric. I do not think it solved the problems of the cold war, nor do I think it was institutionally capable of solving those problems. Nevertheless, I am sure that the fact that it provided a forum within which argument could take place, did take place, and does take place has made an emormous difference in the degree to which the cold war has not warmed up. I have spent three and a half years sitting next to the Russians in the Security Council, by the accident of the alphabet since the United Kingdom follows the Union of Soviet Socialist Republics. Relations are not always entirely cordial. Occasionally we agree. When I do find myself in agreement with my Soviet colleague, I must confess that my first inclination is to reexamine my basic position. But despite that fact, a number of international issues that would not be solved on a bilateral basis are more capable of solution within that particular forum and around that horseshoe.

I will give one example, unconnected with the East-West confrontation, of what I mean. Ominously, just about this time last year, the Turkish government decided it would send a survey ship into the Aegean. The result was to bring Greece and Turkey as near to conflict, I suppose, as they have been for many years, even including the Cyprus crisis in 1974. The Turkish foreign minister and the Greek foreign minister descended on New York, and there was a meeting of the Security Council. It met for perhaps two days and then, as far as the public could see, the issue disappeared from view. During the next two weeks, I happened to be directly involved in intensive discussions in which we all tried to get the Greeks and the Turks to agree on a resolution in the Security Council. Both sides were extremely difficult. It was not really a question of deciding which side was the more difficult. I would spend the morning with Mr. Caglyangil, the afternoon with Mr. Bitsios, the evening recovering, and then the following day going through the whole procedure again. This went on for the best part of two weeks, until we were almost arguing about where the commas went in a resolution. Now an outsider might say, "This is a rank absurdity. It is ridiculous that so many grown men should spend so much time arguing about the semantic details of a resolution that would not have any mandatory effect anyway."

What is interesting, however, is that after those two weeks the Security Council succeeded in passing a resolution. Immediately after it was passed the two foreign ministers met face-to-face, and after that first meeting they agreed to meet again soon. I am not saying that the Security Council solved the difficulties between Greece and Turkey in the Aegean, but I am saying that the possibilities of war in that particular situation would have been very much greater if the UN had not existed and if there had not therefore been a forum within which that type of argument could take place.

When I first came to the UN, without experience as a diplomat, it took me a long time to realize why gradations of language seemed so important. To my rather naive mind, whether one "condemned" something or "strongly deplored" something or "gravely and deeply regretted" something did not seem to make much difference. For the first few months, I was astonished at the amount of energy and effort that countries and people put into changing an adverb or getting "condemn" out and "deplore" in. Then I realized that in such arguments the difference between "condemn" and "deplore" was a victory or a defeat, depending upon which side you were on—and that was distinctly better than sending tanks across a border.

The third major achievement to the UN's credit is the emergence within the last decade of a pattern of global functional cooperation. A quiet revolution in international cooperation has been taking place. A lot of work is being done quickly but effectively through the agencies and through some of the other UN institutions. In the last few years, we have had a series of international conferences on global issues that cut aross or transcend national boundaries. Whether or not the sea is grossly polluted is not the concern of only one nation. It is clearly the concern of all the nations and peoples of this planet. Whether or not the environment of this world of ours can be safeguarded for the future is also something that cuts across national boundaries. The series of major conferences that we have had—on the environment, last year on human settlements, a few years ago in Mexico on the problems of women, and about four years ago in Rome on world food problems—this pattern is a new innovation as far as diplomacy is concerned. It is a relatively recent development that has led the major nations of the world to recognize (and it is primarily the major nations that have to recognize this) that there are indeed some problems that even they are not in a position to solve on an individual or bilateral basis.

According to one estimate, 70 percent of the time of all the diplomats in the world is now spent on multilateral rather than bilateral matters. In other words, most ambassadors, wherever they are posted and with whatever country they are dealing, now spend relatively little of their time on purely bilateral relations between their own country and the country in which they happen to be stationed and spend much more of their time trying to develop a common attitude or a common approach to multilateral fora. I am sure the British ambassador in Moscow, for example, now spends far more time talking to the Russians about things like Belgrade or disarmament or the UN or world food or the environment than he does talking about purely bilateral British-Soviet relations. I am sure this is now true of the larger countries, and the smaller countries have in any event always been more interested in multilateral rather than bilateral diplomacy. One of the things that struck me when I first came here, if it is not slightly patronizing to express it, was the extraordinarily high caliber of the third world ambassadors, until I realized that the UN is the main outlet for international relations and the main diplomatic effort for many third world countries. Therefore, they take very great care indeed to send their very best people to the UN. I sometimes wonder whether we in the West take similar care, or indeed whether perhaps we should not take greater care in the future.

In the present climate of international politics, one cannot realistically expect the UN to solve issues in which the vital interests of one or more of the major powers are involved. It may be able to help, but rarely can it produce a solution. There is an unwillingness to subordinate major national interests to the uncertainties of UN involvement, lest control and direction be lost. One such issue for the United States was, of course, Vietnam; for Britain, a good instance has been Rhodesia. The Security Council has undoubtedly helped by imposing mandatory sanctions, but when a lasting solution seemed possible, the Rhodesian problem has been dealt with primarily by the countries most directly concerned.

The Geneva Conference on Rhodesia

Our experience at the Geneva conference on Rhodesia is therefore a good example of a country unwilling to hand over the conduct of a major international dispute to an international institution like the UN. Since Rhodesia is still technically a British responsibility, we have tried to solve the problem ourselves. I first became involved in this exercise one morning while quietly shaving: I got a phone call from my foreign secretary, who asked if I would like to chair the Geneva conference on Rhodesia. As those of you who have dealt with foreign secretaries or secretaries of state realize, it was not actually intended to be a question, so I said, "Well, thank you very much, yes, I would be delighted to do it, naturally," and took off for Geneva three days later.

Of course, the occasion for the conference was Dr. Kissinger's mission last summer to Africa, and Mr. Smith's broadcast on September 24, 1976, in which he seemed to accept majority rule within two years. Just for a moment, however, one ought to look at the arithmetic and history of this particular problem. There are 270,000 white Rhodesians and 6.25 million blacks. Just over half of those 270,000 whites have gone there since the end of the war. It is therefore false to place them in anything like the same category as the Afrikaners in South Africa who, if one talks to them, will often and proudly tell you how van Riebeck arrived at the Cape in 1652 and that they therefore have been in possession for three hundred years. This is not the situation in Rhodesia; indeed, before 1896, the year Rhodes went there, it was unsettled. It was run by a company until 1923. In the honorable tradition of British colonizing, as the East India Company colonized India, and the Hudson's Bay Company colonized Canada, the British South Africa Company colonized Rhodesia. In theory, the company continued to run it (the police in Rhodesia are still called the British South African Police, and it is a strange sight to see them walking around with shoulder patches that say BSAP—they are still called that rather than the Rhodesian police). But in 1923, it ceased being "corporate property" and became a self-governing colony. From 1923 to 1965, it had a British appointed governor, but we have never run the country, and we have never been responsible for its internal administration. In law, however, Britain is the administering power. In law and constitutionally, Rhodesia is a British colony, and only the British Parliament can make Rhodesia legally independent.

Until 1965, we tried to negotiate that independence with successive Rhodesian governments. Unfortunately, those attempts failed because the white Rhodesian government—of course there were no blacks at all in it—was not prepared to concede political rights to the vast majority of the black population. In 1965 in a document whose opening words I am sure you will recognize (it begins, "When in the course of human events it becomes necessary for one nation to dissolve the bonds which have tied it to another," in a somewhat obscene parody of an earlier document that also had to do with a dispute between Britain and one of her colonies) the Rhodesians purported to declare their independence. They have since been illegally "independent," nobody has recognized them, and the UN has imposed sanctions against them. Therefore, when Dr. Kissinger went there last year, his first task was to try and persuade Mr. Smith and his government to accept the principle of majority rule within a relatively short period of time. Dr. Kissinger apparently left Africa thinking that that had been achieved.

When we got to Geneva, it became clear that there were two major problems to be faced immediately. One was that no African trusted Mr. Smith or believed him when he said that majority rule would come within two years. This mistrust inevitably spilled over into a feeling on the part of the African delegations that the structure of the transitional government had to be such as to remove power from Mr. Smith's hands at the beginning of the transitional period. This could be a process in two stages. At Geneva we would set up a transitional government in which power would be shared. During the transitional period there would be elections, a government would then emerge, and finally at the end of the period we would grant independence to that government elected by a majority of the people. Unfortunately, because nobody believed Mr. Smith's commitment to majority rule within two years, the Africans insisted that power should be taken away from Mr. Smith at the beginning of the period of transition rather than leaving him in a position to interfere with the process. In other words, they were asking for (and they were entitled to ask for) an assurance that the process to majority rule would be irreversible. They said, and there was some truth in this, that on a number of occasions Mr. Smith had apparently agreed to something and then gone back on it. They were therefore not prepared to accept a structure of government during the transition that allowed him the potential to interfere with a process that they wished to be inevitable and irreversible.

The other major problem at Geneva was the fact that the four black delegations were not united. Two of them, Mr. Nkomo and Mr. Mugabe, loosely joined in what became known as the Patriotic Front, while the other two, Bishop Muzorewa and Mr. Sithole, did not. We therefore had four different black delegations saying much the same thing but with four different voices. Jockeying for position was clearly occurring on the black side, and there was total nonnegotiation by Mr. Smith and his people on the white side. Mr. Smith came to Geneva waving a piece of paper saying, "I have a contract with Dr. Kissinger, and I am prepared to implement that contract," and after ten weeks he left Geneva saying, "I have a contract with Dr. Kissinger, and I am prepared to implement that contract." He did not shift one inch from his original position.

By the time that we adjourned at Christmas, it was clear that each side was asking for assurances that were contradictory. The blacks wanted reassurance that the process would be irreversible, and the whites wanted an assurance both that they would have a share of the power in the transitional period and that in an independent country there would be a major role for the whites and guarantees for the white population. An agreement produced by what I would call the normal processes of diplomatic negotiation was impossible. It would have been just as effective to have treated it like the College of Cardinals, locked them up in the Sistine Chapel, and waited for the smoke to come up through the roof.

This impasse was perhaps not entirely surprising. One of our formats for discussion was a round table at which sat Mr. Smith and the heads of the other four delegations. I could not help reflecting that no less than three of those principals sitting around that table had spent more than ten years in prison on the orders of Mr. Smith himself. At the beginning of the conference we did not really know whether any of them were going to be able to sit together around the table. We did not know whether one of the Africans might decide to take his understandable feelings about Mr. Smith out on him in person, and we did not know either how Mr. Smith and his people would react.

It was a somewhat touchy time. I came to the conclusion when we adjourned that there was only one way of squaring this particular circle, and that was for Britain to assume a direct role in the transitional government. We would have to have a British resident commissioner or governor-general, whatever you would like to call him, who basically would be the commander in chief of the armed forces of the country and also, by a system of weighted voting in the various constitutional organs, would be in a position to exercise a veto over either side. I therefore took these proposals to Africa in January and saw all of the parties. I saw the front-line presidents. I saw Mr. Vorster twice, Mr. Smith more than three times (I am not quite sure how many), and all the leaders of the black delegations. The nationalist delegations and the front-line presidents, I believe, would have accepted our proposals as a basic framework for further discussion. Mr. Vorster, while unprepared to accept them, at least gave a qualified blessing to the whole enterprise. Unfortunately, Mr. Smith, much to my surprise and that of everybody with me, turned us down flat on January 25, 1977. I regarded it then, as now, as an extraordinarily shortsighted and indeed foolish action on Mr. Smith's part. It would have been one thing if I had gone there with a detailed set of proposals that I was demanding he sign then and there, but since I went only with a set of proposals that were to be a framework for future discussion in Geneva, his saying no, that he was not even prepared to discuss them further, seemed to me to be the height of foolishness.

The result of that rejection has been threefold. First, the guerilla war has increased. Based on the arithmetic—270,000 whites and 6.25 million blacks—it is impossible, as I see it, for Mr. Smith to win that war. However good the Rhodesian army is—and it is an efficient small army—until yesterday it did not have one black officer. Indeed, there is not one black administrator in the higher reaches of the Rhodesian civil service. It is beyond me, therefore, to appreciate how they hope to get the loyalty of the majority of the population. However good an army it is, it is bound to be stretched too thin to defend properly the borders of the country. Moreover, while a few months ago the guerillas were not numerous or very well-equipped, they are now becoming much more numerous, much better equipped, better trained, and much more skillful; therefore, unless one can get a political settlement soon, I would expect that the war will not only continue but increase. If it does increase, then I think the dangers for the whole of southern Africa are extremely great. My meetings with Mr. Vorster convinced me that the last thing he wants is to get drawn into the dispute, but if large numbers of people are killed the danger is that South Africa might get involved almost against its will and against its better judgment.

We are now trying to approach the problem from another angle. Instead of concentrating on a transitional government, we are now trying, together with the United States, to see whether a general agreement is possible on what an independent Rhodesia, a constitution for an independent country, would look like. I must say that at the moment we are quite a long way from it, but the feeling is that if we get that understanding, then the period of transition will become relatively less difficult and, therefore, the chances for an overall settlement are increased.

One of my problems, too, was the fact that the Geneva conference started on October 18, the United States election was held on November 2, and Mr. Carter was not inaugurated until January 20. To say the least, it is strange and difficult for a foreigner to understand why a great technological society like the United States takes nearly three months to change its government. In Britain we have an election on Thursday, and the new prime minister takes office on Friday. If the Republicans had won the election in November, obviously the difficulty would not have arisen because of the continuity of administration. Unfortunately for me there was a change. I use "unfortunately" purely in terms of continuity; it is not meant as any expression of approval or disapproval of the decision of the great American electorate last November. But it meant as far as I was concerned that American "clout" just was not there at the very moment I needed it because the administration in Washington was on the way out, and the new people had not even been appointed at that stage. It is not for a foreigner to suggest what constitutional amendments might be desirable for the United States of America, but let us hope that if we have another Geneva conference it will take place in the early part of the year, and not in the fall of a year in which an election is going to take place.

It was a difficult time, an infuriating time. I felt that we were nearly on the verge of a settlement; I still believe that we were within a whisker of it. Mr. Smith's refusal to negotiate was in my view shortsighted in the extreme, dangerous for his people, and dangerous for the peace of that part of the world. I only hope that the fact that he turned it down totally in January does not mean that he will turn down any sensible proposals that the United States and the United Kingdom might present in the future.

It is moreover difficult to see with precision the exact role that the UN could play in the process of further negotiations over Rhodesia. There might possibly be a future peacekeeping task that an international body like the Commonwealth or the UN could fulfill, but only as part of a political settlement worked out between the parties themselves. But if I see the UN's usefulness in this area as necessarily limited I am nevertheless moderately hopeful about the future of the UN itself.

Conclusion

The most important set of issues, the most important complex of problems that must be ironed out between now and the end of the century, is that involving economic relationships between the third world and the developed world, and in defining the developed world I would include the Eastern European as well as Western European developed countries. In some ways, the most important test that now faces the international community is whether it is possible to create fundamental and radical changes in world economic relationships by a process of peaceful dialogue rather than by a set of political confrontations, in which the developed countries will find themselves on the wrong side of the argument. The OPEC action raising oil prices was of fundamental importance, not only in economic terms but also in political terms. It was the first time a group of raw material producers managed to stay together long enough to confront the industrialized world and win. It therefore had a catalytic effect on political relationships between the mass of third world countries and the industrialized ones. We have not yet, I think, fully appreciated the fundamental nature of that confrontation or its political effects.

"Interdependence" is, of course, a fashionable word now. It is a somewhat unaesthetic word, but nevertheless it does contain the essence of a concept that is becoming increasingly important. A short time ago in the *New York Times*, Harlan Cleveland wrote an article in which he said that more and more countries are realizing that there is now no such thing as internal affairs, that in fact it is almost impossible for one country to insulate itself from the rest of the world and to pursue policies, whether economic, social, or military, that can be said to be solely in their own national self-interest. Indeed, the perception of what is in one's national self-interest is beginning to change. After all, if there is a bad harvest in the Soviet Union, for example, the chances are that the price of grain in the United States will go up. If Britain finds its policy in Northern

Ireland under attack, the chances are that at some stage or another we will find ourselves arraigned before something like the European Court of Human Rights and be obliged to account for our actions. If the Turks decide to send a ship into what they claim to be international waters, the chances are that those who were or might be affected by it will raise the issue in an international forum like the UN. If South Africa pursues policies of internal repression against its black population, then that is inevitably going to have an effect; it will be raised in these international institutions, and it will eventually find expression in the commercial policies and certainly the political policies of other nations toward South Africa. The degree of intermeshing or interlocking of national policies is now very great and in my view is going to increase.

If that is so, then the international community has to try and provide institutional frameworks to encourage that process of interdependence rather than to discourage it. I am not claiming that this is necessairly going to be an easy task; the larger countries, particularly those that do not depend on foreign trade for their existence, still tend to believe that you can pursue economic policies with a degree of insulation that I do not believe will be possible in the future. While trade makes up about 3.5 to 4.0 percent of the gross national product of the United States, it accounts for 19 percent of ours. Britain has always existed on world trade. We cannot feed all our population; domestically, we can feed only two-thirds of it, however good our agricultural system is, and it is very good indeed. We have to feed the rest of our population by importing raw materials, exercising our manufacturing skills, and then selling manufactured goods abroad in world markets. Therefore, we have a direct, almost a quantifiable interest in seeing world economic relationships change in a peaceful and orderly way rather than in a confrontational and more cataclysmic one.

Interdependence is going to dominate the international agenda from now until probably the end of the century. If we cannot create a new international economic order, not necessarily the one now being talked about in specific terms, but at least a radically different set of relationships between the rich third of the world and the poor two-thirds of the world, then I must say that the future seems somewhat bleak. The importance of the UN is that it may be able to provide the framework for that change to take place cooperatively and peacefully. Our support of it is thus crucial in the years ahead.

The United Nations and United States Foreign Policy

DAVID A. KAY

United States policies toward the United Nations have received increased attention in recent years. This has, no doubt, been spurred by the voluble nature of the United States ambassador to the UN, Andrew Young, and of one of his predecessors, Daniel Patrick Moynihan. The clashes in the UN between the United States and the third world over the shape of future economic relations and highly publicized anti-Israel actions by several UN organs have also contributed to this renewal of interest. The UN is variously viewed, often somewhat inconsistently by the same analyst, as a dangerous place dominated by implacable foes of American interests, a powerless debating society, or the last and best hope of mankind to avoid global chaos.

A rise of interest in United States policy toward the UN, however, is not immediately transferable into approval or support for it as an institution. Indeed, the attention that Ambassador Moynihan gained for the UN was made primarily by attacking the organization and the behavior of a majority of its members. Even in the case of Ambassador Young much of the attention that he has gained in the press resulted from seeming verbal gaffes or controversial statements and not from any ringing defense of the UN or its activities.

It would be convenient to dismiss much of the difficulties recently experienced by the United States in the UN as simply the pernicious influence of a secretary of state—Henry Kissinger—who seemed to dislike multilateral diplomacy that he could not dominate or the equally pernicious influence of two ambassadors with gifts for enlarging on reality and undiplomatic lusts for verbal combat. Such a response, however, would ignore fundamental shifts taking place in the international system and in global multilateral institutions. Quite apart from the phenomena of Henry Kissinger, Daniel Patrick Moynihan, and Andrew Young, the United States since the mid-1960s has found itself frequently subjected in the UN system to actions, both symbolic and operational, by groups of states that call into question the value of these institutions as instruments of international cooperation.

Among these "UN shocks" are increasingly aggressive challenges and opposition to Israeli legitimacy and policies, including the equating of Zionism with racism, the recommendation that states halt economic aid to Israel, and action in the UN Educational, Scientific, and Cultural Organization (UNESCO) to exclude Israel from the European group; support for national liberation movements, including a call for the United States to grant full independence to Puerto Rico; demands for the redistribution of global economic wealth, culminating in a call for the establishment of a New International Economic Order and a Charter of Economic Rights and Duties of States; a general conversion of UN forums into platforms for vitriolic attacks on the West in general and the United States specifically; the seeming inability of even the Carter administration to get minimal changes in the procedures of the International Labor Organization that would lessen its recently highly politicized nature; and such biased and unproductive negotiations at the UN Law of the Sea Conference that Ambassador Elliot Richardson has recommended that President Carter reevaluate whether the United States should continue to even participate in these negotiations.

For the United States, these "shocks" have been particularly unsettling as they have come in institutions that were viewed as having their origin in American initiatives and reflecting, in the case of the specialized agencies, the organized pluralistic nature of American society. It would have been impossible fifteen years ago for such consistent and broad-ranging attacks on United States policy and interests to gain majority support in the UN. Without a doubt the breadth and extent of this shift in United States fortunes account for the attitude of many who are now ready to write the UN off as a viable instrument for international cooperation.

The impact of these "shocks" and related developments is that the UN as an institution often seems adrift from its own principles. Senator Ribicoff of Connecticut, after a year-long study of the UN system by the staff of the Senate Governmental Affairs Committee, concluded: "All too often the organizations headquartered in extravagant and luxurious surroundings, are ineffective, top-heavy, with high-paid officials, underrepresented by United States personnel, uncertain in their purposes, and unduly repetitious of other organizations." Senator Ribicoff's views reflect a more general attitude of disillusionment that international institutions are proving more efficient at supporting their own bureaucracies than at advancing the goals and programs for which they were established.

Although generally masked by the drumfire of contentious political debate in the General Assembly and the associated disillusionment of many Americans with the United Nations, there has been a growing recognition, at least among industrial states, that in areas ranging from monetary affairs to ocean mining, international organizations with administrative, policymaking, and operational responsibilities are an urgent requirement. Economically and technologically complex societies increasingly impinge on one another even in their more mundane and tradition-rooted activities, such as agriculture. The best available alternative to chaos or high-cost autarkical solutions appears to be international institutions with enhanced coordination and policymaking responsibilities.

The entire UN system has been in the midst of a major transformation along these lines in the last fifteen years. It has come from being essentially a center for debate and the passing of nonbinding resolutions largely concerned with security issues to being a major operational center that in 1976 expended over $2.5 billion (not including World Bank lending of over $5 billion a year) and maintains staff and programs in approximately 100 countries. While the political functions of the UN certainly remain and usually manage to dominate journalistic and academic analysis of the system, even a cursory review will make apparent the dimensions of this transformation. In 1960 the total assessed budgets of all the UN agencies amounted to only $183 million and World Bank lending was only $602 million. Even ten years ago, in 1966, the total assessed budgets of all the specialized agencies stood at only $290 million, not including World Bank lending of just over $800 million. During this same period major programs have been created, including UN/FAO World Food Program (1961), World Weather Watch (1963), UN Conference on Trade and Development (1964), UN Industrial Development Organization (1965), UN Development Program (1965), UN Institute for Training and Research (1965), World Intellectual Property Organization (1967), UN Fund for Population Activities (1967), UN Fund for Drug Abuse Control (1970), UN Environment Program (1972), World Food Council (1974), and International Fund for Agricultural Development (1976).

Even as harsh a critic of the operations of the political side of the UN as Daniel Patrick Moynihan has written: "There is no escape from a definition of nationhood which derives primarily from the new international reality. . . . World society matters and world organizations have evolved to the point where palpable interests are disposed in international forums to a degree without precedent. . . . The stakes are considerable. They are enormous."[1] Much the same theme of resigned recognition of the operational role and impact of international programs can be found in the addresses of former Secretary of State Henry Kissinger during his last two years in office. In May 1976 while addressing the fourth UN Conference on Trade and Development, Kissinger noted:

> In the long sweep of history, the future of peace and progress may be most decisively determined by our response to the necessities imposed by our economic interdependence. This is the challenge we have assembled here to address—the urgent need for cooperative solutions to the new global problems of the world economy. These issues dominate the agenda of the evolving relationship between North and South, the industrial and the developing countries.

[1] Daniel Patrick Moynihan, "The United States in Opposition," *Commentary* 59 (March 1975), p. 40.

While program expansion has clearly been the dominant theme of recent UN activity, signs of disquiet and concern with the operational record have begun to be sounded. For example, in his massive two-volume *Study of the Capacity of the United Nations Development System* (1969), Sir Robert Jackson wrote:

> The cumulative impact of this evidence, then, is to show that although the UN development system is delivering a valuable service, it is doing so under a greater strain than is acceptable, that the output is less than optimal, and that the quality and quantity of future performance must be threatened. . . . What can be said with certitude is that the system is seriously overstrained at the present time and that, despite determined efforts from many quarters, there is no evidence that all defects are being overcome. There is, in short, a decline, and its propositions are becoming more serious. Major changes in organization and procedures are therefore imperative.

In addition to the range of organizational difficulties that Sir Robert Jackson and others have pointed out, a different source of concern about the UN has recently become apparent. Contrary to the fundamental assumption behind much of the activity of the organization that international cooperation on economic, social, and technological problems will lead to future cooperation in the political sphere, it has become apparent in the last few years that the functional and technical operations of the UN are becoming more and more politicized with the introduction of issues designed principally to attain political ends extraneous to the substantive and usually technical purposes of these programs. At times, as in the recent case of the UN Educational, Scientific, and Cultural Organization (UNESCO), the World Health Organization (WHO), and the International Labor Organization (ILO), the disruption resulting from the interjection of such partisan political issues into the specialized agencies has been sufficiently severe as to raise doubts about their effectiveness and future.

The essence of the policy problem that faces the United States today concerns the tension between the spreading perception in some quarters that the UN has become, in the words of a recent *Wall Street Journal* editorial, "a dangerous place" and the growing realization even among critics of the UN that medium-term thinking about almost any significant economic, social, or technological issue confronting governments today leads to the realization of the necessity of institutionalized, multilateral collaboration. On the one hand, unless the Carter administration is able to reassure itself, the Congress, and the American public that the UN is not "a dangerous place" and to reverse the level of abuse and misuse to which it is widely believed UN institutions are being put, then the process of multilateral cooperation and institution building will be decisively set back. On the other hand, unless efforts are begun at once to deal, both inside and outside of the UN, with the economic, social, and racial injustices felt by the developing world, then there is little hope that the despair and bitterness engendered by these felt injustices can be kept from destroying most global, multilateral institutions.

In broad brush strokes the options for the United States in meeting this general policy problem can be said to fall into roughly three categories. The first option can be termed the accommodationist option. This option, best reflected in the writings of a former United States ambassador to the UN, Charles Yost, is premised on the assessment that the recent hostility that has met the United States in the UN is principally the result of a lack of American leadership in meeting the demands of the third world in three areas: economic assistance, southern African problems, and the Middle East conflict. Proponents of this option argue that future United States policy in the UN should be forthcoming in attempting to meet the demands of the developing states and that if the policy is indeed forthcoming then hostility toward the United States will diminish and the golden days of United States leadership will be restored.

A second option can be termed the confrontationist option. This option, most forcefully presented by Patrick Moynihan, argues that the United States now finds itself in a world that is basically hostile, that this hostility is deeply rooted in philosophical opposition to the American economic system and wide personal liberties and constitutional restraints on government power. Finding itself in this hostile world and particularly in its global manifestation (the UN) the proponents of this option argue that the United States must be prepared to wage virtually unceasing combat with few allies to defend its interests and principles. The UN of this second option begins to resemble nothing so much as the Roman Coliseum and the United States, the Christian martyrs. The contest is one of conflicting faith and principles with only a very limited area left for mutual cooperation.

The third option is a pragmatic strategy that both seeks accommodation on issues when the United States believes that change can reasonably promise to advance both long-term American and global interests and yet stands ready to resolutely defend vital American interests and principles when attacked in the UN. Proponents of this option seek to avoid both the overreaching approval of the accommodationist of all things that are UN and the similar overreaching hostility of the confrontationist. The heavy burden of this option is that it demands a subtlety and sophistication in its formulation and application that is not generally present in large bureaucracies. It can promise only small successes rather than the alluring appeal of the return to the golden days of American leadership held out by the accommodationist or the heady thrill of combat that the confrontationist relishes.

As a first step in sorting out these options and of probing beyond the high level generalities that they encourage, the essays in this volume set out to assess a wide range of UN activities. While reflecting on the past performance of the organization, the authors have concentrated most of their attention on examining from the perspective of the United States the problems and opportunities for future action on important global issues. While the coverage of topics is broad, no claim is made that it is exhaustive. Indeed, given the burgeoning of the international agenda, it is impossible in a book of a reasonable length to examine every issue area that is likely to soon require some type of multilateral attention. There has been no attempt to force these essays into a homogeneous view of what the future may hold for the UN. Instead, the authors have been encouraged to be clear as to their assumptions and premises so that the bases of their policy prescriptions are clear to all. It is hoped that this volume will provide a foundation for further public discussion and debate on the critical issue of future United States policy in the UN.

The United States Public
and the United Nations

ALFRED O. HERO, JR.

American public reactions to the United Nations system may be fruitfully examined from several frames of reference. This essay will first consider general trends as they have been linked with international and related domestic developments and events since the establishment of the world organization. Next, it will compare trends, especially over the 1960s and 1970s, among major educational, occupational, racial, ethnic, religious, and political groups in the country. Leadership opinion will be briefly compared with mass opinion. Then, attitudes toward the UN in the United States will be contrasted with those prevailing among similar groups abroad insofar as comparable surveys have been conducted internationally. Finally, some policy implications of these findings will be considered.

The UN has fared relatively well in the eyes of the general United States public, particularly in view of the UN's much changed composition, emphasis, and performance relative to perceived American interests since the early 1960s. Though support for continued United States membership in the UN and approval of the organization's performance have declined from their high points during the two decades following the UN's establishment in 1945, periodic declines of public support in the initial decade and a half were comparable in a number of respects to more recent declines.

While the UN was being established and during its first half decade, an overwhelming majority of the American public favored United States membership and active involvement.[1] However, the advent of the cold war in the late

---

[1] For more detailed analyses and documentation for observations herein for the period 1945–55, see William A. Scott and Stephen B. Withey, *The United States and the United Nations* (New York: Manhattan Publishing Co., 1958) and for the period 1954–66, see Alfred O. Hero, Jr., "The American Public and the UN, 1954–1966," *The Journal of Conflict*

1940s, and especially the invasion of South Korea in 1950, dampened public support and optimism about the UN's future performance. Disillusion-ment with and disapproval of the world body increased to a high point since reached only during and shortly after the brief Arab-Israeli war of 1967. By 1955 public approval rose again to approximately its pre-Korean war level, only to suffer a brief decline during the Suez crisis and the Soviet invasion of Hun-gary in the fall of 1956. Public approval rose thereafter until the effects of massive entry of former colonial dependencies, most of which were less de-veloped countries (LDCs) and nonaligned, caused a decline beginning during the mid-1960s.

In November 1974, 74 percent of the general public—a somewhat higher figure than during the early part of the Korean war—felt the United States should remain in the UN. Table 1 shows that this figure had been as high as 86 percent in the early 1960s. The 16 percent who would withdraw, and who

TABLE 1

Responses to Questions on the United States's Membership in the UN

Date	Agency	No.	Stay In	Get Out	No Opinion or Do Not Know
Jan. 1951	Gallup	1,367	72%	14%	14%
Feb. 1951	NORC	1,236	78	12	10
May 1951	Gallup	2,067	75	12	13
Nov. 1951	Gallup	1,962	75	13	12
June 1952	NORC	1,265	85	6	9
Feb. 1953	NORC	1,291	84	10	6
July 1953	NORC	1,291	83	11	6
Nov.-Dec. 1953	NORC	1,301	74	13	13
Oct. 1954	NORC	518	84	6	10
Aug. 1955	NORC	1,262	88	5	7
Apr. 1956	NORC	1,224	88	6	6
Oct. 1956	NORC	1,286	87	6	7
Dec. 1956	NORC	1,295	75	14	11
Jan. 1962	Gallup	1,543	86	9	5
Nov. 1963	Gallup	1,636	79	8	13
Nov. 1963	Harris	1,009	76	9	15
July 1967	Gallup	1,506	85	10	5
March 1974	Harris	1,106	83	7	10
Feb. 1975	Gallup	1,559	75	11	14
Apr. 1975	NORC	1,490	75	18	7
Nov. 1975	Gallup	1,533	74	16	10

Note: Questions of different agencies were somewhat differently worded.

Resolution 10 (December 1966): 436–75. The author is indebted to the Roper Public Opinion Research Center at Williamstown, the Interuniversity Consortium for Political and Social Research at Ann Arbor, and the Institute for Research in Social Sciences at Chapel Hill for survey data provided on the period 1966–76.

also usually preferred that the UN be located outside the United States, have been primarily isolationists. In March 1974, 76 percent felt that "all things considered" the UN was still "worthwhile" after twenty-nine years of existence; only 15 percent thought it was not.[2] The following December, 81 percent felt that the United States's role in the founding of the United Nations was a "proud" rather than a "dark" moment in United States history.[3]

Opinion studies indicate that since World War II most of the public has continued to view the UN mainly in terms of keeping the peace. Therefore, the UN's apparent inability to prevent or settle war is the primary reason for the declining appreciation of its performance. This conclusion is further reinforced by increases in the percentages of people who felt the UN was doing a "poor job" during the early part of the Korean war, the Suez and Hungarian military interventions, the Arab-Israeli war of 1967, and the latter years of the Vietnam war. As table 2 shows, these crises were succeeded several months after hostilities ended by increases in the percentages of those who felt it was doing a "good" or "fair" job. Thus the important decline in perceived UN per-

TABLE 2

Responses to the Question, "In General, Do You Think the UN is Doing a Good Job, or a Poor Job, in Trying to Solve the Problems it Has Had to Face?"

Date	Agency	No.	Good or Fair	Poor	No Opinion or Do Not Know
Dec. 1950	Gallup	1,502	57%	36%	7%
May 1951	Gallup	2,070	54	36	10
Sept. 1953	Gallup	1,613	66	22	12
Dec. 1953	Gallup	1,469	55	30	15
July 1954	Gallup	1,549	59	26	15
Oct. 1955	Gallup	1,500	80	10	10
Nov. 1956	Gallup	1,502	77	11	12
Dec. 1959	Gallup	1,527	87	7	6
Oct. 1960	Gallup	1,589	80	9	11
June 1961	Gallup	1,506	79	11	10
Jan. 1962	Gallup	1,543	78	12	10
June 1962	Gallup	1,512	78	15	7
Nov. 1963	Gallup	1,552	80	7	13
July 1964	Gallup	1,569	81	7	12
Aug. 1967	Gallup	1,503	49	35	16
Sept. 1970	Gallup	1,539	44	40	16
Oct. 1971	Gallup	1,509	35	43	22
Nov. 1975	Gallup	1,533	35	51	16

[2] Louis Harris and Associates, March 1974.
[3] Harris, December 1974.

formance in the summer of 1967 was undoubtedly linked with the fact that large majorities of Americans venturing opinions at the time felt that the UN had not been effective in dealing with the Middle East crisis and that it had not made a significant effort to help settle the Vietnam war.[4]

Although a significant majority has continued to argue that the veto in the Security Council should be eliminated, only a minority of one in five still believes the UN would be more effective if it were reorganized without the USSR.[5] Although a majority opposed membership by the People's Republic of China throughout the 1950s and 1960s, especially if Nationalist China were ejected, this development was finally accepted, as indicated in table 3. By the mid-1970s membership by the People's Republic of China and its behavior in the UN were no longer significant sources of unfavorable United States perceptions of the international body.

Anti-Israeli statements and actions in the General Assembly and in some specialized agencies by coalitions of Arab states, Asian and African LDCs, and Communist members seemed to contribute to at least short-term undermining of United States public perceptions of UN effectiveness. For example, only 9 percent of the United States public approved of the UN resolution in late 1975 claiming that "Zionism is racism and a form of prejudice." When earlier action against Israel by the United Nations Educational, Scientific, and Cultural Organization (UNESCO) was briefly explained, an even smaller United States minority favored that development. The anti-Zionist resolution, like the Arab-Israeli wars of 1956, 1967, and 1973, was followed by an increase in the number who felt the UN was doing "a poor job," as table 2 shows.

Universal membership in the UN has been generally accepted as desirable since China's entrance. The majority that opposed membership by North Korea and Vietnam declined to a minority after the Korean war and, particularly, the Vietnam war became history. A large majority believes that, in principle, nonaligned LDCs critical of the United States should be members.

However, the results of the broadened UN membership and the reduced relative influence of the United States in the UN have been major sources of public frustration and disillusionment with its effectiveness. Thus, by early 1972, 50 percent of the public said their "respect for the UN" was "decreasing as the years go by," while only 18 percent replied that their "respect" was "increasing."[6] In March 1974, 56 percent of Americans felt that "the UN is too much talk and too little action," 43 percent that it "generally passes ineffective resolutions," and 54 percent that it "wastes too much United States money."[7] Six months later, 62 percent considered the UN good in theory but felt that the real way to keep peace was "to have the superpowers agree they will not allow

---

[4] Harris, January, April, May, and June 1967.
[5] American Institute of Public Opinion (Gallup), April 1973.
[6] Gallup, February 1972.
[7] Harris, March 1974.

TABLE 3

Responses to Questions on the Admission of Communist China to the UN

Date	Agency	No.	Favor	Depends	Opposed	No Opinion or Do Not Know
June 1950[a]	Gallup	1,450	11%		58%	31%
Nov.-Dec. 1953	NORC	1,301	12	6%	74	8
March 1954	NORC	535	11	5	79	5
June 1954	Gallup	1,587	7		78	15
July 1954	Gallup	1,549	8		79	13
May 1955	Gallup	1,503	10		67	23
Sept. 1956	NORC	1,263	17	5	73	5
Dec. 1956	Gallup	1,540	11		74	15
Feb. 1957	Gallup	1,507	13		70	17
Jan. 1958	Gallup	1,550	17		66	17
Aug. 1958	Gallup	1,563	20		63	17
March 1961	Gallup	1,550	19		64	17
Sept. 1961	Gallup	1,552	16		64	20
Jan.-Feb. 1964	Gallup	1,631	14		69	17
Feb. 1965	Gallup	1,568	22		64	14
March 1966	Gallup	1,631	25		55	20
April 1966	National	1,479	25		57	18
Sept. 1966	Gallup	1,554	25		56	19
April 1967	Harris	1,105	23		54	23
Dec. 1968	Harris	1,544	31		53	16
Oct. 1970	Gallup	1,597	35		49	16
Jan. 1971	Harris	1,598	39		46	15
May 1971	Gallup	1,509	45		38	17
Sept.-Nov. 1972	SRC	1,372	62		18	20

If UN majority decides to admit Communist China, should the United States go along:

Date	Agency	No.	Favor	Opposed	No Opinion or Do Not Know
July 1956	Gallup	2,105	39%	44%	17%
Sept. 1961	Gallup	1,552	44	39	17
Jan.-Feb. 1964	Gallup	1,631	39	44	17
Feb. 1965	Gallup	1,568	49	35	16
March 1966	Gallup	1,631	49	31	20
Sept. 1966	Gallup	1,554	53	33	14
Oct. 1966	Gallup	1,561	49	31	20
May 1971	Gallup	1,509	58	28	14

If Nationalist China also remains a member as a different country, Communist China should be admitted:

Date	Agency	No.	Favor	Opposed	No Opinion or Do Not Know
April 1967	Harris	1,105	35%	34%	31%
Dec. 1968	Harris	1,544	39	38	23
Jan. 1971	Harris	907	47	32	21

[a]Before the Korean war.

other countries to wage war."[8] By mid-1976, 13 percent of American adults (mostly those who would withdraw from the UN) would have ended United States financial support entirely and 35 percent would have reduced it, contrasted with 37 percent who would have kept support at prevailing levels and 6 percent who would have increased it; four years earlier, these respective positions on financial support were held by 9 percent, 29 percent, 46 percent, and 10 percent.[9]

Nevertheless, generally favorable perceptions of the UN prevailed at the same time. In April 1974, 73 percent of Americans agreed that the UN "provides a forum for open, honest discussion between nations," 65 percent that it is "helping the poor countries develop their economies," 64 percent that it takes "positive steps to keep the peace in the Middle East and elsewhere," and 63 percent that "today's problems require international action that only the UN or other international agencies can take." Only 18 percent accepted the charge that "the UN is pro-Arab and anti-Israel," and only 20 percent believed that "the UN generally works against the interests of the United States."[10] Moreover, a majority has continued to ascribe considerable priority to efforts by the United States and other members to improve the UN's effectiveness, to use it more actively rather than defensively or as a propaganda forum, and to extend its effectiveness into further areas of international concern.

Although the minority arguing for such utopian objectives as converting the UN into a world government declined by the 1970s to around 10 percent, in September 1970, 84 percent of American adults thought it "very important that we try to make the UN a success" and agreed also that they "would like to see the United States become a stronger organization." Table 4 indi-

TABLE 4

Responses to the Question,
"How Important Do You Think it is That We Try to Make the UN a Success?"

Date	Agency	No.	Very	Fairly	Not So	No Opinion or Do Not Know
Oct. 1952	Gallup	3,114	77%	10%	6%	7%
Nov. 1956	Gallup	1,502	85	8	3	4
Dec. 1959	Gallup	1,327	88	7	2	3
Oct. 1960	Gallup	1,589	83	8	2	7
Jan. 1962	Gallup	1,543	83	9	4	4
Nov. 1963	Gallup	1,552	79	9	4	8
July 1967	Gallup	1,511	79	10	6	5
Sept. 1970	Gallup	1,511	84	8	5	3

[8] Harris, September 1974.
[9] Potomac Associates, May 1976.
[10] Harris, April 1974.

cates that these percentages were approximately the average for the period since 1952. In December 1974 only 14 percent considered it "not important" for the United States to "strengthen the United Nations," while 44 percent felt it "very important" and 31 percent "somewhat important."[11] At that time only 13 percent preferred that the role of the UN be "less important" in United States foreign policy and in world affairs than they perceived it to be. Conversely, 53 percent thought it "very important for the United States to be a world leader in international organizations such as the United Nations" and 60 percent that "we should conduct more and more of our foreign affairs through genuinely international organizations."[12]

Specifically, in the fall of 1971, 66 percent favored the establishment of a UN "army of about 100,000 men to try to enforce peace," approximately the mean that, between 1958 and 1964, approved the proposal "to build up the UN Emergency Force to a size great enough to deal with 'brush fire' or small wars throughout the world." (See table 5). In March 1974, 68 percent wanted to see

TABLE 5

Responses to Questions on UN Armed Force

Date	Agency	No.	Good Idea	Poor Idea	No Opinion or Do Not Know
Proposal to build up the UN Emergency Force to a size great enough to deal with "brush fire" or small wars throughout the world:					
Feb. 1958	Gallup	1,474	66%	15%	19%
July 1960	Gallup	1,653	72	12	16
Jan 1961	Gallup	1,502	66	17	17
April 1964	Gallup	1,661	62	19	19
July 1964	Gallup	1,569	66	16	18
Proposal to establish a peacekeeping army of about 100,000 men to try to enforce peace:					
Sept. 1970	Gallup	1,511	66%	32%	2%

the UN do more "to set up peace-keeping forces," 71 percent "to solve the world food supply problem," 68 percent "to solve the world's energy problem," 67 percent to "help clean up air and water pollution in the world," and even 54 percent "to provide aid to developing countries"; in most cases these were slight increases in approval over four years earlier.[13]

Perceptions of the UN's performance, criticisms of its behavior, and reactions to proposals to make it more effective have been parallel to, if not linked causally with, public reactions to international affairs and United States foreign

[11] Harris, December 1974.
[12] Ibid.
[13] Harris, March 1974.

relations in general. When Americans have been relatively optimistic about international affairs—especially about avoiding war—and the United States role in the world, they have tended to be more optimistic about and more in favor of the UN.

Declines over the past decade or so in favorable images of the UN, of its performance, and of the degree to which the United States should help to strengthen it have been smaller than decreases in support for most other United States international involvements and commitments since World War II. For example, 35 percent of Americans in the spring of 1975 and 32 percent in the spring of 1976 felt that "it would be better for the future of this country if we stayed out of world affairs," contrasted with 60 percent and 63 percent respectively who thought it would be "best . . . if we took an active part."[14] Comparative percentages had been 16 percent contrasted with 79 percent in June 1965,[15] and an average of 20 percent contrasted with 71 percent over the previous twenty years.[16] While from 1947 through 1965 a majority was willing to send United States military forces to defend at least the European allies of the United States in case of a major attack by "Communist-backed" forces, by April 1975 only 37 percent would do so to defend Britain, 27 percent to defend Germany, and 42 percent to defend even Mexico.[17] Only in the case of Canada would a majority of 57 percent—smaller than at any time since 1938—send United States troops. NATO, formerly about as popular in the United States as the UN, has likewise lost more public support than the latter. Fifty-seven percent of American adults in September 1973 favored reducing or entirely withdrawing troops stationed in Europe as a part of NATO forces.[18] Declines in favorable public opinion for United States economic and, particularly, military aid have also been more marked than have those regarding the UN.[19] Small majorities of even those isolationists who would "stay out of world affairs," who would not send United States troops to defend Mexico, Western Europe, or Japan, who would cut United States troops under NATO, or who would reduce or terminate nonmilitary aid would nevertheless remain in the UN and have the United States participate in strengthening it and making it more effective.

Social, Political, and Leadership Distribution of Opinions on the UN

The number of years of formal schooling an American has completed remains more intimately associated than any other demographic variable with most

---

[14] National Opinion Research Center (NORC), March and April 1975, April 1976.
[15] NORC, June 1965.
[16] Gallup, October 1945; NORC, January 1950 and March 1955.
[17] Gallup, April 1975.
[18] Gallup, September 1973; NORC, December 1974.
[19] Gallup, Harris, and NORC polls of 1947–76.

"liberal" views on the UN, as it does on international affairs and United States foreign policy in general. At least as early as 1945 relevant knowledge and realistic, factually based views about the UN system have been even more highly correlated with educational attainment.

For example, on most questions about the UN, Americans who did not finish high school have often been three or more times as likely as college graduates to have no opinion. When they do have an opinion, they are more inclined than college graduates to feel that the United States should withdraw from the UN. Less educated Americans tend to favor cutting United States financial support and to oppose channeling United States economic aid and technical help through the World Bank, the United Nations Development Program, or specialized agencies. On the other hand, the better educated have been more critical of the UN performance since 1967, more inclined to feel the world organization has been doing a "poor" rather than a "good" or "fair" job, and more apt to say their respect for it has declined in recent years. However, college educated Americans have also been more apt to feel the United States government should assign a higher priority to making the UN more effective and to using it more constructively as a major vehicle in United States policy.

After education, age remains the next most relevant demographic factor. Americans under thirty have been more consistently favorable than those fifty and older to staying in the UN and to the United States government's assigning a higher priority to working within the UN, improving it, and channeling United States aid through the UN system. Since younger people have a considerably higher average education than the older group, however, educational differences rather than age are probably the more important explanation.

Although women have about the same amount of education as men, they have been less informed about the UN and less inclined to venture opinions about it. However, women expressing views have held opinions somewhat more favorable than those of men. For instance, women have been less inclined to favor United States withdrawal from the UN and to argue that it be moved out of the United States, and they are more apt to agree that it is important to make the body a success and to believe it is doing a "good" or "fair" job.

Among religious groups, Jews were consistently more inclined to favor the UN until the Arab-Israeli war of 1967 than were Catholics or Protestants. However, so few Jews have been in individual surveys that in order to attain reliable comparisons it has been necessary to combine three or more surveys in which the same question has been asked. Where this has been feasible, differences in opinion between Jews and non-Jews since 1967 have been negligible on queries that neither dealt with the Middle East nor took place during or shortly after developments in the UN in regard to a "crisis" in that part of the world. The "anti-Zionism" resolution of the General Assembly resulted in more negative reactions among the small sample of Jews than among non-Jews in the survey dealing with it. The minorities of Jews, however, who have favored terminating

United States membership seem in recent years to be no larger proportionally than those among Gentiles. Indeed, even since 1967, support for strengthening the UN in the respects mentioned above has been about as widespread among Jews as among others.

Though Catholics were either less enthusiastic about the UN or differed not at all from Protestants during the first decade or so after World War II, by the 1970s they were rather consistently more liberal than Protestants on such issues as United States membership, a higher priority for the UN in United States foreign policy, and the gradual extension of the UN's effectiveness into technical, economic, and other fields.

Farmers and inhabitants of small towns have been less favorable toward the UN than citizens in more populous areas. Southerners, especially when blacks are omitted from the samples, have continued to be less favorable than other regional groups. Blacks, though less apt than whites to be informed or to express opinions, have become in recent years more favorable and less critical than whites, at least among those who have ventured views.

Republicans have been somewhat more inclined than Democrats to favor withdrawal from the UN, to feel it has been doing a "poor job," to manifest decreasing respect for it in recent years, and to accord a lower priority to trying to make it a success. However, these partisan differences have been only between 3 and 8 percent. Differences between voters and nonvoters have often been larger, with nonvoters tending to have less favorable views. The most active political minority—including those who have voted consistently and have themselves participated in political campaigns either as candidates or as active supporters or who have followed public affairs regularly in the print media— has been the best informed of the political groups about the UN and the most inclined to favor strengthening it.

Elites in the United States—either those listed in *Who's Who* or the small minority that follow international affairs regularly, hold clearcut, differentiated views on foreign policy issues, and take active roles in foreign affairs, foreign policy analysis and formulation, or mass media coverage of world affairs—have differed in their views on the UN from the general public in approximately the same ways as college graduates, only more so. An inconsequential number of these elites has felt the United States should withdraw from the UN, but a majority of them has argued that the UN in recent years has done a "poor job," has become a "talkfest," is less able to make constructive contributions to world affairs than formerly, is decreasing in relative importance, and is "not important at all" or only "somewhat important" as a goal for United States policy to try to strengthen. On the other hand, these elites have been much more inclined than the general public to channel increased United States economic aid and technical assistance through the World Bank and other UN-related agencies. They prefer more than Americans generally do that the UN "become a stronger organization." They would accord more respect and power to the International Court of Justice, increase the UN budget, "expand its work," limit the powers of the Security Council, and modify General Assembly rules to include weighted voting and to make its deliberations and actions more manageable.[20]

Some International Comparisons

From its beginning until at least the early 1960s the UN enjoyed wider popularity in the United States than in most of the rest of the world. Enthusiasm and optimism about its potential for preserving the peace were especially widespread among influential, articulate minorities, but these attitudes were also extensively held in a vaguer, less differentiated form among much of the general public. However, their enthusiasm was shared by few people, largely liberal intellectuals, in most other countries. More extreme or utopian versions of these attitudes, such as viewing the UN as a major step toward world federation or some other form of international government, were even more concentrated in North America. To some degree these comparative perceptions were offshoots of the United States's preponderant worldwide role as contrasted with the defensive, regional, or special concerns of most of the other independent countries of the period. While much of the rest of the world was significantly damaged—economically and politically, as well as physically—by the most destructive of wars, the United States emerged as the dominant victor, strengthened rather than weakened. This reinforced its own historical experience and produced unrealistic views of and hopes for the UN.

With the decline of more optimistic United States perceptions of the performance and potential roles of the UN that began in the mid-1960s, contemporaneous with more self-assured national perceptions in Western Europe and Japan, these differences between the United States and the rest of the industrialized non-Communist world seem to have narrowed. Meanwhile, aware publics in the LDCs, particularly in the new member states from Asia and Africa, have harbored attitudes and preferred priorities for the UN more divergent from opinions in the industrialized West than the smaller attitudinal differences between the United States and Western Europe.

A worldwide survey of thirty countries sponsored by the Kettering Foundation in 1975-76 found that Western Europeans were much more able than Americans to identify such specialized agencies and activities as UNESCO, UNICEF, WHO, FAO, and UNDP, though only minorities smaller than a third of the adult populations were able to identify any of them in even the most informed countries. Large majorities (66 to 81 percent) in the LDCs could not identify or were little aware of even the UN itself. Between North America and Western Europe, earlier comparisons had by then become reversed in respect to perception of the UN. Forty-two percent of North Americans, contrasted with 46 percent of Western Europeans, felt the UN was doing a "good job," while 36

<hr />

[20] NORC, December 1974; Gallup, September 1973 and December 1975.

percent and 26 percent respectively thought it was doing a "poor job." But in the LDCs, larger majorities of those holding opinions felt it was doing a good job—85 percent in Africa, 74 percent in Asia, and 60 percent in Latin America.

Throughout the non-Communist world, publics aware of the UN and willing to venture opinions viewed "maintaining peace" as one of its central purposes. During 1976-76, 51 percent in North America, 56 percent in Western Europe, 76 percent in Asia, 65 percent in Africa, and 35 percent in Latin America held this view. North Americans were more apt than citizens of any other non-Communist region, including Europeans, to view the promotion of international understanding as a major purpose—60 percent in North America, 28 percent in Europe, 38 percent in Latin America, 20 percent in Africa, and 14 percent in Asia. But North Americans, particularly those in the United States, were even less apt than Western Europeans to view helping underdeveloped nations with technical and economic assistance as a major purpose of the UN (4 percent compared to 10 percent) or, particularly, than publics in the LDCs aware of the UN (an average of 18 percent).

The one comparative study of elites—those from seventy countries listed in *Who's Who in the World* and *The International Who's Who*—in 1973 like-wise suggested narrowed differences in thinking about the UN between elite Western Europeans and Americans since the early UN period as well as significant differences between both those groups and their counterparts in the LDCs. The latter seemed to have a more favorable attitude toward the UN "as time goes on," to want to expand its budget (supposedly for work in the LDCs), to oppose weighted voting in the General Assembly and other UN agencies, and to favor relative importance in world affairs for the organization.

Conclusion

American public opinion as a whole on the UN has remained rather stable in view of the important changes in the UN's composition, tone, and emphases pertinent to the United States's international interests since the early 1960s with the entry of newly independent, largely underdeveloped countries. Though views held by most Americans about the UN are based on relatively little factual knowledge and are therefore not well informed, differentiated, or intensely held, the general level of public awareness has certainly not declined since the initial decade and a half of the UN's existence. The decline in naive enthusiasm for the UN since the 1940s and 1950s has been accompanied by the development of more realistic and pragmatic attitudes about it.

Since about the time of the Middle East crisis of 1967, the public has been more critical of and less optimistic about the UN's performance in world affairs than during the late 1950s and early 1960s. However, previous declines in favorable perceptions, especially during the Korean war, followed rather quickly by "rebounds," suggests that the public could again become more favorable. Whether it does will depend on developments in the UN, the international problems with which it will be confronted, and the behavior of the United States in regard to the UN. Few past shifts in American opinion on the UN have been conclusive.

Most of the public would prefer that the UN become a more effective body, especially in regard to keeping the peace, and most would expand United States support for it, accord it higher priority in United States policy, and work more actively toward improving its performance. Most American citizens accord it higher priority than recent United States policy has. They would have their government leaders make more serious use of the UN, strive more constructively to make it and its specialized agencies more effective and relevant to diverse international concerns, and devote expanded funds to its more promising activities.

Public opinion, however, tends more to follow government policy on the UN than to lead it. From the foregoing data, it is clear that United States policy has been a reflection of public opinion to a quite limited degree. As the change in opinion on membership by the People's Republic of China combined with ejection of Nationalist China suggests, majorities of the public tend to accept changes in the UN, and in United States policy in regard to it, once those changes have taken place, even when only limited minorities favored such change beforehand.

Undoubtedly more important in the domestic body politic are the views of the relatively articulate, better educated, more informed minority who are more apt to influence policymaking either directly, or through the media, diverse organizations, and informal face-to-face relations. This better informed and more politically active minority has been considerably more critical of the UN's performance in the last decade but also more favorable than the mass public to expanded United States efforts to support and strengthen the organization. This heterogeneous elite has largely felt that the United States government should accord the UN a more central role in its foreign relations than has been official practice in the last fifteen years or so. It would generally support, or at least acquiesce in, the Carter administration's channeling more technical and economic aid through its pertinent agencies, and favor greater accommodation with the more legitimate demands of the LDC majority in respect to development, human rights, and most other issues. Indeed, the views of this elite have usually shifted more quickly toward congruence with changes in governmental policy than have those of the general public.

Thus the leadership in Washington has a wide degree of freedom vis-à-vis its electorate and, in particular, the potentially influential nongovernmental elites, should it elect to upgrade its relationships with the UN system. Major obstacles to such change are more apt to come from the executive branch or, perhaps more seriously, from Congress than from the American electorate.

A Non-American Perspective

JOHN W. HOLMES

When President Roosevelt informed the prime minister of Canada how he had proposed the name "United Nations" to Churchill as the latter emerged naked from a shower, "The President mentioned it was like adopting the idea of Seeley's Expansion of England. This was the expansion of the United States. The United States had grown into the United Nations. . . ." Mackenzie King added: "The pride of authorship is one of the strongest of the temptations of most men. . . ."[1] Is there perhaps reflected in this perspective of Roosevelt's the triumph and the fallacy of the United States and the UN? One has only to contemplate the ghastly state the world would be in if the United States had not done more than its share in creating the United Nations system to acknowledge that the game was well worth the hubris. Still the hubris has been and remains a problem as one contemplates the future of that system and the part its strongest and most affluent member will be called upon to play.

The problem is often enough stated by Americans. The proprietary stance, the paternalism, and the assumption that it was the destiny of mankind to become units in the expanding Republic of God (established 1776) are themes that no foreigner need elaborate. Stanley Hoffmann, quoting Jimmy Carter's reference in June 1976 to a framework for peace as one "within which our own ideals gradually can become a global reality," comments that "the more one is convinced of the need for an American policy for world order, the more important it is to understand why it cannot be an American world order policy."[2] As president, however, Mr. Carter told the UN that although the United States could sometimes help others resolve their differences, "we cannot do so by imposing our own particular solutions."[3] No United States leader would, of course, say or intend

---

[1] J. W. Pickersgill, *The Mackenzie King Record*, vol. 1, *1939–1944* (Toronto: University of Toronto Press, 1960), p. 430.

[2] Stanley Hoffmann, "No Choice, No Illusions," *Foreign Policy* (Winter 1976–77), p. 98.

[3] Jimmy Carter, address to the UN General Assembly, March 17, 1977.

otherwise. President Kennedy, answering the question what kind of peace Americans sought, said, "Not a Pax Americana enforced on the world by American weapons of war."[4] But that is at least a partial description of the tragedy in Vietnam.

Americans are being warned by Americans that they can no longer expect to control the UN as they did in its early years. "Leadership without hegemony" is the apt slogan. Out of an American desire to be fair has been created a new legend. The United States, it is said, created the UN and ran it until recently, before the third world took over. Developing countries and the Communists find this thesis convenient, and it is peddled by those arch cultural imperialists, the American revisionist historians, with what Raymond Aron calls their myth of American omnipotence. One reason for the distortion is that most books about the UN have been written by American scholars. American archives are more freely available and the parts played by others hidden from sight. It is not that the United States role has been glorified, just magnified—even by foreign scholars led astray by American domination of political science. Both the pride and the guilt inspired by this tale of hegemony accentuate the American sense of responsibility for world order and the obligation to manage it. It might be easier for Americans to adjust to "leadership without hegemony" if they got a better perspective on what their previous "hegemony" amounted to.

Others present at the creation have reason to feel aggrieved. That the American contribution was most influential is beyond question. However, the UN Charter was a product of international bargaining. It incorporated the bright ideas—not to mention the bad ideas—of many peoples, notably the British. The result was compromise, and compromise is an international act. The USSR deserves credit for opposing full powers to the General Assembly. The charter reflects no national will but a state of international tension, and being based on a permanent reality rather than legal fictions, the UN has survived and grown.

The security provisions of the UN Charter were designed not to ensure American domination but to prevent Americans from running away. The Europeans wanted collective security provisions against aggression because of their deductions from the experiences of 1914 and 1939. The Europeans, however, never had total confidence in the Security Council and provision was made in the charter for defensive action as necessary before the council had established its authority. When it became clear in a couple of years that they could not leave their protection to the Security Council, the Western powers shifted from collective security to collective defense. The important thing was still to get or keep the United States committed. The drive to form NATO came to a large extent from Britain and Canada, motivated partly by their anxiety to thwart the movement to turn the UN into a "free world" organization. The design was established in secret talks in Washington in the early part of 1948 among British, American, and Canadian representatives. The concern was to put forward proposals that

4 John F. Kennedy, address to American University, June 10, 1963.

could catch the support of the United States Senate in an effective guarantee of Western Europe. Changes were made when the other prospective members joined the discussions in the summer of 1948. The security provisions of "the creation" were now functionally distributed between the UN and NATO. This was the will and to a considerable extent the design of Western Europeans and Canadians.[5] The assumption that it was an American security system imposed on others has contributed greatly to the legend of "hegemony."

The purpose of such recollection is not to minimize the crucial role of the United States but to show it as one of leadership and not of dictation. The United States was a better team worker than has been assumed. It was the "leader" because it had the resources and the energy, but its friends and allies were by no means puppets. If the United States had in fact been running the UN, the UN may not have survived. The Korean war, for example, could have ended in disaster if the Allies had not, in association with the State Department resisted pressures within the United States to turn it into a war against China. The whole UN operation in Korea was much more of a combined operation than it may now seem. United States military power and direction were the sine qua non, but the other powers who participated insofar as they could saw the enterprise as a common effort to do what the League of Nations had failed to do over Manchuria and Ethiopia. The United States had to make the crucial decision to intervene because it alone had the capacity to do so, but it had widespread and genuine support in the UN.

In the formative first decade of the UN, the United States could not "command" votes from a subservient majority. On occasions it would exploit its leadership, as when it bullied unwilling associates to support the ill-timed General Assembly resolution declaring China an aggressor in January 1950. United States delegations had to work hard for a majority. What vote-counters forget is that so-called United States resolutions suffered a good deal of compromise to get support. Many of them were strangled at birth. It was not only the other Western powers who curbed the will of the United States and not infrequently took over leadership, it was also the representatives of the developing countries. Their voice was by no means what it is today, but it was not negligible. In UN politics India had the weight of a great power. The pressure of the developing countries was such that during this period of so-called Western domination the switch was swiftly made from liberal internationalist assumptions about economic development to the priority for active assistance, minimal though it was at first. It was that same "Western dominated" UN which took the momentous step in 1955 of admitting all applicants for membership and thereby providing for the end of its own "domination." The admission of new members in 1955 was in

[5] For an authoritative account of the founding of NATO by one of its Canadian participants, see Escott Reid, *Time of Fear and Hope: The Making of the North Atlantic Treaty, 1947–1949* (Toronto: McClelland & Stewart, 1977).

fact a significant case when the resistance of the United States was overcome by a coalition of lesser powers.

When the UN in the mid-1950s moved into conflict resolution and peacekeeping, the United States played a constructive role that was far from dictatorial. It was not easy for Americans to acknowledge objectivity and neutrality as appropriate attributes of a UN that many regarded as a crusade against evil. As they were beginning, however, to grasp the paradoxes of mutual deterrence, Americans came to accept, tacitly at least, the inevitable constraints of the balance of power and the need to search for consensus. When the Suez crisis erupted, the United States used its weight as a great power should, but left the direction of the UN enterprise to others, accepting on pragmatic grounds the principle that the great powers should be excluded from peacekeeping. The United States did, of course, continue to supply the lifeblood. Economic projects could not get under way without American support, and the essential logistics for peacekeeping were usually supplied by the United States. The attitude of the majority was ambivalent. Prospective supporters of the UN Emergency Force (UNEF) in 1956, for example, wanted to be certain that this was not simply a United States scheme, but they also wanted to be sure that the United States was going to support it and thereby make it feasible.

Americans inevitably felt put upon and insufficiently appreciated. It was not surprising that Americans would assume a certain right to manage the UN, not only because they thought they were the ones who paid for it[6] but also because of their tendency to see it as the instrument for extending United States morality to a benighted world. Of course they saw it as an instrument to promote the kind of economic and social development that would strengthen United States security and prosperity, but the faith was strong that the whole "free world" would profit as well. Americans, however, had a way of taking upon themselves responsibility for world order. They would chide and pressure others to pay up and to do their duty by joining committees or leaping into breaches from Cyprus to Vietnam. The United States was not so much a dictator as a governess. Other countries' sense of responsibility for the communal effort was inevitably weakened.

The assumption that good allies should support American resolutions was a source of irritation, especially when these resolutions were sprung on the allies shortly after they had been leaked to the *New York Times* It was difficult to oppose United States proposals in disarmament negotiations for example, but those of whom collaboration was expected frequently saw the proposals on twenty-four hours' notice, with an explanation that they had been the subject of such protracted negotiation among the power bases in Washington there was no

---

[6] The conviction that the United States was paying the shot was partly illusion. The limitation on the gross United States contribution means that an American citizen pays less for the United Nations than does the Canadian or Swede—a fact even more notable in recent years when the United States contribution to aid programs has declined.

possibility of changing them. The issue of consultation among allies and associates in international institutions is, of course, full of paradoxes. None of the NATO allies ever has or ever will properly consult its associates. In any case, countries frequently prefer to complain about not having been consulted than to be consulted and thereby committed in advance. Like many other principles of international cooperation, consultation is better left undefined. If one takes a functional view of power one would have to recognize that there is inevitably differentiation in decision-making. It is wiser for the United States neither to offer nor expect communal decision-making in general terms, for it has to make decisions of its own. What matters is constant awareness of other interests and other perspectives.

What is most frustrating, especially for countries with responsible parliamentary systems, is that no one can speak for the United States in multilateral diplomacy. The division of powers in the United States constitutes, no doubt, a beautiful thing in the eye of the political philosopher, but it is self-indulgent. One must, however, recognize that there is no more hope of reforming the archaic United States Constitution than the more supple UN Charter. The disadvantages increase as the world moves into a period when multilateral negotiation through international organizations is becoming increasingly complex, increasingly crucial, and increasingly inseparable from domestic policies. To the exasperated foreigner it looks like another manifestation of the American conviction that the United States Constitution, United States legislation, and the will of Congress represent a superior level of sovereignty that is not negotiable. For the United States negotiator it provides a constant source of blackmail but also a grave handicap in bargaining.

If the United States was lacking in any kind of generosity it was moral generosity. Few people in the democratic world would fail to pay due credit to the Declaration of Independence and its beneficent influence on the world at large. The assumption, however, that the American way is the only way to the Kingdom is particularly resented by citizens of the Commonwealth—the un-American revolution. Americans have regarded themselves, with some justification, as the godparents of the colonial revolution. Roosevelt saw the pattern for empires in United States policy toward the Philippines. The more effective precedent, however, was set by those who fled the American Revolution to establish in Canada the principle of independence by peaceful means which created the Commonwealth. The leadership and inspiration for the UN's role in overseeing decolonization was provided largely by India.

It was the evolution of the Commonwealth by reason of its own dynamics which started the process, provided the precedent of evolution by consent, and established the formula for the most momentous peaceful transformation of power in history. One has only to look at the fate of French Indochina to comprehend what a difference this formula made. The extraordinary persistence of the Commonwealth as one of the most useful frameworks of consultation between the developing and developed countries is something for which Americans should be grateful because it supplements their own mission and takes some burden away from them. It was at the Commonwealth prime ministers' meeting in Jamaica, for example, where familiarity permits candor to an unusual degree, that the confrontation notable at the spring session of the General Assembly in 1975 began to move toward a concrete agenda at the thirtieth session of the General Assembly. The Commonwealth has been fulfilling its function effectively in the past few years, but like all institutions which seek to bridge gaps between races and continents its survival is highly desirable but not to be counted upon. It is, however, along with the Warsaw Pact, probably the only international organization that has never received either praise or encouragement from American statesmen.

The case of the Commonwealth is presented here not to air a grievance but to suggest that the jealous anxiety of Americans to preserve rather than to share moral leadership with others is a handicap in their effort to achieve leadership without hegemony. Americans talk a good deal, and with justification, about burden sharing, about the impossibility of their accepting all of the primary responsibility thrust upon them. A question always arises, however, whether Americans really want to share direction as well as burdens, whether they are content to let organizations like the Commonwealth, the Common Market, or even the Organization of American States (Southern Division), pursue and accomplish compatible aims without either interference or resentment. To do so will require a change in the attitudes not of isolationists and reactionaries but of the liberal internationalists, men whose consciousness of good encourages arrogance.

The new era for the UN—which really means the new era in world politics—poses particular problems for the United States, in the analysis both of the system and of the American role. The need of international organizations in which to tackle the inescapably complex economic and social issues in an interdependent world need not be restated. The United States could conceivably but very uncomfortably isolate itself, and the temptation to do so must be great when nothing the United States can do will escape denunciation. Public support for a strong UN policy does not seem to be forthcoming, but a major reason may be the widespread misperceptions of the UN. American scholars are performing a laudable service in searching for sensible approaches to international institutions, and one could only wish that they were more widely read by editors and politicians at home and abroad.

The message does seem to be getting through to the Carter administration. The dedication to the development of the system pronounced by the administration is encouraging, but even more encouraging is the fact that the constructive approach was notable before the 1976 elections and is presumably therefore not simply a partisan matter. There was no mistaking abroad President Nixon's dislike of the UN. It was probably necessary for Americans to go through the brief fling at Moynihanism just to show that it was counterproductive.

A changed American approach seems to date from the appointment of Governor Scranton rather than that of Andrew Young. Henry Kissinger was widely regarded as too Machiavellian to espouse anything so beautiful as the UN. What he did see, however, was that the UN, if it is to be healthy, must be a focus of *realpolitik*. Real is beautiful. His direct grappling with the issues of the Middle East and southern Africa may be regarded as acting outside the United Nations or as accepting the responsibility of one of the permanent members of the Security Council to work out solutions that could be submitted in the end for its approval. The secretary general himself has endorsed the second interpretation.[7] Kissinger's speech on the UN in Milwaukee of July 1975, followed shortly by more specific proposals to the General Assembly on the new international economic order, revealed a grasp of UN realities along with some of the old American loftiness. Such statements from American leaders are important in providing leadership elsewhere, for, particularly in Western Europe, the role of the UN system is far less well understood. The way in which Americans have resisted the temptation to a new isolationism after the dreadful experience of Vietnam has reassured and inspired its friends far beyond the narrow "Western camp." As *The Times* of London commented on December 13, 1975, "sinners who seek redemption have more right to speak on the subject than those who deny their sin." If the United States displays a determination to work through the UN system and international institutions in general, then others, even the Russians, have to play that game also.

There are problems of structure to be faced, of course, but first of all perceptions must be clarified. The so-called politicization of UN bodies, for example, requires historical perspective. At the time of San Francisco there was a good deal of enthusiasm for an Economic and Social Council and family that would consider its agenda in pure objectivity. Well, the UN has been a great learning experience. The proper connection between politics and economics is now accepted, at least in the abstract. There remains a strong case, however, against using the specialized agencies and strictly functional committees to fight the battles over Israel, South Africa, or Chile. The selection of victims is inequitable and the pragmatic value of universality is flouted. There is a good argument for making clear by precision boycotting or withholding of funds that results will not be achieved this way. There is, furthermore, evidence that third world countries are recognizing this fact of life. The charter can be interpreted as requiring due regard for the will of the majority, but it did not create a legislature.

Nonetheless, the United States is a late convert to universality. The cold war was often carried into the International Labor Organization (ILO) or the UN Educational, Scientific, and Cultural Organization (UNESCO). Henry Kissinger in Milwaukee warned that "those who seek to manipulate UN membership by procedural abuse may well inherit an empty shell." The procedural abuses by which

---

[7] Kurt Waldheim, address to the conference, "Canada and the United Nations in a Changing World," United Nations Association, Winnipeg, May 12, 1977.

the proper representatives of China were kept out of the UN set some nasty precedents. The apparent attempt by the United States to bargain membership of Vietnam for satisfaction on missing Americans was the kind of linkage rightly deplored when used by other members. Linkage is, of course, a tricky problem not to be dealt with in pious phrases. It is inherent in the whole North-South relationship, less in the nature of threats and deals than in inescapable expectations of favor or disfavor. Linking a refusal to support a UN conference on racism with objections to views on racism expressed by a General Assembly majority seems more defensible than threatening economic retaliation against those who fail to support a United States resolution. On the other hand, those who denounce United States economic imperialism in unrestrained tones ought not to expect benefits. There are no clear rules. The United States and the Western powers in general need patience, imagination, and above all a comprehension of the havoc their whims can wreak on lesser powers.

The "politicization" of UN bodies cannot always be blamed on the side that resorts to militant action. It is tragic that the United States should have allowed the fate of Israel to be linked so inextricably to its relations with the third world. No one has profited from this excessive politicization of an issue, least of all Israel. One cannot ignore the frustration of the anticolonialists over the failure of the United States to act boldly in fulfillment of a unanimous resolution of the Security Council ten years ago. They fail to see, it is true, the genuine idealism in United States support of Israel and regard it wrongly as a matter simply of cold war strategy and American politics. As for the notorious resolution equating Zionism with racism, Americans deserve some blame for escalating this into an issue that has undermined support for the UN in all Western countries. The real complaint against the resolution is that very few if any of the sponsors had the right to call the kettle black. Everyone is to some degree a racist. The leaders of Israel brought with their baggage from Europe attitudes toward Arabs that are more European or North American than Jewish. The Arab objection to Israel is that it is in their eyes a European colony imposed on them by great powers and permitted to spread by conquest. One does not have to agree with that interpretation to understand why the opposition to Israel is due to anticolonialism rather than anti-Semitism. The efforts of both the Ford and Carter administrations to see more clearly that there is right on both sides is heartening. By simply lowering the temperature the United States might produce a better climate for settlement or at least remove Palestine as a major obstacle to negotiations of supreme importance. It is inevitable in a lively democracy that political pressures will affect policy, but the stature of the United States is undermined when, for example, its position on Cyprus seems attributable to the greater attention Congress pays to the Greek than the Turkish vote. Legislatures in other countries are just as susceptible to domestic pressures. It is, however, the misfortune of the United States that its vote counts for more and its politics are so highly visible.

The popular perception of the UN as a failed world government must be corrected. The problem, of course, always has been that the perfervid defenders and malevolent critics have the same misunderstanding. They are concerned with structure rather than with function. What might correct this misunderstanding is the involvement of far more people in the functions for which the UN system exists. Fishermen, air travellers, and the executives of multinational corporations cry out for international regulation, even though they may at the same time deplore interference. However much one would like to live by the less exhausting principles of international free enterprise, there is no escaping the need for some kind of management. The difference, however, between management that is regulatory and what might be called international administration has to be borne carefully in mind, in order not to frighten off the free enterprisers or bury the UN Secretariat under a load no international institution could sustain. More precise calculation and fewer general slogans are required in determining exactly what it is advisable and possible to expect of the UN system.

A better perspective is gained by starting from the agenda rather than by concerning oneself primarily with the preservation or improvement of the structure. Roosevelt deliberately launched the UN with a conference dealing with the practical question of food. The United States was as much responsible as any country for seeing that agencies dealing with relief, international monetary and financial questions, and civil aviation were tackled before San Francisco. The UN in wartime had to be created in the abstract, but it was no Wilsonian philosopher's dream. Then as now there were things to be done, and institutions were devised or improvised to cope with them. The great powers started out with plans for a "World Council" to which the General Assembly and other bodies would be subordinate. The lesser powers insisted that this so-called World Council be limited in function to security, a specific purpose for which the great military powers might have special status. They argued against the hierarchical and for the functionalist principle according to which institutions for certain purposes should be run as much as possible by those with special interests in the subject. They opposed central control from the great powers in council, and there emerged a UN that is more a system or a constellation than a government.

Looking back on these provisions of the charter after three decades, one is impressed by the basic strength and resilience of the framework created. The checks and balances made necessary by the incipient confrontation among the great powers have prevented secessions. The lack of centralized direction encouraged organic growth that would have been stifled at birth by a more high-minded, all-embracing, and utopian charter. NATO and then the Warsaw Pact could take shape and by assuming major responsibility for security save the UN from an impossible burden. When the Economic and Social Council (ECOSOC) proved little more than a propaganda forum for the East-West debate, the developing countries established UNCTAD. To begin with there was an assumption that the three principal organs must create functional bodies and nominate the members. When the UN Atomic Energy Commission and the Commission on Conventional Disarmament, as set up by the main organs, failed to find solutions for the insoluble, the General Assembly created ever larger commissions, ending up with the total absurdity of a plenary committee to deal with disarmament. Rather than abandon the search, however, those principally responsible for disarmament—the members of NATO and the Warsaw Pact—created in Geneva, with UN facilities but without the strict laying on of hands, a body composed of representatives of the two opposing alliances, later joined by representatives of a "third force." The test was not its legitimacy but whether it worked. The world is not yet disarmed, but this body, composed to suit its task, has moved as far as the state of international politics would allow. The creation of international institutions is a continuing exploration. Some serve a temporary purpose only and some blossom into continuing institutions. When it became obvious that representatives of North and South had to sit at a table to bargain, the Conference on International Economic Cooperation (CIEC) was set up in Paris in 1975 with a composition arbitrarily but functionally and equitably selected. It made some progress on the agenda, but the subject, not the institution, thwarted agreement. The experiment was useful. Whether CIEC continues, reforms, or winds up will be determined by the requirements of the dialogue.

Nothing, of course, can prevent the General Assembly from surveying actions of such bodies and telling them what to do. Whether a body that performs a useful service is within or without the UN's writ need not be a primary consideration, although there is an important value to be kept in mind. The devising and negotiation of schemes must, in the UN as in national governments, take place in countless formal, informal, and usually ad hoc sessions of people appointed or self-appointed for the purpose. Unchecked proliferation, however, especially when the purpose is consistently that of evading the will of UN bodies, could in due course undermine and disparage the system.

From this perspective it can be argued that the UN, far from dying, has been in a period of extraordinary organic growth. There are countless new processes and new uses of established organs. Special conferences and sessions of the Assembly have opened up the major social issues of the time: population, pollution, and housing. The slow laboring to establish international regulations and international law has developed into one of the most ambitious projects in the history of man, the universal Law of the Sea Conference. That extraordinary body has itself been remarkably inventive of new procedures to reach consensus. Special interest groups like the Organization of Petroleum Exporting Countries (OPEC) or the Organization for Economic Cooperation and Development (OECD) spring up when they are needed. They have their special interests but they never have the field uncontested. They serve to channel international dialogue and rescue it from cacophony. Such organizations tend to be more conscious of the basic facts of interdependence than are their members singly, and more aware, therefore, that they cannot simply impose their will.

UN purists are somewhat unhappy. If one insists, however, on the need to reform the structure of the UN or on a UN mandate for all that is done in the world, one only strengthens the argument for its futility. Instead, concepts must be adjusted to recognize the values of the galaxy. The UN would collapse if it became too pretentious and assumed an overweening authority. International life is managed to a very large extent by private international bodies—grain exchanges and money exchanges, giant regulatory organizations, and corporations with resources far beyond that of the whole UN budget. What is needed is to incorporate a consciousness of these networks into the designs for world order rather than capture them for an international administration that is simply not mature enough to cope—and possibly never will be. There is an important and sufficiently dignified role of surveillance for the UN, with power of intervention to propose changes required in equity. The problem of world order is always in finding the appropriate equilibrium between organic growth and pollution.

This loose functional system that must now be accepted as the UN provides for the United States great opportunities, responsibilities, and some of the old temptations. The complexity of the agenda and the intricate and shifting balancing of power defy control by any power or group of powers, and yet firm hands are needed. The great powers must see that the UN is committed to restraint. Participation by the United States on almost every level and in almost every corner of the system would be hard to resist because it is still by far the strongest military and economic force in the world and its resources are the most multifarious. There might be something to be said, however, for resisting when possible and moving in when urged to do so.

How much has United States power or control changed in the new era? Its grip on bodies like the World Bank and IMF where it did exercise real hegemony could not remain undiluted and the United States administration has been adapting well to the shifts of power that have been taking place. The test, of course, will be whether Congress and business accept the policies that flow from the adjusted institutions. As for such agencies as UNESCO or the ILO, the United States retains the kind of "control" it has always had, a limited capacity to block because of the intimidating size of its contribution. The Security Council and the various bodies dealing with arms were never "controlled" by any one power. The United States now has to use its veto because majorities are harder to line up. Americans, however, are more sophisticated in the politics of consensus than they were when they thought of unconditional surrender. Voting power in the General Assembly has, of course, shifted. The superpowers are, however, moving back toward their 1945 consensus on the authority of the Security Council. Where the United States finds itself weak in the General Assembly is in the face of declaratory resolutions. These matter, of course, but their effectiveness is now determined less by the total score than by the breadth of their support. In any case, the United States still is in a position to determine the success or failure of most serious resolutions of substance by its participation or abstention. Here, too, they have a reluctant ally in the Soviets who do not approve of the General Assembly as a legislature either.

Manipulation is the name of the game in the present international system. Multilateral diplomacy is a nicer term, but the world will survive, one must acknowledge, only through an intricate pattern of brokerage. Americans are susceptible in such a predicament to the dream of the single computer, the direct-ing hand, when the infinite complexity of it all suggests that simple solution. The voice of the engineers, economists, and world federalists will be heard in the land—men who know the problems, are confident of their answers, and recognize their mission to manage the world for its own good. What others fear is, as the authors of *Agenda for Action* put it, "the oft-revealed interventionist and tech-nocratic positivist tendencies within American society."[8]

There are mixed feelings about the new crusade for human rights. There is a widespread opinion that it is high time that the West stood up for principles which are not just prejudices but which were hammered out over centuries and through many civilizations. This time the convictions of rightness in Washington seem less blinkered and there is a cautious approach to ways and means that reveals how much American policymakers have learned from experience. Still, one is always nervous about Americans when their eyes have seen the glory. Manipu-lation in the name of the Lord is more like hegemony than leadership. When a group of distinguished Americans, in presenting "A New US Policy Towards the UN"[9] speak of the need for "synchronized diplomacy," one pauses to wonder. "Responsible UN behavior" of a country is cited as a criterion for United States blessing, responsibility to be determined not by such things as the payment of debts but by the voting record on issues that the United States regards as salient. The United States has as good a right as any country to crusade for righteousness, not because of its own unblemished record but because of its capacity for self-correction. President Carter's note of humility will have to be sustained, how-ever. The West must bear in mind that although it is sensitive about the rights of the individual it has been somewhat careless of the rights of people en masse, when execution takes place by bomb, napalm, or an adjustment in the grain market.

There is a dilemma here that cannot just be blown away by rhetoric. Multi-lateral diplomacy does require something like "synchronized diplomacy." Bar-gains must be struck, payoffs arranged, and diverse causes linked if intricate mul-tilateral negotiations like the Law of the Sea Conference and the Tokyo Round of GATT are to be successfully concluded. This must be done not just to further the national interest but to lay the infrastructure of world order. A special responsi-bility for the institutions is expected of the United States because other major powers, Japan and the incoherent European Economic Community, for example, take a less serene approach. Americans are expected to be the champions of good causes even by those who denounce them. It is idle to pretend that the course between leading and imposing is easy to distinguish. There is no formula, just a prescription for eternal vigilance and infinite calculation.

Should the United States seek to act in the UN system as leader or partner of

[8] Overseas Development Council, *The U.S. and World Development: Agenda for Action 1976* (New York: Praeger, 1976) p. 31.
[9] *New York Times*, April 21, 1976.

the Western or industrialized powers and encourage greater coherence? If so, perhaps the allies should be encouraged at least to perform their historic UN role as a check and balance. An Atlantic Council of the United States working group on *The Future of the UN* calls for a "coalition of the willing." It was such a coalition that set up NATO and thereby rescued the UN from the burden of collective security; so there is a time and place for such action—but only in extremis. Such coalitions should be ad hoc and never so exclusive as to require members to avoid other coalitions. On certain precise issues the interests of NATO countries are either common or coincidental, but on other issues their interests are contrary. An Atlantic coalition on the law of the sea could well be denounced as a politicization of a functional conference. The continuing health of the UN depends not on the elimination of blocs but on a spreading pattern of blocs in constant formation, dissolution, or reformation. There are times and places for combined action or united fronts—in seeking a negotiating position in the Conference on International Economic Co-operation, for example, or in seeking uniform rules for the export of nuclear reactors and uranium. The call for a united Western front, however, is a counsel of despair, based usually on the dubious conviction that the second and third worlds, working as a team, have isolated the Christians.

The most promising feature at the moment is that everybody is so healthily disillusioned. In three decades the world has worked its way through most of the illusions about international organizations and come to see them as instruments and learned a great deal about how to use them. United States policy has been through many phases and has perhaps entered a new one, but the change can be overdramatized. Doing what comes naturally might be a better guide to policy than striking any of the familiar but meaningless postures—internationalism, isolationism, and hegemony. Mr. Earl C. Ravenal sees the key for the United States in "the concept of equanimity," explaining, "This is not an attitude of negligence or unconcern or rejection; it is an acceptance of situations and consequences."[10] There is much to be said for withdrawing from a too forward position, contemplating more and listening more, leaving initiatives to others whenever possible. United States policy in the UN will be more arduous than ever because it requires more suppleness. American power cannot be described in abstractions. It depends upon the effective application of various resources, including those of diplomacy. As for strengthening the UN, this can be done not by praising it as a charitable organization but by using it as the agenda requires without ever losing sight of the design being spun. One may, of course, be facing the failure of this century's grand effort to manage international institutions. There is no guarantee of success, although optimism is essential. There might be less danger of failure if there was less glib talk about success. What is "success"

[10] Earl C. Ravenal, "The Case for Strategic Disengagement," *Foreign Affairs* 51 (April 1973): 505–21.

in finding a "solution" for the gap between rich and poor nations for which the orators plead? The UN can save the world, if at all, by adjustments, improvements, and expedients. To provide the leadership it can hardly escape, the United States needs a steady hand, a clear head, a sense of humor, an unexcitable conscience, and equanimity. President Carter has set a good tone by his rejection of the apocalyptic style.

The International Protection
of Human Rights

DANA D. FISCHER

A moral commitment is not worth the paper it is *not* written on, according to an old quip. Even if true, it does not necessarily follow that written law will reinforce virtue. True or not, this conviction seems to characterize the human rights policies of the United Nations over the last thirty years. Resistance to this approach has rested on a slight but important variation on the relationship between moral commitment and law. This is the desire on the part of states to make the behavior of others predictable while keeping maximum freedom for themselves. The UN practice in human rights illustrates the push and pull of this basic paradox in the behavior of states.

With few exceptions, prior to 1945, there was universal acceptance of the view that how a state treated its citizens was its own concern. The individual, alone or collectively, was considered merely an object, not a subject of international law. All of this followed from the broader assumption that international law was a law between states and that consequently states were its sole subjects. Traditionally, only the state of which an individual was a national could sue in an international court or protest through diplomatic channels. It was not a question of the protection of human rights. Injury to a national was deemed an injury to his state; hence it was the state and not the individual that enjoyed the right of protection. The individual injured by his own state was without recourse because no other state could press his claim. When speaking of the protection of human rights, one is considering the position of the individual and efforts on the part of the UN and other intergovernmental organizations (IGOs) to fashion ways in which he can proceed directly or through an international agency, possibly even against his own state.

The international protection of human rights means a new source of rights for the individual with legal remedies against their violation. Over the last thirty years the UN has been responsible for a steady growth of international law and institutions designed to articulate and protect these rights.[1] The charter itself lists the promotion of human rights among the major purposes of the organization. The Universal Declaration of Human Rights, adopted in 1948 with little opposition by a still Western-dominated General Assembly, spells out more specifically what the member states promised to promote in the charter. The declaration, however, is not a treaty and contains no implementation machinery.

Since the declaration, a rather imposing network of UN sponsored treaties has emerged. These treaties deal with particular problems, such as genocide, forced labor, abolition of slavery, protection of stateless persons, refugees, racial discrimination, and apartheid. Of greatest moment are the Covenant on Civil and Political Rights and the Covenant on Economic, Social and Cultural Rights. Together, these two documents have translated the general principles proclaimed in the declaration into precise legal language with detailed elaborations of exceptions, limitations, and restrictions.

The remedies against violation of the rights enumerated in the entire arsenal of declarations and treaties are like ecclesiastical doctrine in that the more rigid and demanding they become, the more the faithful leave the fold. The implementation procedures generally impose on states the duty to report compliance but not the duty to remedy violations.

In a few instances, the individual has had direct or indirect access to the international arena. Under the Convention on Racial Discrimination, complaints from individuals and nongovernmental organizations (NGOs) are allowed. Under procedures in effect since 1970, the Human Rights Commission may receive complaints from individuals and groups through the Subcommission on Prevention of Discrimination and Protection of Minorities. This involves a process of confidential hearings on evidence of gross and continuing violations of human rights. Only through this process can the UN launch a study or investigation without permission of the country involved. The most glaring weakness is that the confidentiality of the procedure often serves to protect the worst violators. For instance, the 1977 session of the commission was distinguished by a refusal to take any action on the reported massacres in Uganda, a state represented on the commission.

The two covenants have come into force largely because of their extremely weak implementation procedures. The primary method is government reporting of measures taken in compliance with the treaties. Each covenant has its own reporting system. The Covenant on Economic, Social and Cultural Rights requires the submission of state reports to the Economic and Social Council and

---

[1] Space does not permit discussion of the non-UN regional efforts to protect human rights. The European Convention for the Protection of Human Rights and Fundamental Freedoms is the most important. The more recent American Convention on Human Rights is closely modeled on the European treaty and the institutions it establishes to implement it.

through it to the Commission on Human Rights. The Covenant on Civil and Political Rights establishes a separate body, the Human Rights Committee, whose function is to "study" the reports submitted by the parties and make "general comments" to the states regarding their reports. This body may be able to provide some leadership and supervision, but it is mandated to be no more than a fact finder, a source of good offices, and a conciliator. The Covenant on Civil and Political Rights does not permit one state to complain about violations in a second state unless the latter agrees. Acceptance of complaints from individuals and groups claiming violations is also optional and contained in a separate protocol requiring special ratification.

Clearly, UN efforts to protect human rights contain serious flaws centering on the weakness or lack of implementation procedures. On the other hand, before 1945 there was no international system whatsoever for the protection of human rights. The individual was flatly denied recognition as a subject of international law—an entity with rights as well as duties. Such a denial would be more equivocal today, a denial in fact if not in law and followed by hundreds of footnotes for which the UN sponsored efforts would be partly responsible.

United States Policy

Despite early interest and leadership, the United States has largely remained outside the international human rights program. Until recently it has been for this country a peripheral aspect of its UN activities, not taken very seriously and the responsibility of officials remote from the seats of power and the major concerns of United States foreign policy. This attitude is clearly antithetical to the Carter administration. At the outset, it was announced that human rights considerations would play an integral part in the formulation of foreign policy, and an inadequate bureaucracy was modified to make that possible.

Until recently, a common lament was that the State Department did not give human rights issues the professional attention and resources commensurate with their growing importance. Indeed, there is enough evidence to suggest that the executive branch dealt with human rights matters largely on an ad hoc basis.[2] In theory, this situation was changed by the International Security Assistance and Arms Control Act of 1976, which provided for the creation of a new human rights bureaucracy in the State Department and required the government to report publicly on human rights conditions in states receiving United States military aid and on what the United States is doing to improve them. The first report was made in the last days of the Ford administration, but the Carter administration has expanded the policy and provided a bureaucracy to implement it.

The argument that prevailed in the final formulation of the 1976 act was best

---

[2] Thomas Burgenthal, "International Human Rights: U.S. Policy and Priorities," *Virginia Journal of International Law* 14 (Summer 1974): 611, 615.

stated by Tom J. Farer. He reasoned: "New offices unencumbered by hostile precedent and linked to formerly unrepresented constituencies are more promising avenues of reform, particularly when one takes into account the bureaucratic log-rolling which is such an important determinant of national policy. Offices exclusively concerned with the human rights implications of national security policy will claim, and surely obtain, some piece of the decisional pie."[3] In the long run, this will probably be true.

The new office is headed by a coordinator for human rights and humanitarian affairs and situated directly under the deputy secretary of state. It is intended that the coordinator operate on a policy level, and the resources equivalent to an assistant secretary make this technically possible. In the first year of the Carter administration, however, the new office has constantly battled with the old bureaucratic establishment whose reaction to the new human rights policy seems to range from bemusement to hostility.

Routine consideration of the human rights implications of a policy is made possible by the full- or part-time presence of human rights officers in all the regional and functional bureaus of the State Department and at some level of every United States embassy. In April 1977 the Interagency Committee on Human Rights and Foreign Assistance was established and chaired by the deputy secretary of state. Loan applications from international banks in which the United States is represented, bilateral United States economic aid programs, and the United States Export-Import Bank, which finances the sale of American equipment abroad, fall under the human rights review process of this body. The administration is also reviewing applications for licences to export weapons even when no government financing is involved in the sales. In addition to the machinery activated or created by the Carter administration, the Office of Human Rights Affairs in the Bureau of International Organization continues to exist, and since 1974 there has been an assistant legal advisor for human rights.

Concern for human rights was a primary theme in President Carter's UN address in March 1977, in which he made several concrete proposals. He revived the idea of a UN high commissioner for human rights and pledged to seek the ratification of the Genocide Convention, the Racial Discrimination Convention, and the two human rights covenants. He also proposed to return the UN Human Rights Division to New York from Geneva and back to the scrutiny of the international press and interested NGOs and to strengthen the Human Rights Commission.

Under these new circumstances, what can the United States realistically expect the UN to accomplish in the field of human rights, and what kind of United States policy will advance this effort? First, any expectations must be modest. Even an aggressive United States policy must begin with several givens that are

---

[3] Tom J. Farer, "United States Foreign Policy and the Protection of Human Rights: Observations and Proposals," *Virginia Journal of International Law* 14 (Summer 1974): 623, 645.

unlikely to change in the future and will be difficult even to modify. The most obvious is the fact that the vast majority of member states cannot be considered free societies in the sense that their citizens enjoy political and civil rights. This suggests a continuing conflict between the two quite different approaches to human rights embodied in the covenants. The sets of political and civil rights attach themselves to the individual and essentially constitute prohibitions on government. The economic, social, and cultural rights are more collective in nature and require government action. Although the United States has traditionally associated human rights with political rights, the majority of the member states will place hope of an improved standard of living over fear of a lack of freedom. They will have less concern for political representation than for honesty, stability, and efficiency in government.

Another given is that President Carter's proposals must be approved by the General Assembly, whose majority now opposes any autonomous human rights body and, with a few notable exceptions, seeks to avoid publicity on rights violations. This all portends a continuation of the much discussed double standard restricting the existing machinery to those issues in which the majority has a direct political interest.

Finally, one can expect an escalation of doublethink in the human rights questions as a result of the ratification of the covenants by the Soviet bloc. The treaties have enough escape clauses to legitimize what would clearly be a violation. For example, Article 12 of the Covenant on Civil and Political Rights has been used to restrict emigration for reasons of "national security" and "public order."

The time is long past when the United States could advance a position in the UN and expect blind acceptance by others. The alternative, however, need not be powerlessness. It has been argued that the United States should begin to think of its objectives in the UN as much in terms of shaping the agenda for action as in settling the problems themselves in the world body.[4] This would mean a human rights policy geared to small gains over the long run.

The United States should continue to improve the effectiveness of its representatives on the Human Rights Commission. The Carter appointee to the 1977 session appears to have done quite well in broadening the debate beyond South Africa, Israel, and Chile, if not in securing action on important issues. The goal should be to place human rights issues in a routine, bureaucratic structure that would allow the commission to focus on a less grievous offense without its being perceived as an unfriendly act.

Some bargaining chips ought to be expended for support in shoring up the complaint procedures available to the Human Rights Commission. Since 1970, under the new procedures, a subgroup of the commission reviews thousands of rights complaints from individuals and NGOs to spot a "consistent pattern of

[4] Charles William Maynes, "A U.N. Policy for the Next Administration," *Foreign Affairs* 54 (July 1976): 804, 812.

gross and reliably attested violations." The subgroup then forwards its confidential findings to a subcommission. Eventually, after months and even years of review and updating, some of the findings reach the commission itself, which can call for an official inquiry, although it has never done so. Clearly, many states do not object to the fact that the commission is hamstrung by a maze of procedural obstacles. However, the United States should work to establish a "due process" standard for handling individual and group complaints as well as procedures to guide investigations that would protect both sides and thus discourage politicization. As it now stands, a petitioner is told the UN has received his complaint but does not know whether it is being considered. If it is rejected, the petitioner is not told when or for what reason. The International League for Human Rights has proposed that the United States should work for improvements like supplying complainants with copies of the government's reply, providing a hearing procedure for complainants, ensuring that supplementary material on complaints is appended to existing complaints and not treated as a new complaint requiring a great loss of time, requiring action on complaints within a reasonable period, and informing the complainant of action taken on the complaint.[5]

Perseverance by a major power on procedural issues could well be successful in the long run. In the immediate future, however, the challenge may be simply to preserve the existing imperfect procedures. The entry into force of the covenants appears to have inspired a movement by the Eastern European bloc to eliminate the procedures because, it is argued, the covenants supplant them. The United States must resist these efforts. The covenants cannot replace the complaint procedures for two very good reasons: (1) only ratifying states are bound, not all member states of the United Nations and (2) the Optional Protocol, allowing for petitions from individuals, has been accepted by only a few states.

The escalation of doublethink in human rights by the Soviet bloc may well serve an active United States human rights policy in the UN. Russell Baker of the *New York Times* observed that the USSR has handed Carter the human rights championship of the world by accepting his definition and thereby putting themselves in the weaker position. They could have distinguished political from economic and social rights, and individual from collective rights, but they did not. One of the assistant legal advisors of the State Department has termed it "knee-jerk stupidity" for the USSR to have chosen a strategy that requires it to prove that the West's record on human rights is worse than the East's. At the very least, it provides a rich source of debating points for the United States. But a UN policy actively searching for ways to build bridges to moderate elements in the third world should be able to parley it into something more.

---

[5] Roberta Cohen, "Recommendations for United States Policy at the U.N. in the Human Rights Field" (Paper presented at the Human Rights Committee, Confeerence of United Nations Representatives, Council of Organizations, UNA-USA, March 31, 1977).

The search for common ground on human rights issues in Africa is by no means hopeless. For some time now, several African leaders have demonstrated interest in human rights in general and a particular contempt for the situation in Uganda. The meeting of the Commonwealth states in London during June 1977 may well prove to be a turning point. For the first time, thirteen African heads of state or their representatives openly discussed the status of human rights in another African country at an international forum and publicly passed a harsh judgment on a colleague. In addition to this important development, it seems possible that the United States for the first time may be in a position to compete for the respect and friendship of the African states as a result of the Carter-Young policy in southern Africa. Until the first months of the Carter administration, it would have been difficult to find a knowledgeable observer inside or outside the diplomatic community who could conceive of anything but a bloodbath sooner or later in sorting out the issues related to majority rule in southern Africa. It now appears at least a possibility that a nonviolent resolution could evolve. A twofold dividend would be the opportunity to reduce the intensity and frequency of confrontations between the West and the third world and the possibility that a less rancorous environment would allow progress on other issues as well.

However, any leadership the United States wishes to exercise in the human rights area will be undercut if it does not ratify the UN sponsored treaties. The Carter administration's increased concern with human rights has thus far resulted largely in either unilateral action or international initiatives outside the UN. Offending countries have been put on notice that human rights violations will cost them something. It is true that human rights restrictions in United States law obliquely tie the United States to the international protection of human rights by reference to "internationally recognized rights." However, those same restrictions reflect the United States's preference for political over social and economic rights in international dealings. Strategically, it would seem wise for the United States to take care not to appear to be imposing American values when raising human rights issues with other countries whether bilaterally or in the UN system and to rely instead on international standards set forth in the human rights covenants.

Securing United States adherence to the treaties has been a great problem in the past and continues to be obstructed by a sizeable number of senators. The original resistance in the early 1950s coalesced around Senator Bricker's attacks on the human rights conventions the UN had already adopted and the proposed Covenant on Human Rights that seemed at the time to be nearing completion.

Between 1952 and 1957, there were various efforts to amend the United States Constitution with respect to the making and effects of treaties and other international agreements. Although the wording of the proposals varied widely over the years, the psychology behind the movement that continues to have a dampening effect on the acceptance of human rights treaties is best illustrated by the 1952 version of the so-called Bricker amendment. It provided that "no treaty or executive agreement shall be made respecting the rights of citizens of the United States protected by this Constitution" and that "no treaty or executive agreement shall vest in any international organization or in any foreign power any of the legislative, executive or judicial powers vested by this Constitution in the Congress, the President, and in the courts of the United States respectively."

To avert a constitutional amendment, Secretary of State John Foster Dulles made a commitment on behalf of the Eisenhower administration to withdraw the United States from participation in human rights treaty-making. A policy statement to this effect was formally communicated to the UN. Although this has long since ceased being United States policy, the attitude that supported it has left a lasting mark. Particularly in recent years, Congress has been keenly interested in human rights but the enthusiasm has favored cutting off assistance rather than in adhering to treaties.

Objections to accepting international human rights obligations via treaty have ranged from frivolous to reasonable concerns about conflicts with United States law that could be handled by reservations. One long-standing objection is that a state's treatment of its nationals is a matter of domestic jurisdiction. For instance, the American Bar Association maintained for many years with particular reference to the Genocide Convention that the definition of crime and presciption of punishment was a purely domestic concern and therefore outside the treaty-making power. There have been fears that the treaties would authorize what the Constitution prohibits even though the Supreme Court has always upheld the Constitution when there was a conflict. The dominant view in the UN reflected in some of the treaties that human rights include those of an economic, social, and cultural character have inspired charges of "socialism by treaty." Another theme concerns interference of a treaty with the division of powers between the states and the federal government—that is, obligating the federal government in an area constitutionally reserved to the states.

None of the four treaties cited in President Carter's UN address will be approved easily by the Senate. The Genocide Convention has been in various stages of oblivion since President Truman signed it in 1948. This treaty provides that genocide, whether committed during peace or war, is a crime under international law. Genocide is defined as the commission of certain enumerated acts "with intent to destroy, in whole or in part, a national, ethnical, racial or religious group, as such." To be guilty of the crime of genocide, an individual must have committed one of the specified acts with the specific *intent* of destroying, in whole or in part, one of the covered groups. With three understandings and a declaration (as opposed to reservations) attached, the treaty will come before the Senate once again sometime in 1978. The prospects look more hopeful since the American Bar Association reversed its previous position in 1976 and now supports adherence. It is believed that there are sufficient votes to break the inevitable filibuster, but it is not at all certain that the necessary two-thirds can be mustered to ensure passage.

Although the International Convention on the Elimination of All Forms of Racial Discrimination was signed in 1966, the administration did not even bother to send it to the Senate largely because there had been no agreement on the Genocide Convention. This treaty prohibits racial discrimination, which it defines as "any distinction, exclusion, restriction or preference based on race, colour, descent, or national or ethnic origin" having the purpose or effect of "nullifying or impairing the recognition, enjoyment or exercise, on an equal footing, of human rights and fundamental freedoms in the political, economic, social, cultural or any other field of public life." A ratifying state is obligated to enact whatever laws are necessary to ensure nondiscrimination in the exercise and enjoyment of fundamental human rights listed in the treaty.

Unlike the Genocide Convention, some parts of this treaty do conflict with the United States Constitution. For instance, characterizing the dissemination of ideas advocating racial superiority as a criminal offense conflicts with the constitutional right of free speech. Difficulties of this kind can be handled by reservations. However, resistance to the treaty will be vigorous. The fact that the two-thirds vote required for ratification of treaties is an even greater hurdle than the simple majorities necessary for civil rights legislation does not harbinger well for ratification.

The kind of resistance encountered by the Genocide Convention and anticipated for the Racial Convention suggests trouble ahead for the covenants. Getting acceptance of the Covenant on Civil and Political Rights will be difficult enough even though the rights covered by the treaty are attuned to those guaranteed in the United States Constitution. Problems with the concept of economic and social rights will be formidable. The Constitution is silent on economic and social rights. In the American tradition the right to life has meant the right to the protection of a policeman, not to the services of a physician. Nevertheless, it is true that with the coming of Medicare and Medicaid and the proliferation of federal and state social welfare legislation, the whole tenor of the Covenant on Economic, Social and Cultural Rights is becoming more palatable to Americans than it would have been only a generation ago when the drafting began.

The Office of the Legal Advisor of the State Department has scrutinized the covenants, and any specific conflicts with United States law have been covered by draft reservations. It is a matter of education now on a scale so imposing that it is highly unlikely that the Carter administration will see the covenants ratified.

The long-term costs to the United States in not ratifying the human rights treaties in general and especially the covenants are not widely understood. The various treaties have been seen as designed for other states. Even those who have strongly favored adherence have often seen ratification more in terms of an encouragement to other less virtuous states or perhaps as providing a justification for intervention in the affairs of a violating state. As long as these are perceived to be the main advantages, the costs of nonadherence are rather easily absorbed. The far more serious cost is that the United States is prevented from playing a role in the interpretation and application of the treaties.

The Genocide Convention was directly inspired by the terrible events during World War II, and adherence is often seen as a purely symbolic act for this reason. Since 1965, however, at least five instances of genocide or massive ethnic killings bordering on genocide have occurred—in Indonesia against the Chinese in 1965, in Nigeria against the Ibos in 1968, in Pakistan against the Bengalis in 1971, in Burundi against the Hutus in 1972, and in Iraq against the Kurds since 1975. Pakistan and Iraq have adhered to the Genocide Convention. For all practical purposes, the treaty leaves the punishment of offenders to national courts. Although a government practicing genocide will not try or extradite one of its nationals accused of genocide, a successor government might well take such action. Even though successor governments have occasionally done so voluntarily, a widely accepted treaty obligation is harder to ignore. As a state that did not ratify the treaty the United States is in no position to exert pressure in this direction.

Not ratifying the Racial Convention is far more serious from the point of view of the development of human rights law. The Committee on the Elimination of Racial Discrimination that enforces the treaty has more extensive powers than those the Covenant on Civil and Political Rights confers on the Human Rights Committee. In existence since 1970, the committee consists of eighteen individuals elected to serve in their personal capacity by the states that are parties to the treaty. In the course of reviewing the reports of signatory states on measures taken to comply with the treaty, the committee has made formal and informal rulings interpreting the convention, thereby building up a substantial body of law bearing on the meaning of the convention. As Thomas Burgenthal has pointed out, a majority of the experts sitting on the committee come from states more inclined to take strong positions on racial discrimination issues, but they lack a comparable enthusiasm when it comes to enforcing civil and political rights. These very states predominate among those that have ratified the Covenant on Civil and Political Rights and therefore will control the Human Rights Committee.[6]

The Human Rights Committee was established in September 1976, and its first two sessions in the spring and summer of 1977 have been dominated by procedural matters. It is within this body that the covenant will be interpreted. The fact that the United States is not represented means one more arena where

[6] Thomas Burgenthal, "Human Rights Covenants Become Law: So What?" *American Society of International Law Proceedings* (1976), pp. 97, 99.

Americans will be excluded from shaping the global human rights law of the future.

Conclusion

There is an abiding skepticism about the viability of making a commitment to human rights a fundamental tenet of United States foreign policy. It has inspired consternation among friends and foes alike. Friends invoke images of Woodrow Wilson and a foreign policy founded on evangelical didacticism. Foes charge that to press human rights issues is to declare ideological war with serious consequences for détente, including most seriously a future arms limitation agreement. Efforts to internationalize an activist human rights policy through the various UN institutions are criticized because of the belief that there is no connection between policy and action in bodies like the Human Rights Commission where nearly three-fourths of the member states charged with trying to improve human rights conditions in the world are themselves accused of violating the rights of their citizens.

The claim that the present place of human rights in United States foreign policy is the spiritual descendant of Wilson's crusade to make the world safe for democracy overlooks some important changes in the international system. Louis Henkin has described the most fundamental difference between 1920 and the present: "The existence of the United Nations, the language of the Charter and its dissemination among all peoples, the adoption and invocation of the Declaration and mountains of documents and years of discussion have made human rights a subject of international concern, and indelibly established human rights in the aspirations of peoples, even in the consciences of governments. Governments may continue to claim that how they treat their inhabitants is of concern to them alone, increasingly it is a losing claim with little hope that it will prevail in politics if not in law."[7] Once an idea commands such attention, it cannot be delegitimized, although it may appear to falter in the often self-serving rhetoric so common in international forums.

Clearly, it is of major importance that a great power now pursue an active human rights policy. Up to a certain point, human rights are important because the president of the United States defines them as such. Only a great power cultivates a network of foreign relations of sufficient intricacy and magnitude for a commitment to give human rights a higher priority to make any difference for a significant number of states.

Some blame an uncomfortable automobile trip on Detroit, some on a poor road surface. It all depends on how one sees it, and one should not underestimate the alacrity with which perspectives have been radically altered within the

[7] Louis Henkin, "The United Nations and Human Rights," *International Organization* 19 (Summer 1965): 504, 506.

forum of the UN system. Quite a few ideas, like the 200 mile economic zone, have been considered to be borderline madness by many states at first, but have achieved legitimacy rather quickly. The idea of international accountability for the observance of human rights standards has been in the pipeline for some time without much attention from the United States. The active support of a member state as important and powerful as the United States might well exert a surprising influence on its progress.

The United Nations and Political Conflict: A Mirror, Amplifier, or Regulator?

HAROLD K. JACOBSON

Does the United Nations inhibit, moderate, and resolve international political conflicts, or does it promote and exacerbate them? This is the central question of the renewed and sometimes strident debate within the United States about the role and the utility of the UN. This debate has been provoked by actions that have been taken within the UN, particularly those concerning the Middle East conflict between Israel and the Arab states, decolonization and policies toward the white regimes in southern Africa, and the creation of a new international economic order.

In 1975 the General Assembly adopted a resolution determining that Zionism was "a form of racism and racial discrimination."[1] This was done in the context of evolving a program for the Decade for Action to Combat Racism and Racial Discrimination, the purpose of which is the "total and unconditional elimination of racism, racial discrimination and *apartheid*."[2] The General Assembly reaffirmed the inalienable rights of the Palestinian peoples to self-determination, to national independence and sovereignty, and to return to their homes and property. It also established a committee to make recommendations for implementing these rights and called for inviting the Palestine Liberation Organization to participate "on an equal footing" in any deliberations or conferences on the Middle East.[3]

---

[1] UN, General Assembly, 30th Session, *Elimination of all Forms of Racial Discrimination* (Resolution 3379[XXX]), November 10, 1975.

[2] UN, General Assembly, 30th Session, *Implementation of the Programme for the Decade for Action to Combat Racism and Racial Discrimination* (Resolution 3377[XXX]), November 10, 1975.

[3] UN, General Assembly, 30th Session, *Invitation of the Palestinian Liberation Organization to Participate in the Efforts for Peace in the Middle East* (Resolution 3375[XXX]), November 10, 1975.

The General Assembly maintained its pressure against Southern Rhodesia and South Africa by adopting a resolution strongly condemning "the actions of those states and foreign economic and other interests which continue to collaborate with the racist régime of South Africa." It strongly urged "the main trading partners of South Africa, particularly the United Kingdom of Great Britain and Northern Ireland, the United States of America, France, the Federal Republic of Germany, Japan and Italy, to cease collaboration with the racist régime of South Africa and to co-operate with the United Nations in its efforts to eradicate *apartheid*."[4]

Finally, the General Assembly continued in 1975 to endorse the basic concepts of the Charter of Economic Rights and Duties of States and of the Program of Action on the Establishment of a New International Economic Order that had been adopted the previous year. In these documents the General Assembly asserted the right of states to nationalize foreign property and to use their own national laws rather than international law as the standard for action and compensation. It also endorsed both the right of states to collaborate in organizations of primary commodity producers and the concept of indexing the prices of primary products to those of manufactured goods.

These and other concepts in the charter and the program of action were anathema to the United States, which voted against the adoption of the above resolutions and many others as well. In fact, as shown in figure 1, while the United States voted with the winning side on roll call votes roughly two-thirds of the time in the first sessions of the General Assembly, by the 1970s (from the twenty-fifth session on) this proportion had dropped to about one-third. Meanwhile, the positions of the USSR and the United States relative to the majority within the General Assembly had reversed. The USSR usually voted against the majority in the early years of the UN, but by the 1970s it was voting with the majority in about two-thirds of the roll call votes.

Consequently, the United States began to feel itself besieged within the UN. Some United States policymakers and some segments of the public began to feel that the UN tended to fuel international political conflicts rather than contribute to their solution. Individuals wondered whether the UN could play any role in working toward a world order acceptable to the United States. Although the minority favoring United States withdrawal from the UN did not increase, dissatisfaction with the UN's performance grew substantially, and numerous suggestions were made to reform the UN and to revise United States policies toward it.

It is certainly appropriate to evaluate the UN in terms of its relationship to international political conflicts. According to its charter, one of the UN's principal functions is to maintain international peace and security and to prevent and remove threats to the peace. However, a proper evaluation ought not to be based

---

[4] UN, General Assembly, 30th Session, *Policies of Apartheid of the Government of South Africa* (Resolution 3411 G [XXX]), December 10, 1975.

FIGURE 1

The Position of the United States and The USSR in Relation to the Winning Side of Roll Call Votes of the General Assembly

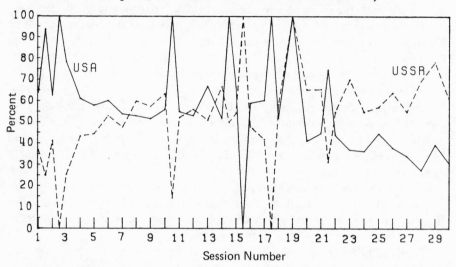

solely on an examination of whether particular resolutions of the General Assembly accorded with the prevailing United States policies, but on an appreciation of the role of conflict in society and on a clear understanding both of the nature of the UN as a political institution and of its place in the global political system.

Conflict and Political Institutions

In the sense of disagreement and struggle over the distribution of status, power, wealth, scarce resources, and other values, conflict is present in all human relations; thus, it is inherent in international politics. Moreover, one would not want to eliminate conflict for it provides the dynamic force for social change and, through social change, for human betterment. It is both possible and desirable, however, to limit the means by which conflict is pursued, and one instinctively judges political systems according to the extent to which they have achieved the goal of limiting the violence and coercion associated with conflict.

Different political systems have had varying success in dealing with conflict. By suppressing conflict, some have successfully maintained order occasionally for long periods, but the repressed forces have eventually erupted, often with great violence and chaotic results. Conflicts have been managed most successfully in loosely structured and pluralistic political systems that allow conflict to be expressed among a variety of contenders in a variety of places. Such systems have concentrated on defining the appropriate means of pursuing conflict, rather than on eliminating it, and by allowing conflict to be openly expressed they have hoped that the result would be many crosscutting cleavages instead of the polarization of divisions. The fluidity of such political systems has facilitated regular change at a moderate pace and has avoided the cataclysms endemic to more repressive systems. In the latter, those who dissent from particular policies are led to see the overthrow of the whole system as the only means of attaining their specific goals; thus, individuals with diverse grievances are aided and perhaps even forced to unite in revolution.

Of course, the societal context in which political institutions exist influences their ability to restrain the violence and coercion associated with conflicts, to channel their energy in constructive directions, and to settle conflicts authoritatively and with perceived legitimacy. The success of political institutions in managing conflicts depends on the development and maintenance of a widely shared commitment to some common goal or goals. At a minimum there must be a determination to preserve the political system. Divisions within society can be either deep and polarized or shallow and dispersed; clearly, the task for political institutions of managing conflict is considerably easier in the latter case.

The prevalence of political conflict in the UN should not be surprising. Successfully functioning political institutions characteristically mirror to some extent the conflicts in the societies of which they are a part. Since sharp political conflicts undeniably exist in the world society, a proper evaluation of the UN would probe its contribution to and its potential for the management of conflict. One then asks whether the UN has helped limit the violence and coercion associated with conflict, helped channel conflict in constructive directions, and helped achieve accepted solutions to conflict. Regardless of its record, what is the potential of the UN as a political institution to contribute to the management of conflict? United States policies toward the UN and toward the issues that the UN addresses must be considered because, as its most influential participant, what the United States does inevitably affects what happens within the UN.

The UN in the Global Political System

As a political institution embracing almost every state and empowered by its comprehensive mandate to consider virtually any issue, the UN occupies a unique position. Its position in the world is similar but not analogous to that of national governments within states. Understanding the differences between the UN and a national government is crucial to understanding what the United Nations might be expected to accomplish.

Unlike national governments, the UN has very little autonomy. For instance, it depends on the assessed and voluntary contributions of member states for its funds. Even if a state fails to pay its assessed contributions it loses no more than its right to vote in the General Assembly. Also, military forces are available to the UN only if member states assign them to the world institution. The UN must depend on the voluntary cooperation of its member states to achieve its purposes. In contrast, national government can tax individuals and has the means to compel compliance with its decisions.

Another major difference between the UN and a national government is that the latter is generally only one of several established political institutions. Political systems within states generally include interest groups, political parties, and courts, as well as legislative and executive bodies, while the UN, despite its several principal organs and substantial bureaucracy, stands alone within the global political system. This fact particularly influences the raising and defining of political issues, since there are no global institutions truly analogous to national interest groups and political parties.

Because of these fundamental differences the United Nations should not be expected to contribute to the management of international political conflict in the same way that a government contributes to the management of internal national political conflicts. Normally, the UN can merely propose solutions and recommend that national governments take particular actions. Since the global political system does not contain true counterparts to national interest groups and political parties, activities of the type that would occur in these settings frequently occur in the UN, it being a conveniently available forum. Activities carried on within interest groups and political parties often have a tendency toward hyperbole. The fact that UN resolutions lack binding consequences allows or perhaps even encourages this tendency to become operative.

The role of the UN is also molded by the doctrine of sovereignty, the fundamental principle on which the contemporary global political system is organized. Sovereignty postulates that each national government has supreme authority for the internal and external affairs of the state. Given this principle, membership in international governmental organizations like the UN must be confined to states, and it is difficult if not impossible to devise an acceptable basis of representation other than to accord one vote to each sovereign state. Formal arrangements can be devised to skew influence—for example, by requiring that majorities include all or a number of the more powerful states or by reserving certain categories of decisions to organs containing disproportionate numbers of the larger and more powerful states. Such arrangements, however, tend to gain broad acceptance only when the more powerful states make them a condition of their committing substantial resources to the institution. Without the promised resources, the smaller and less powerful states see little to gain by relinquishing their voices and votes.

Although other outcomes might have been possible, the General Assembly, in which each member state has one vote, has clearly become the most salient organ of the UN. Regardless of which other organs of the UN may deal with an international political conflict, the General Assembly is certain to become involved and, once involved, its role tends to overshadow that of the other organs. The prominence of the General Assembly means that the most visible decisions of the UN are made on the basis of one vote for each member state.

As a consequence of decolonization, the creation of new states, and their admission to membership, the composition of the UN and of the General Assembly has changed sharply since the organization's formation. Table 1 illus-

TABLE 1

The Composition of the UN by Geographical Area

	1946		1976	
	No. of Countries	% of Total	No. of Countries	% of Total
Africa	4	7.8	49	33.3
Americas	22	43.1	29	19.7
Asia	8	15.7	33	22.5
Eastern Europe	6	11.8	11	7.5
Western Europe	9	17.7	20	13.6
Oceania	2	3.9	5	3.4
Total	51	100.0	147	100.0

trates the dimensions of this change by grouping the UN's members in geographical categories and comparing the membership in 1946 when the General Assembly opened its first session to the membership at the end of 1976 upon the recess of its thirty-first session. These categories portray the political texture of the General Assembly only in the most general way: they include South Africa with all other African states, both north and south of the Sahara, Israel in Asia along with the Arab states of the Middle East, Japan in Asia despite its high level of economic development and membership in such bodies as the Organization for Economic Cooperation and Development, and Canada and the United States in the Americas. Nevertheless, table 1 clearly shows the dramatic increase in the number of African and Asian states in the UN. In 1946 African and Asian states constituted less than 25 percent of the UN's membership, but in 1976 they accounted for more than 55 percent. In 1946 the UN contained more states from the Americas than from any other geographic region, but in 1976 Africa was the predominant region while the number of Asian members also exceeded that of American members. The African and Asian states became a majority of the UN's membership in the mid-1960s as decolonization progressed. As early as 1961, Asian, African, and Central and South American states constituted more than a two-thirds majority. Since General Assembly resolutions require only a simple or a two-thirds majority, starting in 1961 the third world had the votes to pass virtually any resolution that it might desire. As the number of African and Asian members of the UN has increased, the task of mobilizing a victorious third world coalition has become progressively easier.

In theory a large number of small, poor states, constituting only a tiny proportion of the world's population and contributing only an infinitesimal amount to the gross world product, could compose a majority in the General Assembly.

This has seldom happened in practice, however; the General Assembly majorities in the 1970s have almost always included states representing a majority of the world's population. The distribution of votes in the General Assembly roughly accords with the distribution of the global population according to income levels; in 1973 more than 60 percent of the world's population lived in countries that had per capita GNPs of less than $500, and only 25 percent lived in countries that had per capita GNPs of $2,000 or more. In this sense the one state, one vote system is a fair method of representation. However, it accords too much influence to Africa and Central and South America, which have a large number of small states with limited populations and too little to Asia, which has several large states with substantial populations. Table 2 compares the distribu-

TABLE 2

A Comparison of UN Voting Strength and Population

	Voting Strength (1976)	Population in millions (1973)	% of Total
Africa	33.3%	392	10.2
Americas	19.7	535	13.9
Asia	22.5	2,131	55.6
Eastern Europe	7.5	378	9.9
Western Europe	13.6	379	9.9
Oceania	3.4	21	.5
Total	100.0	3,836	100.0

tion by broad geographic areas of voting strength in the General Assembly in 1976 with the distribution of global population in 1973 estimated by the World Bank. The table is misleading in that the populations of the United States and Canada constitute more than 40 percent of the population of the Americas, while the other twenty-seven states contain slightly less than 8 percent of the world's population and hold more than 18 percent of the votes in the General Assembly.

The central issue of the debate in the United States about the role of the UN in international political conflicts stems directly from the changed composition of the world body. Daniel Patrick Moynihan raised the issue sharply in his widely noted article in *Commentary*, "The United States in Opposition," asserting that "the simple and direct fact is that any crisis the United States takes to an international forum in the foreseeable future will be decided to the disadvantage of the United States."[5] The third world states that now dominate the UN, he argued, are united by an ideological commitment to what he called British socialism, a doctrine in his view strongly opposed to the institutions and policies of the United States. He recommended that the United States should go into opposition in the UN and directly, forcefully, and loudly defend liberalism and liberal policies. He enthusiastically put this recommendation into effect when

[5] Daniel Patrick Moynihan, "The United States in Opposition," *Commentary* 59 (March 1975), pp. 31-44, p. 42.

he became United States ambassador to the UN. Leonard Garment, who served as United States representative to the UN Commission on Human Rights, argued the case in more pragmatic terms. He maintained that "for strategic political reasons, an abnormal preponderance of nations are determinedly hostile toward the West,"[6] and attributed their hostility to the fact that their expectations had not been realized after they gained their independence. The West was a convenient scapegoat for their frustration.

Others have taken a more optimistic view. Senator J. William Fulbright, for instance, maintained that the attitude of other countries in the UN "reflects criticism, not a built-in hostility,"[7] and claimed that most countries wished to have good relations with the United States and to share the modern technology that it has developed.

The United States and the third world majority in the UN have visibly and undeniably clashed in the 1970s, but the reasons for the conflict remain unclear. The actions that the UN has taken in international political conflicts might indicate whether the third world states that predominate in the UN are in some sense unalterably hostile toward the West and the United States in particular, or whether their attitudes and policies are responsive to actions that the United States has taken and might take.

Whatever one's attitude on this issue, the nature of the UN and the characteristics of its membership ensure that it will amplify the positions of the world's poorer states. The UN provides a platform where these states can articulate their positions as well as coalesce, while the resolutions they propose and adopt can give their positions a certain legitimacy. The voice of the poorer states in world affairs would surely be less audible without a global forum like the UN. Therefore, if one role of a political institution successfully managing conflict is to ensure an adequate opportunity for the presentation of all points of view, particularly the grievances of the disadvantaged, then the UN clearly makes an important contribution. Particularly in a loosely structured political system, such as the global political system, that depends on voluntary action, the amplification of grievances may be a prerequisite for corrective action. Moreover, the detestable discrimination suffered by black people in the modern period and the presence in Africa of the greatest number of the world's poorest states perhaps justify the amplification of the voice of Africa.

The UN and International Political Conflicts

In assessing the UN's past responses to international political conflict and inferring from this the UN's capacity to manage conflict, one must consider not just certain resolutions or even all resolutions adopted in a particular year, but rather the sum of all actions taken by the UN over substantial periods of time.

[6] American Enterprise Institute, AEI Forums, The Future of the United Nations (Washington, D.C.: AEI, 1977), p. 20.
[7] Ibid., p. 15.

The UN has devoted considerable effort to buttressing the charter's prohibition of force and its requirement for the peaceful settlement of international disputes, and it has adopted resolutions and declarations elaborating these norms. The UN has also provided a setting in which arms control agreements have been negotiated and in which such agreements negotiated elsewhere have been given broad legitimacy. On several occasions persons acting on behalf of the UN have mediated in international disputes and have promoted solutions or at least have helped to prevent escalation, while UN peacekeeping forces in the Middle East and Cyprus have served as buffers between hostile forces to inhibit the renewal of violence. The United States has generally supported these actions, despite its concern that struggles for national liberation have always been exempted from the exhortations against the use of violence; it has, in fact, played an instrumental role in several of them, particularly the creation and the continuation of peacekeeping forces.

It is difficult to gauge the effects of these UN actions with any precision. Unquestionably, however, they have contributed somewhat to limiting the violence and coercion in international political conflict, and any such accomplishment should be assessed in light of the fact that consensus within world society probably does not extend far beyond the proposition that nuclear war must be prevented. The tentative and limited unity of world society, the fragility of the UN, and its relative youth as a political institution make its contribution a significant accomplishment. The UN has in some measure succeeded in regulating international political conflicts in general.

However, its success in regulating particular conflicts has been more controversial. To be sure, UN peacekeeping forces have been vitally important in inhibiting the renewal of violence in the Middle East. Moreover, the UN has been an arena in which the various sides could present their positions. By providing a forum for the Palestinians, however, the UN has given some legitimacy to their position, and its tone has been unquestionably anti-Israel. Yet, if a lasting solution to the Middle East conflict depends on a settlement that addresses the Palestinians' aspirations, then focusing attention on this issue may be an important contribution.

Although the United States has consistently opposed UN actions taken in regard to the Palestinians, it has become more favorable toward including the Palestinians in any negotiations and has gradually taken a more positive view on various aspects of their position. If UN actions have contributed to this shift in United States attitudes, and if this shift facilitates a lasting settlement, then the UN will deserve credit for instrumentally contributing to the management of this conflict.

The UN has also been long committed to the creation of governments in southern Africa open to the full participation of all of the countries' inhabitants, regardless of color. This commitment has been stated in stronger and stronger terms as the number of African states in the UN has increased, and powerful historical forces are surely moving in the direction of this goal.

The United States fully shares the UN's goal but has often argued that a more conciliatory approach would be more likely to lead the existing governments to introduce change. Also, the United States has not always been willing to follow UN recommendations for specific actions. The Byrd amendment, for example, precluded United States participation in the UN boycott of Rhodesian chrome. Here also, however, United States policy has changed, perhaps as a consequence of the actions of the UN. In 1976 the United States assumed a more active role in trying to bring about change in Southern Rhodesia and South-West Africa, and there is every indication that the Carter administration will be at least as actively involved in promoting such change as was the Ford administration in its final months. It is yet unclear whether change can occur in southern Africa without substantial violence. Here, too, one cannot yet reach a final judgment on the UN's ability to regulate conflict.

The third major conflict with which the UN is preoccupied differs from the other two because it does not focus on a specific geographic area but instead concerns the structure and functioning of the global economy. The danger of violence is less immediate, partly because this conflict is so diffuse, but the conflict is at least as serious as the other two, for it ultimately involves the domestic economic stability and the potential for economic growth of virtually every country. The developing countries have long desired to narrow the gap between their per capita gross national products and those of the developed countries, and in the 1970s they have more insistently reiterated this goal and have obtained UN endorsement of several specific steps to implement it. The 1973 oil embargo and the price increases have reflected the coercive power available to the third world to attain its goals.

The United States has regularly endorsed the general goal of narrowing the gap in per capita GNP between the developing and the developed countries and has contributed substantial funds through multilateral institutions and its own bilateral programs to facilitate the growth of the economies of developing countries. Within the UN, however, the United States has consistently been confronted for more than a decade with resolutions suggesting that the United States and the other developed countries take actions of which it at least initially disapproved. The United States has regularly voted against these resolutions. Yet in some instances the United States has taken or is inclined to take the action that it initially opppposed. For example, the United States Trade Act of 1974 provided for a "Generalized System of Preferences" for developing countries, although the United States strongly opposed this proposal and voted against it when the Final Act of the first United Nations Conference on Trade and Development first recommended it. Also, the United States has indicated a willingness to consider measures to stabilize earnings from the export of primary commodities, even though it consistently voted against such resolutions throughout the 1960s and early 1970s.

Thus, a familiar pattern appears: confrontation and disagreement within the UN is followed by change in United States policies. Again, a judgment of the

UN's role as a regulator of conflict must be deferred until the ultimate outcome is clear.

In another respect, however, a partial judgment of the UN's performance as a regulator of conflict is warranted. Unquestionably, the major contemporary international political conflicts are thoroughly aired in the UN. This is at least a first step in the management of these conflicts. The existence of an institution with such a capacity should be regarded as important progress in the development of the global political system.

Choices for the United States

What should be United States policy on the UN and international political conflict? How accurate is Daniel Patrick Moynihan's diagnosis and how appropriate is his prescription?

The third world clearly has the voting strength to dominate the political processes of the UN and often uses this strength to push through resolutions that the United States opposes. It is much less clear, though, that an ideological commitment to British socialism actually unites the third world. Political structures in the third world are often primitive and fragile, and governments face staggering problems of poverty. The populations of these countries are increasingly literate and urbanized and hence increasingly mobilized for political action. In view of these conditions it should not be surprising that few of these governments are democratic in the sense in which that word is understood in North America and Western Europe. Indeed, most of them curtail civil liberties in some fashion, and more than 60 percent of them have political systems in which competition among political parties is limited or nonexistent. On the other hand, almost half of these countries have capitalist economies, and only about 20 percent of them intervene in their economies sufficiently to be classified as socialist systems.[8]

African countries, composing the largest single geographical group within the UN, are clearly united by their commitment to eliminate discrimination against black people and to end regimes based on such discrimination. However, their own economic and political systems and ideologies differ greatly. Similarly, the Arab states of the Middle East share a hostility toward Israel, but their unity is limited. Some have significant numbers of Palestinians within their borders, while others do not. The economic and social structures of these countries also differ widely, as do their ties with the West. Although relatively poor countries would prefer to be richer, no single measure would equally benefit all of them.

In view of these many differences, Moynihan's diagnosis seems at best only superficially valid. The normal legislative process of logrolling might be

[8] This summary analysis is based on Raymond D. Gastil, "The Comparative Survey of Freedom—VII," *Freedom at Issue*, no. 39 (Jan.-Feb. 1977), pp. 5-17.

just as plausible an explanation for the apparently united hostility of the third world in the UN toward the United States. A further difficulty with Moynihan's prescription is that its imputation of ideological unity to the third world may lead the United States to take defensive actions that themselves might increase the cohesion and the very ideological unity within the third world that he decries. Similarly, Leonard Garment's assumption of strategic hostility could also become a self-fulfilling prophecy.

Moynihan's strategy of opposition, based on a parliamentary analogy, may credit the UN with more political authority than it has. The UN seldom performs as a legislative body would in a domestic political system. Rather, it often resembles the annual convention of an interest group. Such actions are serious, but they do not have the same consequences as those of a legislative body. The General Assembly's system of representation, giving each state one vote, is adequate for framing broad exhortations, but the distortions inherent in this system of representation would create serious deficiencies if the UN were given greater authority. However, no alternative system of representation would be broadly acceptable. The United States thus has no interest in crediting the UN with more authority than it has.

An alternative course for the United States would be to adopt a more pragmatic and positive stance. By taking initiatives rather than concentrating on opposition the United States might alter its position in the General Assembly. The United States shares a variety of interests with many third world states. Furthermore, when the United States simply reacts negatively, it facilitates the USSR's aligning itself with the third world. The USSR is not called upon to act, but merely to join in condemnation. When the United States advances positive proposals, the question of what the USSR will do to assist the third world is less easy to evade. Figure 1 shows that the United States's position in relation to the third world majority in the General Assembly was more favorable in the early and mid-1960s when it pursued a more active policy than it has more recently. A more active and positive United States policy might produce crosscutting cleavages rather than polarizations in the General Assembly.

The global political system is loosely structured and relies on voluntary coordination. Even though the ties are growing among the sovereign states that are the basic units of the system, central political institutions with substantial authority are not an immediate prospect. The UN is more an instrument for communication among states than a legislative, executive, or judicial body. It would perform a useful function in the global political system even if it only mirrored the positions of the opposing sides in international political conflicts and amplified the voice of the weaker parties. Its role in regulating international political conflicts probably in most instances will remain limited to defining general principles, while solutions may be achieved through actions taken unilaterally or negotiated in ad hoc bodies created to reflect more accurately the interests at stake.

Polarization in the General Assembly might not destroy the UN, and its consequences would surely not be as serious as they would if the world body had greater authority, but it would nevertheless be harmful. In the long run, polarization would probably hinder and perhaps make impossible other activities of the UN, such as peacekeeping and technical assistance, and it would hamper attempts to frame legally binding conventions that are important for arms control and the regulation of activities that are important for arms control and the regulation of activities in new environments, such as outer space and the deep sea. Restraint of the use of violence and coercion, would be weakened. Finally, if the United States concluded that General Assembly resolutions would ignore and oppose its interests, no matter what it did, the United States would pay less and less attention to these resolutions and be less inclined to alter its policy. To the extent then that third world states see United States policy as crucial to the solution of international political conflicts, they share its strong interest in preventing polarization from becoming a permanent characteristic of the General Assembly.

The author gratefully acknowledges the assistance of William Domke and Peter Scherer in the preparation of the statistical material in this essay.

The Apportioning of Political Power

ROBERT W. GREGG

More than thirty years ago the basic outlines of the United Nations system emerged from major organizational conferences held in such places as San Francisco, Bretton Woods, and Hot Springs. Approximately fifty sovereign states, barely one-third of the UN membership in 1977, participated in these conferences. The institutions created not only reflected the prevailing aspirations for the international order, but also attested to the prevailing distribution of power. The original UN system has remained fundamentally intact, but the world of the late 1970s differs markedly from that of the mid-1940s.

Like an old house to which each new occupant adds a new wing, however, the UN system has also grown and changed. The result is a jumble of structures and processes that reflects contemporary membership and issues but also preserves values and constraints from another era. Not surprisingly, this situation generates considerable tension within the UN and its affiliated agencies. Some governments have tried to preserve the essential features of the original UN system in order to maintain stability in an increasingly chaotic and unpredictable world and to impede unwelcome change. Other governments have tried to redesign the UN system and convert it into a vehicle for change in the structure of world order, especially in the realm of international economic relations.

At issue in this conflict is the apportionment of political power within the UN system. Although there are several dimensions to this conflict, it is primarily between North and South. The "North" is the industrialized and relatively affluent states of North America, Western Europe, Japan, Australia, and New Zealand, and the "South" is a large and diverse group of less developed countries (LDCs) from Africa, Asia, and Latin America. These two groups not only use the UN institutions as an arena for confrontation and negotiation about the shape of the international economic order, the rights and duties of the economically privileged and underprivileged, and the transfer of resources from the

North to the South. They also vie for control of the institutional machinery itself to shape the structures and processes of the UN system for the future. Member governments behave as if they agreed with Graham Allison's dictum that "organization matters," since organization confers power.

The organization of the UN system affects the structure, content, and legitimacy of a new international economic order, and the manner and speed of its emergence. As a result, the contest over the organization or the apportionment of political power is vigorous and sometimes bitter. Despite their differences, the developing countries share a conviction that the existing apportionment of power within the UN system is unacceptable. Not only does it impede their efforts to establish a new economic order but it is also unfair because it reflects an old international economic order that they entered late, whose rules they had no part in drafting, and in which they now find themselves at a distinct disadvantage. Therefore, one of the principal elements in both the North-South dialogue and the projected new order is equal participation by developing states in the decision-making process. The global fairness revolution is concerned with the structures of the international system as much as it is with the structure of international economic relations. The developing countries not only want substantially more control, commensurate with their needs and numbers, of the processes and structures of redistribution and rule making in a new order. They also want more control now to facilitate the creation of the new order.

The LDCs view this demand for reapportionment of political power within the UN system as a matter of right, rooted in the principle of juridical equality among sovereign states. Reapportionment would reflect more accurately the changed realities of power in the world than do the anachronistic arrangements of the postwar years. Although the LDCs have worked hard in many forums to reapportion power within the UN system, they remain dissatisfied and frustrated. However, the United States and the other developed countries believe, with varying degrees of ideological conviction and self-interested concern, that the earlier apportionment of power, whatever its shortcomings, is preferable to the reapportionment that the LDCs want to institute. The developed countries, the United States foremost among them, argue that economic importance and its attendant responsibility, rather than the mere fact of sovereign statehood, should confer power. They are dismayed by the misappropriation of the Western concept of egalitarianism for use in international forums and resent the spectacle of new, small, underdeveloped states, few of which are concerned with domestic equality and fewer still with liberty, coalescing to manipulate the machinery of multilateral diplomacy and to confront the large, industrialized, and well-established custodians of a stable international order with unrealistic demands for drastic change in the structure of international economic relations.

As the Western countries see it, the decisions reached at Bretton Woods and San Francisco regarding the distribution of power within the UN system are still valid in the real world of international relations. They have worked hard and with some success to preserve those organizational arrangements or to contain modifications within acceptable limits; therefore, like the LDCs, they are dissatisfied with the UN and consider it a prism that distorts.

Some Salient Institutional Issues

The conflict over apportionment of political power within the UN system is a complex phenomenon that assumes many forms. While the developing and developed states do not normally oppose one another as monolithic blocs, they do tend on many issues to cluster at opposite poles. It is relatively easy to identify and label the position of the Group of 77 (G-77), consisting of more than one hundred LDCs, on most apportionment issues. On those same issues it is just as easy to generalize about at least the principal developed countries. At the risk of oversimplification, the North and the South may therefore be contrasted with respect to the following structural and procedural issues affecting the distribution of power within the UN system.

Deciding the locus of decision has taken as much energy as many of the substantive issues. This central institutional question of the North-South debate has three aspects: whether authority within the UN system should be strongly centralized or scattered among a loose confederation of organizations and programs; whether deliberations should take place and decisions be made in forums with a broad, general mandate, or in more specialized functional forums; and whether the preferable forum is a large one with a universal membership, or a relatively small one involving only those states that have a direct interest in the issue and that may be said to have special responsibility for it.

A major issue dividing developed and developing countries within the UN system has been the degree to which authority should be concentrated. The developed countries have generally favored a decentralized system with the UN itself no more than *primus inter pares*. Each specialized agency and international financial institution would remain unchallenged in its respective sector and would maintain its policy independence, rather than be subordinate to the General Assembly. The LDCs are much more disposed to want development priorities and strategy centrally defined and to want the General Assembly and perhaps the United Nations Conference on Trade and Development (UNCTAD) to review or oversee the rest of the UN system.

Related issues concern the appropriate focus and size of the institutions responsible for the critical decisions regarding a new international economic order. The developing countries have sought universal forums with broad and general mandates, specifically the General Assembly. The developed Western states have preferred relatively small, functionally specific forums and have remained at best ambivalent about the General Assembly.

These differing emphases today are a matter of choice for both groups and no longer the result of an uneven distribution of expertise, although some of the LDCs with limited manpower no doubt find it difficult to function effectively in the more technical areas. The specialized forums with more limited membership tend to focus on technical aspects of economic issues, as the developed countries favor, and the larger and more general forums focus on normative issues, as the developing countries prefer. The dialogue over a new international economic order thus involves a challenge by one value system of another, and the General Assembly and UNCTAD are better suited to that challenge than, for example, the World Bank and the International Monetary Fund (IMF), or the more specialized commodity forums.

From the perspective of the developed Western countries, smaller and more specialized bodies are more likely to involve those states that have a real stake in the outcome of the deliberations and that consequently come prepared for serious and detailed negotiation leading to realistic and concrete results. Large, general-purpose bodies only encourage ill-informed participation by states uninvolved in the issue at hand and thus increase the likelihood of irresponsibly politicizing the agenda. Conversely, the LDCs realize that their strength comes from their numbers. They therefore want full participation by as many states as possible and consider this an appropriate acknowledgement of the global community's shared stake in the outcome of negotiations on the international order.

The positions of the developing countries on these institutional issues constitute a case for the supremacy of the General Assembly as a universal, general-purpose political forum, dominated by foreign ministry generalists. The developed countries prefer the opposite, a decentralized system with the decisive action occurring in relatively small, functionally specific, technical forums dominated by finance ministers and other specialists.

Perhaps the most obvious issue in the conflict over the apportionment of power concerns the manner of arriving at decisions. Developing countries constitute the overwhelming majority of the membership in every UN organization. Quite predictably, they want the institution to reach decisions by majority vote, according one vote to each state regardless of its size, financial contribution, or economic importance. The developed countries, decidedly outnumbered, want to restrict the number of institutions and situations in which the majority can decide an issue. The United States, Japan, and the Federal Republic of Germany do not want Burma, Mauritius, and Guinea, for example, to make vital decisions regarding international economic relations.

Although the principles of one state, one vote and of decision by a simple majority are recognized in the charters of most UN institutions and are too well established to be challenged successfully, the minority of developed states has tried to persuade the developing state majority to abjure voting in favor of consultation leading to consensus. Experience has demonstrated, however, that consensus decisions, as in UNCTAD, are not from the Western point of view necessarily preferable to decisions by the G-77 majority. Frequently they are coerced by deadlines and subsequently disavowed through reservations by the developed countries. Even consultation has to be approached circumspectly and not codified as a required part of the decision process, lest the majoritarian principle be undermined. UNCTAD's formal procedure for consultation has never been invoked;

indeed, a proposal to establish consultative procedures, as recommended by a prestigious panel of experts in 1975, has been one of the major stumbling blocks to restructuring the economic and social sectors of the UN.

The developing states, on the other hand, have tried to introduce more egalitarian methods of deciding issues into institutions that use weighted voting, such as the World Bank and the IMF, and into new institutions as they are created, such as the International Fund for Agricultural Development (IFAD). Since weighted voting is an anachronistic vestige of an old and discredited order, the G-77 demands that the new order be egalitarian. The objectives of the New International Economic Order (NIEO) explicitly include modifying the decision-making formulas of the international financial institutions.

The method of deciding issues in international organizations is therefore basic to national preferences on forums. The developed Western states feel more comfortable in the World Bank and the IMF, the developing countries in the General Assembly and UNCTAD. It is a matter of control.

Developed and developing countries are also divided over the scope and authority of UN bodies. Generally, the more economically developed states of the Western world want these institutions to provide a forum for exchanging views on international economic issues, for raising consciousness, for gathering and analyzing data on specific aspects of international economic relations, and for performing regulatory or service functions as their constitutions stipulate. The LDCs, however, want UN forums to go beyond discussion of a new order and actually to negotiate its elements, not merely advocating resource transfers to developing countries, but actually effecting them. The developing countries thus support a more authoritative UN system. The issue, however, is not whether the General Assembly and other forums are exceeding their authority, because they rarely do so; rather, it is whether their majorities can assign them new and more controversial functions over the strenuous objections of the Western minority. The common strategy has been for UN organs, urged by the G-77, to establish new positions on controversial issues and then to maintain them until repetition and the acquiescence of former critics eventually confer legitimacy.

Closely related to the issue of authority is a matter that may be loosely termed the taxation issue. Many new and relatively poor countries are making claims on the UN system, and more and more resources are needed to satisfy them. While the overwhelming majority of the developing countries in UN institutions can vote budget increases to satisfy those claims, the "tax" burden falls most heavily on the developed Western states, whose payment of assessments is not discretionary.

Both North and South have supported the trend whereby the UN system has taken on operational responsibilities, but these responsibilities have become increasingly controversial as they are performed in lieu of, rather than in addition to, traditional headquarters functions and by the agencies with regularly assessed budgets rather than by the voluntarily funded UN Development Program (UNDP). Recently, the Food and Agriculture Organization (FAO) and the

World Health Organization (WHO) have shifted substantial funds from their assessed budgets into development assistance; to Western eyes, this unjustifiably extends the "taxing" authority.

The growth of the UN and the attendant problems of coordination and management remain one of its chronic institutional issues. The UN system has recently experienced rapid and basically unsystematic growth. This proliferation of new institutions is due partly to the emergence of new issues and the new salience of old ones, but it also reflects disenchantment with existing structures. The developing countries, for example, created UNCTAD and the United Nations Industrial Development Organization (UNIDO) as a result of their frustration with the failure of the existing machinery, especially the Economic and Social Council (ECOSOC), to fulfill expectations. The older organizations were often considered too conservative or too limited in membership. Most recently, however, the Western states have also contributed to this trend. Unwilling to meet the demands of the G-77 for substantial resource transfers or to abandon some of the fundamental principles of the existing international economic order, the developed countries, the United States foremost among them, have instead tried to demonstrate good faith by offering institutional initiatives. Dr. Kissinger's address to the Seventh Special Session of the General Assembly illustrates this approach.

While both developed and developing states share responsibility for the proliferation of UN programs and institutions, they differ over the management of this complex system and on the need to monitor its further growth. Much more than the LDCs, the Western countries are preoccupied with failures of coordination, administrative inefficiencies and corruption, and the absence of a systematic evaluation of programs. The UN is experiencing rampant growth, and it seems to trouble the minority of developed states that pay the bills more than it does the majority of developing states that are the primary beneficiaries. The recent UN debate on restructuring illuminates this difference. The big contributors hope to restructure the system in order to improve its efficiency and effectiveness, but the G-77 considers restructuring a means of giving the LDCs greater control of the UN machinery and thus of creating a more just international economic order.

Another focal point of the North-South conflict over the apportionment of power within the UN system has been the secretariats of these organizations. Although the authority of the secretariats is far less extensive than that of their counterparts in most nation-states, their executive heads and senior subordinates occupy prestigious positions and posses power within each institution, especially with respect to their budgets. These positions confer power, if not in each instance, then collectively.

In the hands of articulate and purposeful officials with a common organizational ideology, international secretariats can significantly affect the programmatic thrust of an institution. It is thus no accident that UNCTAD is widely regarded as the G-77's institution, spearheading efforts to implement some of the major elements of the New International Economic Order. The G-77 has quite literally captured the UNCTAD secretariat; the secretary general and his top directorate are frequently its spokesmen. Western antipathy to UNCTAD is due primarily to a conviction that its secretariat is not even-handedly international but hopelessly biased. On the other hand, Western nationals have maintained leadership in the Department of Economic and Social Affairs. This has disenchanted the G-77 and contributed to the decline of New York, relative to Geneva, as a vital center of the organization's economic and social activity. The most likely "reform" to result from that slow-moving UN restructuring exercise will probably be a new high level secretariat post that will permit an LDC national to outrank the French under secretary for economic and social affairs and perhaps the American administrator of UNDP as well.

Historically, the developed Western states have argued that the size of national contributions to the organization's budget should provide the primary basis for entitlement to secretariat posts and that specific recruitment should be based primarily on merit. Developing countries, however, initially drawing on a smaller talent pool and confined by economic circumstances to much smaller assessments, have argued that financial contribution should receive relatively less importance and that geographic distribution should be the major consideration in apportionment and recruitment. As the number of developing countries and their percentage of total membership in the UN have grown, the struggle over staff recruitment has intensified. The UN and its agencies have modified their rules for allocating positions in order to accommodate the demands of the new member states, increasing their "representation" at the expense of the Western states.

Recent reports by the U.S. General Accounting Office and the Senate Governmental Affairs Committee reveal the importance that governments attach to this continuing struggle. They vigorously complain that the United States, despite placing more nationals than any other country in UN system secretariats, lacks its fair share in these international posts.

A final factor important in discussing the apportionment of power within the UN system is the cohesiveness of the two major "parties" to the dialogue over the international economic order. The most remarkable example of bloc politics in the UN has been the capacity of the LDCs to develop common policies on international economic issues and to maintain their solidarity despite widely divergent economic interests. G-77 now contains over one hundred members as economically diverse as semi-industrialized Brazil, oil rich Saudi Arabia, and impoverished Bangladesh, but its members have preserved a common front on such complex issues as commodities, where they have demanded a common fund for buffer stocks. They have also imposed their collective will within the Conference on International Economic Cooperation (CIEC).

The LDCs' ability to function as a bloc has transformed the North-South dialogue. The G-77 itself is an issue, as the United States and some other Western states try to dissolve the bloc and persuade its members to vote according to their individual economic interests. But for the present, political considerations have triumphed over economic ones. The LDCs are convinced that this strategy greatly enhances their leverage. The economic policies of a bloc of more than one hundred states with varying needs and interests must be couched in quite general and even ideological terms. The Western states continue to ask the LDCs to be specific, and the LDCs continue to avoid specifics in order to preserve their fragile solidarity.

Solidarity has been somewhat more difficult to maintain among the developed countries, although their economic interests may coincide more than do those of the LDCs. The Scandinavians and the Dutch in particular have been more flexible on most questions than, for example, the United States and the Federal Republic of Germany. Moreover, the requirements of the European Economic Community delay and complicate the definition of bloc positions among the developed countries. Yet the developed Western states do function more or less as a bloc. This combines with the solidarity of the LDCs in the G-77 to give the UN some characteristics of a two-party system. The Communist states are only peripherally involved. One reason the developed countries prefer the World Bank, the IMF, and the GATT for negotiating the difficult North-South issues is that bloc politics is much muted, and economic pragmatists are in charge. Elsewhere, blocs are much in evidence and the stage is set for continued confrontation.

Institutional Case Studies

A series of brief case studies may illustrate the effect of the major aspects of the conflict over apportioning power in the UN on the dialogue between developed and developing countries and the shaping of a new international economic order. A major element of the new order is an integrated program for commodities; it has been fashioned under the aegis of UNCTAD, where a common fund for buffer stocks is now being negotiated. UNCTAD has virtually all of the characteristics that simultaneously attract the LDCs and repel the developed states. It has a broad mandate and, prodded by the G-77 and an ambitious secretary general, seems bent on absorbing more and more of the agenda for international economic relations. It has asserted its authority as the premier UN negotiating forum for trade and development issues and brings to that assignment universal membership and a secretariat openly serving the G-77. Nowhere else in the UN system are bloc politics more evident.

UNCTAD has been the most conspicuously confrontational of international organizations, and confrontation has been most acute of late in the case of the common fund. The compromises within the G-77 designed to gain the support of all its members for the common fund proposal have all but precluded meaningful negotiation between the G-77 and Group B (the OECD countries). Bargaining between the two groups threatens to unravel the carefully constructed package of the G-77; some of the LDCs are hurt by almost any conceivable compromise. As a result, the dialogue remains on a plateau of symbolic generalities while the G-77 charges the Group B countries with a lack of political will, and

OECD members complain of the unwillingness of the LDCs to talk about important matters of substance.

In sum, UNCTAD's handling of the common fund negotiations confirms the worst fears of the Western states about the use of political forums for economic problem-solving, the decline of objectivity in international secretariats, and the irrationality of group politics. For the LDCs, UNCTAD has not yet produced a common fund but has seized on a critically important issue, produced a major reform proposal with the overwhelming support of the developing countries, and initiated a negotiating process that the developed countries must take seriously and on which they have begun to give some ground. The LDCs clearly believe that their strategy will ultimately prevail.

On the other hand, the developed countries have greatly desired a less confrontational forum than UNCTAD or the General Assembly to lay the ground for true negotiations. They seek a more intimate forum in which a smaller number of states could pursue some of the critical aspects of the North-South dialogue in relative privacy. The CIEC and the Development Committee of the IMF and the World Bank have heightened expectations for this possibility.

The Development Committee is the less ambitious undertaking of the two. It is a small body designed to generate movement toward the resolution of difficult development issues within the World Bank and IMF community. With the failure of CIEC, it has begun to attract more attention.

CIEC has been one of the more intriguing institutional failures in the history of multilateral diplomacy. Combining a Western desire for an energy forum and an LDC insistence that such a forum have a much broader agenda, CIEC has demonstrated the inherent difficulties in seeking an alternative forum. It was flawed by its separation from the UN system and by a membership that lacked legitimacy and was inappropriate for some purposes; it was also handicapped by a frenetic schedule and the absence of an institutionalized secretariat. Designed to occupy an intermediary position between universal and functionally specific forums, CIEC in fact fell between two stools.

Despite its general failure, the very presence of CIEC stimulated progress in North-South negotiations simply because multilateral institutions occasionally exist symbiotically. For example, support for the International Fund for Agricultural Development (IFAD) reached the breakthrough target of $1 billion because there was a pressing need in a crucial CIEC session to show results and to claim some credit for progress toward realization of a new order. Moreover, the CIEC experience has helped clarify the requirements and limitations of the small forum. Its demise indicates not that smaller institutions necessarily cannot serve as catalysts or even conduct successful North-South negotiations but that the relationships between smaller forums and the General Assembly must be thought through more carefully and universally approved.

The creation of IFAD is a fascinating case study in building institutions during a transitional period in the UN system. Although the World Bank could have provided grants and loans on concessional terms in the agricultural sector, such an arrangement was not attractive to the developing countries. They considered the World Bank dominated by the Western powers and representative of the established economic order. Moreover, it was hoped that a new institution could tap new funding sources, especially among the oil-rich OPEC states. Thus IFAD incorporated, almost from its inception in a recommendation of the World Food Conference in 1974, the principle of shared financial responsibility between traditional donors and OPEC.

The critical issue was whether control of this new and prospectively significant fund would be vested primarily in the donor states by weighting votes or shared equally among all members, according to a new order objective. This issue might have divided governments along North-South lines, but in the end the OPEC states chose to behave first like donors and only secondarily like members of the G-77, much to the dismay of the other developing countries. Consequently, IFAD was created with a tripartite system of membership and control. The three groups of developed donors, developing donors, and developing recipients have an equal number of votes, but each group may apportion its votes as its members choose. The developing country recipients opted for equality, but both groups of donors decided on weighted voting.

This outcome tends to confirm the proposition that where international institutions have large sums of money to distribute on a discretionary basis, the principal donors will insist on essential control of the distributive process. Therefore, such institutions will function more conservatively than the forum institutions. While it may prove to be a unique experiment, IFAD does suggest alternative ways of resolving some of the contentious institutional issues on the agenda of North-South relations.

Although some of the UN specialized agencies have long maintained their own programs of development assistance, partially funded by their regularly assessed budgets, the predominant practice within the UN system has been for such assistance to be funded through and coordinated by the UN Development Program (UNDP), with the agencies then executing the projects. The developed donor countries have preferred this system because it has meant that the decision to support development assistance and the level of that assistance are discretionary with the donors. Moreover, by concentrating responsibility for coordination in UNDP, the donors have felt that their contributions are being used more rationally.

Several factors challenge this arrangement. As a result of mismanagement, UNDP nearly suffered a financial collapse in 1975. Also, some of the agencies, anxious to protect their share of development assistance and pressed by the LDCs to increase resources available to developing countries, took steps to earmark more of their regularly assessed budgets for technical cooperation. FAO and WHO have provided such funds by reducing headquarters staff and by curbing meetings and publications. A 23 percent staff reduction at WHO will permit their development assistance to increase from 51 percent of the assessed budget to

60 percent by 1980–81, and FAO has diverted savings to technical cooperation equal to approximately 10 percent of its budget.

The LDCs warmly support this trend, but it is strongly opposed by most of the developed states because it shifts assessed funds to a purpose that they believe voluntary contributions should support and because it increases development asistance against their wishes and at the expense of universally beneficial activities. Such a trend also undermines the coordinating role of UNDP, thereby violating canons of good management that the developed states have tried to encourage within the UN system. In 1977, this issue very nearly produced a decision by the U.S. Congress to withhold that percentage of funds used for technical cooperation from American contributions to the specialized agencies. This case illustrates the capacity of UN institutions to redirect their efforts in response to the demands of one group over the objections of another. Although it is only the latest in a series of such shifts, the element of taxation could transform it into a crisis comparable to the one involving expenditures for peacekeeping forces in the 1960s.

Conclusions and Projections

The dialogue as well as the conflict between North and South over a new international economic order will continue to have an important institutional component. Both groups will seek an apportionment of the limited power of UN organizations that helps realize their own objectives. Although the current trend favors the developing countries, this corrects an earlier imbalance favoring the developed countries more than it inexorably shifts the UN to an LDC dominated system. The developed states still possess advantages in this contest, particularly their financial contribution to the system.

A number of generalizations about the UN system seem valid in 1977. First, the diversity of issues that preoccupy the UN agencies and the vested interests of so many governments and officials in preserving the sectoral autonomy of those agencies will prevent the centralization of the UN system. The General Assembly, however, is assuming a more central role. Increasingly the direction and scope of change, and to some extent its pace as well, will be centrally defined.

The conflict over the preferability of small technical forums or large general forums will not be resolved in favor of either. The former are necessary for negotiating the specific and usually intricate agreements required if the new order is to have other than rhetorical content. However, such deliberations will be productive and without ideological confrontation only if they operate within the context of consensus on policy guidelines enunciated by the large forum of the General Assembly.

Membership in international organizations will increasingly be determined by the principle of self-selection, rather than universality or election to a prescribed number of seats. The recent conversion of UNCTAD's Trade and Development Board illustrates this. If there is a general international consensus on the work of a given institution, only the directly interested parties will actively participate. In the absence of such a consensus, states without a direct interest in or knowledge of the issues may participate and possibly undermine the deliberations.

Weighted voting is still the rule in multilateral institutions that dispose of relatively large sums of money through direct resource transfer. In these cases, the donors insist on more control, and the recipients acquiesce to obtain the money. Efforts to put organizations such as the World Bank on an egalitarian footing, or to effect large resource transfers through egalitarian forums such as FAO or WHO, risk losing the confidence of their major contributors and a subsequent decline in funds.

The LDCs will jealously guard the principle of majority rule, but the prevailing practice is to produce consensus resolutions and to develop uncodified procedures for consultation in order to achieve that consensus. These techniques are potentially very useful for defusing confrontation if the opponents agree that progress is being made. Artificial consensus, like the UNCTAD IV decision on a common fund, only sharpens the confrontation between North and South.

Management issues that concern the developed countries will almost certainly become more important for the system as a whole. The Geneva Group of major Western financial contributors is growing impatient with the lack of effective coordination and evaluation. The developed countries must convince the G-77 that more effective management of the UN system is necessary for progress on important substantive issues. New confrontations could arise here.

Competition for influence in the UN secretariats continues, with the LDCs now heading many (such as UNCTAD, UNEP, FAO, and UNESCO), holding a preponderance of key staff positions in these and others, and expecting to acquire additional top-level posts. This situation need not exacerbate North-South relations, but it probably will if steps are not taken to improve the quality of some of the secretariats and if blatant bias is not contained and moderated.

The group phenomenon and especially the solidarity of the LDCs cannot be exorcised by anything short of major concessions by the developed countries on some of the new order propositions favored by the G-77. The absence of substantive progress and attempts to persuade LDCs to vote their divergent economic interests only reinforce, at least publicly, the solidarity of the G-77. The LDCs will resist efforts to divide the G-77, but the developed countries must address the question of how to draw the more advanced members of that group into a more fruitful partnership with the OECD countries without challenging their credentials within the G-77. The orderly evolution of the international economic order may well depend on the success of this effort.

The institutional status quo of the postwar years is facing its most severe challenge. However, the LDCs have raised this challenge within the UN system rather than challenging the system itself. Thus, the institutional aspects of a new order should be basically familiar, in principle as well as in form, even if power is somewhat differently apportioned.

The "Politicization" Issue in the
UN Specialized Agencies

GENE M. LYONS
DAVID A. BALDWIN
DONALD W. MCNEMAR

In recent years, the United States has faced increasing difficulties in pursuing constructive policy goals in the specialized agencies of the United Nations, and its commitment to these agencies has declined. The problem, it is often asserted, is that the agencies have become "politicized," that is, that highly controversial issues not always relevant to the agencies' work are introduced by nations to further their political interests. Those who charge "politicization" infer that the agencies are being used as forums for political debate rather than the functional tasks for which they were founded.

Precisely because the charges and countercharges regarding "politicization" affect both the work of the agencies and the direction of American foreign policy, this concept requires careful examination. While the analytic usefulness of the concept of "politicization" may be questioned, the political impact of such charges has already been recorded. This essay examines both the concept of "politicization" and the place of the specialized agencies in American foreign policy. It focuses on the background of United States relations with the specialized agencies, the nature and significance of the alleged "politicization," the agencies' responses to charges of "politicization," and the strategic alternatives available to United States foreign policymakers.

The problem of "politicization" has loomed most seriously since the early 1970s, the years of the oil crisis, the heightened tensions in the Middle East, and the coalescence of the third world behind the concept of a new international economic order. In 1975, for example, the United States served notice that it would consider formal withdrawal from the International Labor Organization (ILO) in 1977, partly because of "politicization."[1] The rupture had

---

[1] In its letter to the director general of the ILO, giving notice of the intention to withdraw,

festered for years, however, as the spread of state-controlled central planning regimes tended to invalidate the original basis of a tripartite system of representation in which labor and management groups sat independently of government representatives.

In 1974 Congress had prohibited payment of the United States contribution to the United Nations Educational, Scientific, and Cultural Organization (UNESCO) until certain anti-Israeli resolutions passed by the UNESCO General Conference were modified.[2] Although UNESCO programs have always been vulnerable to political and, especially, ideological differences, this split was less profound than in the ILO. Both of these cases, however, were only two of the more serious breaches between the United States and the UN agencies. In almost all of the agencies, the United States increasingly found itself in the minority in governing bodies dominated by developing countries using their voting strength to seek support for their own national development and to promote a new economic order in the world.

At least three other factors have exacerbated the situation. First, the call for a new world economic order is an issue through which the USSR can ally its own aspirations with those of the third world and thus seek to isolate the United States and other Western industrialized states. In Marxist-Leninist terms, this strategy is part of a historical process shifting from a Western-centered world system. Second, the drive for a new world order also attacks the vestiges of colonialism and the continued domination of world markets by Western political and economic interests. Finally, while the United States has viewed attacks on apartheid in South Africa and support for liberation movements in Africa and the Middle East as distortions of the purposes of the UN agencies, developing countries with Soviet support have seen these actions within a conflictual theory of international politics as part of a broader strategy to change world politics.[3] What appear to be political tactics to achieve limited ends are really indicators of broader and more fundamental changes. The United States has been increasingly on the defensive in UN forums. Traditional public support for the UN in the United States has been shaken, and conservative opposition to UN agencies in Congress and elsewhere has been reinforced.

Although a residual commitment to the United Nations and its agencies

---

the United States specified four reasons: the erosion of tripartite representation; selective concern for human rights; disregard of due process; and the increasing politicization of the organization. The letter is found in: U.S., Congress, House, Committee on Appropriations, *Second Supplemental Appropriation Bill, 1976, Hearings before a subcommittee on the Departments of State, Justice, and Commerce, the Judiciary, and Related Agencies,* 94th Cong., 2d sess., 1976, pp. 11–15.

[2] In 1976, the 19th session of the UNESCO General Conference reversed one of three anti-Israeli resolutions; this action, together with other changes, has led the executive branch to recommend to the Congress that the United States contribution be restored.

[3] It has been suggested that the Middle East and southern Africa issues are unique and constitute especially aggravating problems for the UN. While this may be true, the UN agencies, with or without these issues, provide forums for controversy for those who follow a conflictual theory of international politics.

has survived since the early postwar efforts to encourage the American people to accept full participation of their government in the UN and thereby in world affairs, the UN was undoubtedly oversold by American poliymakers haunted by the isolationism of the interwar years. At least since the Korean case in the early 1950s the UN has played only a secondary role in United States foreign policy. At the same time, a myth developed that economic and social programs were "nonpolitical" and that the specialized agencies should not be "politicized." American delegations increasingly argued that political issues should be sent to the General Assembly and Security Council and not debated in the specialized agencies.

In some respects, this thesis of "depoliticization" is consistent with the concept of "functionalism" that motivated many of the founders of the specialized agencies. In simplest terms, the functionalists argued that it was unrealistic to expect governments to agree to give substantial authority to international organizations in areas that involve their important political and security interests.[4] Rather, governments needed encouragement to engage in cooperative arrangements to perform functions, such as airline routings, river navigation, and weather forecasting, that served their citizens but needed to be carried beyond national boundaries. It was further hypothesized that the cumulative effect of "functional" commitments would tend to influence the political aims of governments toward more cooperative, less conflictual relations. Certainly, international involvement increases the costs of breaking off cooperative enterprises in order to pursue national interests through conflict, although these costs may be tolerable, especially for major powers. But functionalism does not ignore politics; indeed, its ultimate purpose is to change the incentives in the international political system.

Moreover, functional programs are established through essentially political intergovernmental agreements. Their execution, financing, and effects therefore evolve through systems of relations in which political, economic, and social factors are indistinguishably intertwined. Certainly, factors under certain circumstances other than the political may be overriding: humanitarian reasons may prevail in a UN program designed to respond to natural disasters such as a drought or earthquake, while the need for scientific exchange may underlie a worldwide program to conquer diseases. Yet, even in cases such as these, the centrality of humanitarian or scientific purposes has to be protected by written or tacit political agreements restraining national interests that could jeopardize international cooperation.

The American desire to "depoliticize" the UN agencies is thus a weak basis for national policy. Even if "depoliticization" were possible in an "objective" sense, it is incomprehensible to a Marxist view of world affairs and irrelevant to countries, especially those in the third world, for which these agencies are a major forum for mobilizing their combined forces to argue for systemic

---

[4] For the classic statement on functionalism, see David Mitrany, *A Working Peace System* (Chicago: Quadrangle, 1966).

change. Moreover, since the UN is a secondary issue in American foreign policy, the United States position itself in the specialized agencies often reflects wider political interests in which the UN is the "dependent variable." Thus, the United States response to anti-Israeli resolutions in the specialized agencies follows the needs of United States political and military strategy in the Middle East, and the agencies remain "hostage" to the resolution of external political conflicts. Moreover, there is evidence that the United States pursued special political purposes in the specialized agencies when it possessed the means of critically influencing the votes of other governments and the decisions of agency executives.

During the 1950s and 1960s, for example, the United States felt that it was appropriate to introduce cold war issues into the ILO arena by opposing the admission of Communist China and by keeping such issues salient in ILO debates, even though "the continuing prominence given to cold war issues in ILO debates conflicted with the growing demands of less-developed countries that priority be given to their problems."[5] For that matter, the appointment in 1970 of a Soviet as assistant director-general triggered congressional action to withhold the United States contribution from the organization. At the same time American spokesmen often contrast the World Bank with the ILO as *the* example of an "unpoliticized" functional organization. Yet since its president has always been an American and its voting system is weighted to reflect American financial importance, the bank turns out to be highly influenced—some would say dominated—by the United States. Other nations are less likely to describe it as "nonpolitical" and indeed sometimes describe it as an "instrument" of American foreign policy.

To the extent that it shapes United States policy parameters, "depoliticization" is more than just a tactic in the absence of positive policies and purposes; in effect, it becomes United States policy. Is it true, as Daniel P. Moynihan has suggested, that the United States will have to accept its minority position and assume the role of the "opposition" in UN governing bodies? Does its minority position reduce United States policy in UN agencies to one purely of reaction? Does it eliminate the possibility of leadership or of developing new coalitions?[6] Before addressing these questions, a closer look at the concept of "politicization" is in order.

The Concept of "Politicization"

The statement that decision-making in the specialized agencies has become increasingly "politicized" combines empirical and normative elements that inhibit objective analysis. The term "politicization," like "exploitation" and

---

[5] Robert W. Cox, "ILO: Limited Monarchy," in *The Anatomy of Influence*, ed. Robert W. Cox and Harold K. Jacobson (New Haven: Yale University Press, 1973), p. 135.

[6] Daniel P. Moynihan, "The United States in Opposition," *Commentary* 59 (March 1975), pp. 31–44.

"imperialism," is so loaded with pejorative connotations that serious questions arise about its analytic utility. The fact that nations rarely if ever describe their own policies as attempts to "politicize" an issue should be enough to arouse one's suspicions. It thus seems prudent to ask who uses that term to refer to what situations, and why.

The association of functionalism with the specialized agencies makes the charge of "politicization" almost inevitable when something seems to go wrong. At the heart of the functionalist argument lies the contention that collaboration in technical, economic, and social spheres leads to improved cooperation in political spheres. Both the ambiguity and pejorative connotations of "politicization" are imbedded in functionalist theory. As James Patrick Sewell has stated:

> The functionalist antipathy toward politics is evidenced not only by disparaging comments and the lack of any sustained discussion of the political but also by a certain amount of ambiguity when the term is employed. In the functionalist literature "political" is generally used to denote that portion of the universe of human relations which lies beyond the functional pale. As such the functional is by definition the non-political, and this is synonymous with "non-controversial" or "technical" in terms of procedure, and "economic" or "social" in its substantive aspect. Politics is a residue.[7]

To the extent that the specialized agencies are thought of in functionalist terms, it is not surprising that dissatisfaction with their performance is often expressed in charges of "politicization."

Such charges often imply disapproval but do not provide an explicit description of the problem. How is "politicization" to be recognized? One view sees "politicization" as the pursuit of "political"—sometimes "narrowly political" or "short-run political"—goals in "nonpolitical" arenas like the specialized agencies. If the foreign policy goals of nations could be clearly labeled "political" or "economic," this method might have some merit; unfortunately, a foreign policy goal is not intrinsically one or the other. These are extrinsic qualities dependent on the particular situation: "the ends of politics may be anything."[8] Conflict gives foreign policy goals their political quality. If everyone agrees that including the Palestinian Liberation Organization (PLO) in the deliberations of a particular functional agency is appropriate, then such an act is routine and by definition nonpolitical. Organizations become "politicized" to the degree that the issues that they deal with become controversial. When organizations become extremely "politicized," their very structure and future existence become controversial matters.[9] If the term "politicization" is to be use-

[7] James Patrick Sewell, *Functionalism and World Politics* (Princeton: Princeton University Press, 1966), pp. 43–44.

[8] Quincy Wright, *The Study of International Relations* (New York: Appleton-Century-Crofts, 1955), p. 132.

[9] Cf. Robert O. Keohane and Joseph S. Nye, "World Politics and the International Economic System," in *The Future of the International Economic Order: An Agenda for Research*, ed. C. Fred Bergsten (Lexington, Mass.: Lexington Books, 1973), pp. 116–18.

ful, it should be confined to describing the degree to which an institution is characterized by controversy.

Increasing controversy in the specialized agencies, however, can be viewed from at least three standpoints. "Politicization" can be viewed as an organizational defect to be corrected, an indicator to be understood, or a bargaining tactic to be dealt with. Examination of these perspectives should help explain why debates over "politicization" so often end where they began.

Those who see "politicization" as an organizational defect are likely to accuse "irresponsible" states of distorting the purposes of a specialized agency by attempting to place inappropriate controversial items on the agenda. This view implies that there is a consensus on organizational purposes or that the purposes of a specialized agency are enshrined in the constitution. Inis Claude, Jr., however, has warned that such a view hinders understanding of the political aspects of international organizations. After offering the "blunt assertion that the United Nations has no purposes—and can have none—of its own," he observes that "the political process within the organization . . . is, in essence, a continuous struggle between the advocates of conflicting purposes or between those whose conceptions of the proper order of priorities are different, a struggle to determine which purposes and whose purposes the United Nations will serve. This is what politics is all about, and this is the fate of political institutions."[10] For a functionalist, of course, specialized agencies are not and should not become political institutions, and "politicization" of a functional institution is by definition an organizational defect.

A second orientation considers "politicization" an indicator of forces bearing on the organization—that is, as a function of the environment within which the institution operates and of the problems it addresses. Those who study "politicization" in specialized agencies in this way claim that attempts to amend constitutions or establish agenda control committees focus attention on symptoms while obscuring the underlying causes of the problem. According to Robert O. Keohane and Joseph S. Nye, " 'politicization' is an important concept because it casts light on the process of agenda formation."[11]

International organizations should and do reflect the realities of the international system. If specialized agencies are becoming more "politicized," one should ask whether this is a reflection of trends in the international system or a peculiar trait of certain institutions. If "politicization" is increasing in the international system, one should account for the increase and determine its significance for international organization.

"Politicization" in specialized agencies may arouse concern, but it does not

---

[10] Inis L. Claude, Jr., *The Changing United Nations* (New York: Random House, 1967), p. xvii.

[11] Robert O. Keohane and Joseph S. Nye, Jr., "International Interdependence and Integration" in *Handbook of Political Science*, vol. 8, ed. Fred I. Greenstein and Nelson Polsby (Reading, Mass.: Addison-Wesley, 1975), p. 397.

follow that tinkering with the organizational machinery of such agencies will eliminate it. Rather, one may plausibly argue that many of the economic and social issue-areas with which functionalists have been concerned have become increasingly "politicized."[12] Managed economies, third world restlessness and dissatisfaction, the cold war, rapid technological change, and the growing number and importance of multinational corporations all have contributed to increased "politicization" of the international system. From this perspective the sudden disappearance of the Arab-Israeli dispute and the southern Africa imbroglio would not necessarily signal the end of the "politicization" of international functional agencies.

As an indicator of trends in the international system, increased "politicization" has ominous implications for functionalism. Functionalists assume that issue-areas relatively free from controversy can be identified and that cooperation in these areas will then gradually spread to other arenas; if the existence of the specialized agencies depended solely on functionalist justifications, their future could be seriously in doubt. There are, however, other justifications for such institutions that conceive of them as an integral part of the international political system.

"Politicization" can be viewed not only as an organizational defect or indicator of systemic trends, but also as part of a planetary bargaining process in which the third world nations negotiate with the developed world regarding the relative importance of various global problems. At least since 1949, the history of the United Nations has been marked by the attempts of poor nations to convince rich nations that the concerns of the third world deserve a higher priority on the agenda of global problems. The rich nations, however, have considered the cold war, arms control, and the maintenance of peace and stability more important issues. The inability of poor nations to convince rich nations of the importance of developmental problems in the third world led to frustration and protest. Protest, according to some students of American politics, "is correctly conceived as a strategy utilized by relatively powerless groups in order to increase their bargaining ability."[13] Likewise, the "politicization" of the specialized agencies could be viewed as an attempt by frustrated and relatively powerless nations to increase their bargaining ability.

From this perspective, "politicization" of the specialized agencies does not necessarily mean that such institutions are malfunctioning but may indicate that they are playing a role in a planetary bargaining process whose significance extends beyond the specific technical goals of the organization. For example, one could view the confrontations in specialized agencies as part of a continuing process to "widen the circle of international decision-making" or to "integrate dissatisfied powers into the central management of the interna-

---

[12] Cf. Keohane and Nye, "World Politics and the International Economic System," pp. 118–33.

[13] Michael Lipsky, "Protest as a Political Resource," *American Political Science Review* 62 (December 1968): 1157.

tional system."[14] Robert W. Cox and Harold K. Jacobson have suggested that international organizations may be conceived of as "sensitive communications networks within which the power holders in world affairs . . . may receive and respond to signals from the less powerful without abandoning the control of action to them."[15] They go on to suggest that "over their longer history, the greatest potential for change from international organizations may lie in the opportunity they give the less powerful to influence the climate of opinion and the accepted values according to which action is determined."[16] Thus, the current "politicization" of various functional agencies may be part of the global process of transition incorporating third world nations into the international decision-making system.

In sum, "politicization" of the specialized agencies may be viewed as a defect to be corrected, as an indicator to be understood, or as a bargaining situation to be dealt with. None of these perspectives is "wrong" or nonsensical, and each deserves recognition. One should recognize, however, the potential for hypocrisy in the "organizational defect" viewpoint, a danger especially likely to occur when a powerful nation like the United States complains that "politicization" is undermining the effectiveness of institutions that it has traditionally dominated. Since controversy requires at least two parties, no single nation can "politicize" an issue or agency. Neither third world demands nor American intransigence provides an adequate explanation for the increasing "politicization" of UN agencies.

Responses of Specialized Agencies

The specialized agencies vary in the degree of their involvement in controversies that may lead to charges of "politicization." A continuum of "politicization" of the more prominent specialized agencies would resemble the diagram below, with the agencies to the left of the continuum more likely to have controversial issues introduced in their governing bodies.

"Politicization Continuum"

Most Politicized						*Least Politicized*
UNESCO ILO	WHO	FAO	WORLD BANK		IMF	IAEA

---

[14] Charles William Maynes, "A U.N. Policy for the Next Administration," *Foreign Affairs* 54 (July 1976): 808. Maynes is referring to the North-South confrontation in general, not to politicization in specialized agencies; but the material is quoted here to suggest that a similar line of reasoning could be applied to such agencies.

[15] Cox and Jacobson, p. 428.

[16] Ibid.

This arrangement is based on an estimate of the incidence of controversial decision-making, but it closely parallels the relative degree to which the agency has been attacked by the United States on grounds of "politicization." For example, the United States Congress withheld funding from UNESCO in 1974, charging that the agency had been "politicized" by the passage of three anti-Israeli resolutions. The United States also based its statement of intention to withdraw from ILO on the "increasing politicization of the organization." The United States ambassador to the UN accused the World Health Organization of "politicization" when it became involved in a controversy over health care in the occupied territories. Ambassador Scranton then insisted that "the absence of balance, the lack of perspective and the introduction by the WHO of political issues irrelevant to the responsibilities of the WHO do no credit to the United Nations. Indeed, this is precisely the sort of politicized action which decreases respect for the United Nations system."[17]

The factors differentiating agencies along the "politicization continuum" seem to include the specificity of the technical task assigned to the agency, the professionalism among the delegates, and the level of professionalism within their secretariats. The broad and pluralistic mandate of UNESCO contrasts with the highly technical, task-oriented functions of the International Atomic Energy Agency.[18] The size and composition of the membership are also relevant variables, as the complexity of building coalitions increases with the number of members. Thus the World Bank and the International Monetary Fund are insulated, in many respects, by selective membership, as well as weighted voting. "Politicization" may also arise from the different perceptions of member states regarding potential benefits from participation in the organization.

In all of the agencies, normally technical and routine items on the agenda may nevertheless assume intense political saliency, thereby dramatically increasing their potential for controversy. While it is thus difficult precisely to explain varying degrees of "politicization," Cox and Jacobson suggest in their study of eight agencies that "insofar as functionalist theories are valid, it might be assumed that those international organizations that are most technical, functionally specific, and essential would be least affected by patterns of conflict and alignments and by the nature of political regimes."[19]

In recent years, the specialized agencies, particularly those at the most "politicized" end of the continuum, have responded to "politicization" by develop-

---

[17] "Statement by Governor Scranton on Action Taken by the World Health Assembly," Press Release USUN-58 (76), May 21, 1976.

[18] The International Atomic Energy Agency (IAEA) is not a specialized agency reporting to ECOSOC, but rather an autonomous agency which reports directly to the General Assembly and, when appropriate, to the Security Council. The IAEA is frequently associated with the agencies and is included here to illustrate the broad range of functional organs operating under the aegis of the UN.

[19] Cox and Jacobson, pp. 33–34 and 419–23.

ing procedures for protecting their functional tasks from interference by controversial activities. Such practices have included negotiating and drafting committees, consensus adoption of working group proposals, compatible committee memberships, and separation of political resolutions.

The General Conference of UNESCO in Nairobi in October and November of 1976 formed a special committee of twenty-five member states to negotiate and draft controversial resolutions before discussion and action on them by the full conference. Given the intense reaction to resolutions regarding Israel adopted at the General Conference in 1974 and the explosive potential of such agenda items as freedom of the press, the 1976 conference developed this procedure to prepare resolutions in a committee that still reflected the various cleavages among its members but was a more manageable working group. This negotiating group facilitated the work of the conference both by improving preparatory work on agenda items and by indicating the parameters of acceptable policies, which minimized controversy over the final resolutions of the conference.

UN organs have increasingly adopted proposals by consensus rather than by recorded votes.[20] Such a process permits intense negotiation in working groups, while final action is *pro forma* approval in a plenary session. This technique also promotes general consensus on acceptable international action while preventing proposals that produce intense division among the members. The emphasis is on creating documents that command universal assent rather than forcing some nations into negative votes that would jeopardize the consensus for action by the agency.

Varying committee membership for regional activities is one way to minimize the problem of having disputing nations in regional committees. Tensions between Israel and the Arab states have been handled in this way, while UNESCO has permitted regional groups to vote on their own membership, resulting in Israel's inclusion in the European group. WHO simply has two subcommittees for the Middle East region. One consists of twenty-three members, including all of the Arab states and carrying out most of the regional activity and another composed of Israel and friendly Western states with interests in the region.

Specialized agencies have also separated resolutions on political issues from programmatic actions. Issues of particular political content may be placed together in an omnibus resolution or restricted to the preamble in resolutions. The passage of such separated political resolutions satisfies the domestic needs of instructed delegates while not interfering with the specific functional tasks of the agencies.

Although the Western nations urged these procedural adaptations, only the initiatives of the secretariats of the agencies and the support of the third world

[20] For an analysis of the use of such procedures and their impact on the outcome of the World Food Conference, see Thomas G. Weiss and Robert S. Jordan, *The World Food Conference and Global Problem Solving* (New York: Praeger Publishers, 1976).

member states made them possible. Moreover, this support is related to changes in both the leadership and the policy direction of the specialized agencies. Third world leaders now assume increasing responsibility within the agencies (Amadou-Mahtar M'Bow of Senegal is now director-general of UNESCO, for example, and Edouard Saouma of Lebanon is the executive head of FAO), and third world governments are interested in supporting the initiatives of the new directors-general. The orientation of the agencies, already shifting toward development, increasingly reflect the move toward a new international order. The statements and programs of directors-general emphasize the requirements of self-reliance in developing countries and the reallocation of resources to third world recipients. Perhaps most dramatically, a WHO resolution has called for increased assistance to less developed countries by devoting at least 60 percent of its regular program budget to "technical cooperation and provision of services."[21]

In reassessing its position on the specialized agencies, the United States must examine these changes in the agencies, as well as understand the complexities of "politicization" and the procedural responses of the more vulnerable agencies. These shifts suggest a changing role for international organizations in a world of increasing interdependence and new opportunities for multilateral diplomacy in the pursuit of United States foreign policy.

A Political Strategy for the United States

Keohane and Nye have suggested that viewing "international organizations as incipient world governments" is "archaic." One should think of international organizations, they continue, "less as institutions than as clusters of intergovernmental and transgovernmental networks associated with the formal institutions. Governments must be organized to cope with the flow of business in these organizations; and as governments deal with the organizations, networks develop that bring officials together on a regular, face-to-face basis. International organizations may therefore help to activate 'potential coalitions' in world politics, by facilitating communications between certain elites; secretariats of organizations may speed up this process through their own coalition-building activities."[22]

This approach to international organizations underscores the limits of functionalism without denying its role in developing new bases for international cooperation. It also opens up new opportunities for American foreign policy to engage in coalition-building with the third world through active and positive

---

[21] United Nations, World Health Organization, *Official Records*, No. 233, Twenty-Ninth World Health Assembly, Geneva, 3–21, May 1976, Part I Resolutions and Decisions, pp. 30–31 (WHA 29.48). For comment on the impact on WHO of this establishment of a fixed percentage of budget for a particular purpose, see Lawrence K. Altman, "W.H.O. to Cut Staff in Shift of Goals," *New York Times*, January 30, 1977.

[22] Robert O. Keohane and Joseph S. Nye, *Power and Interdependence: World Politics in Transition* (Boston: Little Brown, 1977), p. 240.

participation in the specialized agencies. The new international economic order is rapidly becoming the dominant theme of the programs and administrations of the agencies. As this theme is strengthened, developing countries are motivated to pursue moderate policies in the agencies and to resist controversial issues that threaten dissension, especially ruptures in North-South relations. The incentive toward moderation is further enhanced as third world leaders assume increasingly responsible roles and encourage consensual and professional techniques in agency operations.

The specialized agencies are a permanent feature of the changing world system regardless of changes in their organization and direction. The United States must either actively participate or risk isolating itself from the developing structure of organized relations, although some commentators suggest that the United States might choose to participate selectively in agencies and activities where its influence is greatest.[23] Effective participation demands a political strategy that anticipates changes in the UN system of specialized agencies and regards the flexibility of the system as an opportunity for political initiatives in constructing creative and stable economic and social relations. However, the American approach to the agencies remains rooted in the short-lived perspectives of the immediate postwar years. It has not fully incorporated the spread of different socioeconomic systems, the rapid rate of decolonization of the third world, the diffusion of power in a world of military stalemate between the superpowers, the disparate possession and disposition of economic resources, and impending ecological dislocations.

The absence of a political strategy reflecting changes in the world has led the United States, by default, to pursue "depoliticization" in the specialized agencies at the expense of more positive and creative initiatives. Under such circumstances, "politicization" has been perceived more as "an organizational defect" than as "an indicator" of broader systemic change or as "a bargaining tactic" of developing countries. Such an approach emerged from the almost exclusive priority of East-West relations in United States foreign policy and from disappointments with multilateral diplomacy as viewed against a limited functionalist perspective.

The UN agencies provide one means of developing cooperative relations among governments for the systematic resolution of complex economic and social problems in an increasingly interdependent world. Any new United States policy must take into account the following factors: the new opportunities and political requirements of "functionalism"; the alternatives available to the UN agencies through regional and bilateral arrangements for constructing long-term economic and social relations, especially with developing countries; the nature of "interdependencies" in a world shifting from the Western-centric system; and, most important of all, a positive assessment of the imperatives of United States involvement in world affairs.

[23] Cf. Maynes, pp. 812–19.

The Role of the United Nations in Economic Negotiations

SIDNEY WEINTRAUB

The United States looks to the United Nations primarily for its sometime political value or as a peacekeeping body when the major powers are not directly in conflict with each other. The United States will tolerate the involvement of the UN in economic activities, since it has no choice, but its tolerance is not always gracious. The UN is rarely the chosen instrument of the United States for economic negotiation and only infrequently for economic debate. If one looks at the structure of the State Department, its international organization bureau is set up essentially for dealing with political issues in the UN. Economic issues are handled elsewhere, and the people dealing with these matters are immersed primarily in the workings of other international economic organizations, such as the International Monetary Fund (IMF), the World Bank, the General Agreement on Tariffs and Trade (GATT), and commodity groupings. The UN is a place where the United States is expected to give concessions. In these other bodies, it sometimes seeks concessions as well.

The developing countries, on the other hand, see the UN primarily as a forum in which they can promote their economic objectives. Political pressure is used as the conduit to seek economic concessions by the developed countries. One citation will demonstrate this. Mahbub ul Haq, in summarizing the results of the fifteenth world conference of the Society for International Development, asked the following questions: "Would there be changes in world power structures which would then be reflected in changes in UN institutions, including Bretton Woods institutions? Or would it be possible through an ordinary dialogue to restructure the voting rights and democratize these institutions and put much greater economic powers within the framework of the UN so that it can gradually evolve more and more into a world development authority?"[1] A United States policymaker would not ask these questions.

[1] Mahbub ul Haq, "Towards a Just Society," *International Development Review* 18 (Winter 1976), p. 5.

When perceptions of the protagonists are so diametrically different as to the purpose of an institution, conflict is inevitable. To borrow a term from Graham Allison, the United States has one "conceptual lens," the third world another, and the Communist countries still others.[2] The conflict is not necessarily unhealthy, since there is a dialectic at work: proposal, conflict, and synthesis. It may be possible to make this process a bit less acrimonious. More basically, since some acrimony between rich and poor is probably inevitable if change is to occur, it is worth asking how the United States should view the UN in the economic arena and what this implies for United States-third world interaction. That is the theme of this essay.

The UN involves more than the Security Council and the General Assembly. There is often disagreement among nations in the specialized agencies dealing with technical issues, but in general the World Health Organization, the Food and Agriculture Organization, the International Civil Aviation Organization, and so on, are not arenas for the central themes in the current North-South conflict. Nor is the Security Council relevant to the kind of economic conflict involved in this North-South debate. It is the General Assembly and some of its appendages, such as the United Nations Conference on Trade and Development (UNCTAD), that are the foci of this conflict, and it is these that will be examined.

The Interplay Between Substance and Institutions

Causality in institution building runs in two directions simultaneously: a problem is perceived and an institution is formed to deal specifically with it; or, based on some vague disquiet or dissatisfaction, an institution is created to seek out its problems. Thus, if a substantive vacuum is not filled by the first sequence of problem-perception leading to institution-creation, it almost certainly will be by the second sequence of institutions in search of unattended-to problems or areas where they believe they can do better than the existing organizations. Institutional explosion is inevitable under this process of dual causality, and this has occurred internationally.

The creation of the IMF was a clear example of the first sequence. The problem perceived was the beggar-thy-neighbor practice of the 1930s and the desire to have some discipline among nations, particularly the developed nations, in the alteration of exchange rates and in practices affecting trade in goods and services. These issues were important to the then leading nations, particularly the United States and Great Britain. The world monetary system matters directly to the United States, Europe, and Japan in that exchange-rate relationships affect trade, capital movements, and even income and employment. The world trading system similarly is of some import. The level of tariffs, those of the United States and other nations, particularly of the developed countries, are of direct conse-

[2] Graham T. Allison, "Conceptual Models and the Cuban Missile Crisis," *American Political Science Review* 63 (Sept. 1969): 689–718.

quence to United States producers and workers. GATT was the result of a per-ceived problem seeking an institution.

The creation of the International Bank for Reconstruction and Development (IBRD) was a hybrid in this sequential process. In a system devised by developed countries, issues of concern to these countries were given primary attention and there was no doubt that reconstruction of Europe came first in the conception of the IBRD. It was only later, after reconstruction was no longer a vital issue, that the development aspect of the IBRD came to the fore. The International Development Association (IDA) was not even created until 1960.

UNCTAD was an example of the second sequence. The disquiet among developing countries with the functioning of the GATT had become evident by the early 1960s. These countries viewed the GATT as an institution in which developed countries negotiated primarily among themselves and reduced tariffs on products in which developed countries trade but remained little concerned with reducing these duties on processed or labor-intensive goods in which the developing countries had some comparative advantage. True, a tariff reduction negotiated in the GATT among developed countries was generalized to less developed countries under the most-favored-nation principle, but receiving hand-me-downs, particularly those that did not precisely fit, was not the same as buying directly in the store. The problem of hand-me-down concessions un-doubtedly was compounded by the less developed countries themselves, since they were not generally active participants in the GATT tariff negotiations. They demanded nonreciprocal privileges without meaningful participation of their own, and the outcome was predictable; they got the hand-me-downs be-cause they were not prepared to buy in the store.

When UNCTAD held its first conference in 1964, the big issue was the developing country drive for generalized, nonreciprocal tariff preferences for manufactured and semimanufactured goods exported to developed countries, which eventually was achieved. As UNCTAD searched for additional functional areas to dominate, the one outstanding issue waiting for some overall direction was that of trade in primary commodities. Issues of major concern to developing countries were not ignored when the post-World War II international economic structure was devised, but they were of secondary importance to the founding fathers. Lord Keynes prepared a seminal document on the international monetary system that was studied and acted on, and when all the negotiations were completed, the IMF was created and ratified. Keynes also prepared a thoughtful document on the use of buffer stocks and other mechanisms to seek to stabilize primary commodity prices in international trade, but it was quietly buried until recently when some of its ideas were revived by UNCTAD. The Havana Charter for an International Trade Organization (ITO) contemplated some regulation of primary commodity trade, but this aspect fell by the wayside when the United States made it clear that it would not join the ITO.

The General Assembly is the prime example of an institution seeking an economic purpose. Slowly but inexorably as its dominant membership altered from developed to less developed countries, the central UN bodies concerned themselves more and more with economic issues. This concern came to a climax following the dramatic events of late 1973 and 1974, when the OPEC cartel successfully raised oil prices and ideas of commodity power were in the air. Simultaneously, world grain prices soared. The developed countries were going through a synchronous recession—the worst since World War II—and this recession inevitably affected the poor countries. This was the atmosphere when the resolutions on a New International Economic Order (NIEO) were adopted in mid-1974 by the Sixth Special Session of the General Assembly.

Some people have quipped that the NIEO is something like the Holy Roman Empire in that it is not new, not international or certainly not universal in the countries on which it makes demands, not predominantly economic in its objectives, and would hardly create order. But this misses a key point. To cite Haq again: "Let us make quite clear in our future negotiations that what is at stake here is not a few marginal adjustments in the international system: it is its complete overhaul."[3] The NIEO is part of the dialectic, but on a grander scale than seeking a few marginal concessions, such as the UNCTAD drive for tariff preferences. The central issue in the NIEO relates to the processes of international decision making. The NIEO deals with the classic kind of conflict between those who seek more—more growth, more power—and those wishing to preserve their vested interests.

The UN was the logical place for launching such an effort or, more precisely, for intensifying it since it had always been there. The weighted voting system of the IMF precluded the developing countries from gaining a majority there. In addition, international monetary affairs are not grist for the everyday mill of the diplomat, as is the UN, but rather a domain for the technician; it is hard to arouse the conscience of the world by talking about adjustable pegs, floating exchange rates, or even a link between the issuance of special drawing rights (SDR) and development assistance. The World Bank group also operates under a weighted voting system. Its sphere is limited to development assistance, to lending mainly for specific projects. The GATT does not have weighted voting, but many GATT decisions are self-implementing in the sense that a reciprocal tariff reduction does not require any collective vote.

No other institution had near universality of membership, a voting system that clearly gave control over resolution passing to the developing countries, and also a mandate to deal comprehensively, with money, trade, aid, investment, debt, technology, and so forth, that the UN General Assembly enjoyed. The voting system and the inherent underlying substance of the other relevant international economic institutions were such that they remained under the effective control of the developed countries. The explosion of sovereignties meant that dominance in the General Assembly had passed from the developed country

---

[3] Mahbub ul Haq, *The Third World and the International Economic Order* (Washington, D.C.: Overseas Development Council, 1976), p. 11.

creators to the numerical sovereign majority of developing countries under the one nation, one vote system.

In this process of the interplay between substance and institutions, there are some general principles that seem to be at work. First, the structures of institutions do influence the ways they evolve. The weighted voting institutions have developed differently from those in which sovereignty is the only weight. One writer has noted that in the thirty-odd years of its existence, the General Assembly has adopted something like 3,500 resolutions. Most of these have since been forgotten. "Resolution therapy" he called it.[4] In most instances, the process has been that a majority of nations passes a resolution and a minority with the resources to carry it out ignores it. This may be tyranny of the majority, as United States spokesmen have at times charged, but tyranny that can be ignored is not very stringent. On the other hand, a vote in the IMF approved by the properly weighted majority involves a decision that generally will be carried out by the very majority that approved it. The same is true in the development banks.

Second, substantive vacuums are filled, sometimes proceeding from substance to institution creation and sometimes from institution to appropriation of the substance. A corollary of this generalization is that institutions adapt to prevailing circumstances, which can involve substantial alteration in functions. Albert Hirschman in *Development Projects Observed* notes that the main benefits from a project may be different from those originally expected. The evolution of the World Bank group of institutions also illustrates this. So does the emphasis on UNCTAD in recent years on primary commodity issues.

Third, a dynamic division of labor among institutions develops. This is not just a question of the substance, since to a certain extent the substantive focus of each institution is planned (for the IMF to deal with exchange rates and correction of balance-of-payments disequilibriums, the GATT with tariff levels and other types of trade restrictions, the World Bank group with development finance), but also whether an institution is controlled by the vested interests or the aspirants to power, influence, and benefits. The UN institutions are aspirant controlled, the IMF vested-interest controlled.

There are significant implications of this principle. Each group of countries will wish to negotiate issues of importance to it in the institutions that it dominates. The developed countries will not wish to negotiate tariff reductions in UNCTAD, whereas most developing countries would be quite pleased to move these negotiations there from the GATT. If an institution becomes too large and unwieldly, there will be a tendency to move key negotiating aspects to some smaller body. This is particularly true of the behavior of the developed countries. Even though they were the dominant powers in the IMF, many of the critical negotiations on exchange-rate issues or on balance-of-payments support among its group were conducted by the developed countries in the Group of 10. In theory, the three summit meetings of developed country heads of government

[4] Andrew Boyd, "The United Nations Thirty Years On," *International Affairs* 52 (Jan. 1976), pp. 67-75.

at Rambouillet, Puerto Rico, and Downing Street could have taken place under the auspices of the OECD, but apart from having too many members (twenty-four), the OECD also has some nations that often consider themselves to be part of the developing country bloc.

When the Conference on International Economic Cooperation (CIEC) was created in 1975, the motive was to find a body smaller than the General Assembly and outside the UN where "the participants in the dialogue [would] subordinate ideological debate to constructive and cooperative work."[5] There was always an intrinsic question of the durability of the CIEC because even though it substituted a smaller, nonvoting body for the General Assembly (27 countries instead of 155), it still left the majority in the hands of the developing country-OPEC combination. The debate may have been made more effective by the smaller size, but the structure removed domination from the vested-interest group of developed countries and therefore did not make it a propitious body for them for serious negotiations. Like the UN, a CIEC negotiation did not involve quid pro quos. The logical alternative to handle the substance covered by the CIEC is the joint IMF-World Bank Development Committee. This has only twenty members representing major individual developed countries (the United States, the United Kingdom, France, the Federal Republic of Germany, and Japan) and fifteen constituencies emcompassing the remaining members of the two underlying institutions. Thus, its membership is dominated by the vested-interest countries. It does not directly control resources, but is an amalgam of two bodies that do. One understandable basis for the birth of the CIEC while the Development Committee existed was that the foreign affairs agencies wished to control the North-South debate (the dominant United States agency in the CIEC was the State Department, and in the Development Committee it is the Treasury Department.)

The recently created International Fund for Agricultural Development (IFAD) has a voting structure of one-third developed countries, one-third members of OPEC, one-third developing countries, and it is being hailed by the latter two groups as a harbinger of the future for other financial institutions, such as the World Bank. Dialogue is useful, but control is crucial in how different groups view the various international organizations.

Fourth, one other principle that seems to be at work is that general-purpose organizations made up both of status quo and aspiring nations that possess resolution-passing but no other substantive power, with resolution-passing divorced from control over resources, tend to become radicalized. (The word *radicalized* would not be used by a spokesman from a developing country; such a person would instead stress the need for change now, economic freedom now,

---

[5] Statement by Charles W. Robinson, Under Secretary of State for Economic Affairs, before the House International Relations Committee, State Department news release, February 19, 1976.

and decision-making power now.) This is the way the United States government views the General Assembly, UNCTAD, and the United Nations Industrial Development Organization (UNIDO). The same polarization process took place in many inter-American organizations where voting on economic issues often was the United States on one side and all the rest on the other side.

Evolution of Institutions

Both the process and the substance of negotiations differ in those institutions dominated by the vested-interest countries from those controlled by the aspirant nations. In the GATT, to take an example where this is self-evident, the articles of agreement were framed on the basis of mutual rights and obligations. A negotiation involved some exchange, a tariff reduction for a tariff reduction, a binding of a tariff level involving compensation when the binding was breached in exchange for the same from another contracting party. Negotiation involved mutual consideration. This has been altering. In practice, if not literally in the words of the articles, the developing countries never granted much in the way of reciprocity. They also complained that they received little in the way of benefits. Part IV of the GATT enshrined the principle of nonreciprocity in the articles. The current round of multilateral trade negotiations accepts this concept of nonreciprocity, although with a caveat: "The developed countries do not expect reciprocity for commitments made by them in the negotiations to reduce or remove tariff and other barriers to the trade of developing countries, i.e., the developed countries do not expect the developing countries, in the course of the trade negotiations, to make contributions which are inconsistent with their individual development, financial and trade needs."[6] The current effort in the GATT of the developing countries is to achieve "special and differential treatment" in all GATT matters—that is, to secure nonreciprocity across-the-board.

As the GATT has developed, therefore, it came to be made up of two classes of countries, one that exchanges rights and obligations and a second that seeks rights but is willing to accept few obligations. The argument for this is that inequality of economic power does not permit equality in negotiation and that unilateral concessions by the developed countries will eventually redound to their benefit as the developing countries become better markets for the goods and services of the richer countries.

The emergence in practice of two classes of members in the GATT has been a complicating negotiating factor. One group of members is prepared to negotiate on the basis of quid pro quos, whereas the other group, which is not so prepared, wishes to have a voice on the content of the former negotiation. A group of experts in the United States has recommended that the GATT be altered formally to have two concentric groups of countries, one willing to take on additional

[6] Declaration of ministers approved at Tokyo on September 14, 1973.

obligations in quid pro quo negotiations, which then would be generalized to all other members, and a second group not so prepared to negotiate.

The IMF, in theory, treats all countries alike in its articles, although in practice special provision is made for the developing countries. The extended fund facility, which is not even in theory operated separately from the remainder of the fund, is designed exclusively for developing countries. The trust fund, using the profits from the sale of some IMF-held gold, is specifically earmarked for the poorest countries, although a trust was set up in order to retain the legal purity of equal treatment of all members.

The General Assembly is an exhortatory body. When spokesmen from developing countries assert that they wish to negotiate specific changes in trade, monetary, and other economic rules there, they do not generally mean that they should provide a quid pro quo. When the United States uses the slogan "cooperation and not confrontation," as it did frequently after the Sixth Special Session, what it really means is cooperation in the UN (that is, less voting) but negotiation elsewhere. There are periodic recommendations that the General Assembly and its affiliated bodies should devise some means of conciliation before voting in order that this cooperation rather than confrontation can be achieved. These efforts have not been successful, and there really is serious doubt that they can be in any fundamental sense. Conciliation of differences involves negotiation in a form that implies an exchange of rights and obligations. When one of the two negotiating sides is not prepared to undertake new obligations, there is a process of concession and not negotiation as it is normally understood in the United States.

This process of providing special privileges to countries that have been disadvantaged over time is neither unique nor necessarily inappropriate. It is an extension to countries of affirmative action programs in favor of individuals. It would be hard to maintain that the past international economic system has not had its elements of exploitation. The tariff structure of developed countries that protects domestic labor most in those very areas in which less developed countries are competitive (and thereby, in effect, exports unemployment) and distribution of international monetary reserves under the system that has developed are technical examples of this.

Even if one accepts the concept of affirmative action domestically, the transference of this concept internationally does involve conceptual problems. Richard Cooper has noted that there is a fallacy in anthropomorphizing nations. Special concessions to Brazil or Mexico or India, for example, might not translate into special concessions for the most needy people in those countries. Most special concessions to all developing countries—a self-designated category—are more likely to benefit Brazil and Mexico and other rich developing countries whereas the most serious problems of poverty are in the very poor countries unable to take much advantage of such "benefits" as trade concessions since they have little to export.

What to Expect in the United Nations

The foregoing analysis of how institutions operate and of how countries negotiate in different organizations depending on their dominant groups can help explain a good deal that has happened in the UN in recent years and what should be expected for the future. If bargaining in the UN is essentially a device for obtaining concessions, this makes the dialectic cited earlier a natural one. Countries seeking concessions propose, but they will be ignored for the most part until they confront, and then there will be a synthesis in which a concession is achieved. This may not be precisely what was proposed but some variant of it. The actual concession is unlikely to be negotiated in the UN, but rather in one of the dominant-nation controlled institutions. Many writers have analogized the UN process to the organizing phase of labor unions or the civil rights movement in the United States, both of which also required a process of proposal and confrontation. If one accepts that privilege is not normally graciously and unilaterally abandoned, then this process of confrontation is necessary. Gamani Corea, the secretary general of UNCTAD, recently made this point forcefully in describing how structural change can be brought about: "One [technique] is the notion of cooperation by the developing countries for the purpose of improving their collective bargaining power vis-à-vis the outside world, of mobilizing countervailing pressure, of acquiring muscle and applying leverage."[7]

Some illustrations of this process at work can be cited. Corea, in the speech and article from which the foregoing citation was taken, was discussing the outcome of UNCTAD's fourth plenary conference in Nairobi, where the key theme was the developing countries' insistence on a common fund for financing primary commodity buffer stocks. When UNCTAD first proposed this a few years earlier as part of its integrated commodity program, the United States was inclined to dismiss the idea. By mid-1976 at UNCTAD-4, the United States was still not prepared to accept the principle of a common fund but was at least prepared to favor a meeting to discuss the issue. By the time of the Downing Street summit in May 1977, the principle of a common fund was accepted, although not necessarily as proposed by UNCTAD, under which the fund would be set up by contributions in advance of reaching the underlying agreements for which buffer stocks and other financing might be necessary. It now seems certain that there will be a common fund, most likely to be built up as underlying individual agreements are reached, with a control structure that will be a compromise between developed-country dominance and developing-country control. The United States will probably seek to keep the common fund institution outside the central UN framework.

One need not rely on prediction for illustrations. IDA, the concessional loan

---

[7] Gamani Corea, "UNCTAD and the New International Economic Order," *International Affairs* 53 (April 1977), p. 184.

affiliate of the World Bank was born out of developing country pressure in the UN to set up a special UN fund for economic development. That was the proposal, and the confrontation followed in the UN. The synthesis was to set up the new facility in the World Bank, where weighted voting and developed country dominance prevailed. The IMF's compensatory financing facility grew out of pressure in the UN. It was a restricted facility when first established in 1963, was further liberalized in 1966, and then liberalized again in 1976 following the meeting of the IMF Interim Committee in Jamaica. This second liberalization grew out of proposals made by the United States at the Seventh Special Session of the General Assembly when the United States was looking for techniques to blunt other specific aspects of the NIEO.

The combination of the Sixth and Seventh Special Sessions are worth examining from the viewpoint of this dialectic. The Sixth Special Session was a diplomatic catastrophe for the United States. As it had done on UN economic issues whenever it possibly could, the United States sought to ignore the session. It expected that the session would make a series of demands on the developed countries and that most of these, if not heeded, would go away over time. The United States, however, had misjudged the context; the demands were made, they were given a slogan of the NIEO, and they caught on in the third world. The United States complained about voting tyranny, about the uselessness of the divorcement of voting power from the provision of resources, and of the need of consent by those powers being importuned.

When the Seventh Special Session came along, this meeting was not ignored. The United States made proposals, most of them not new. They included giving major attention to the ongoing multilateral trade negotiations in the GATT, looking at primary commodities on a case-by-case basis and even reaching formal agreements when appropriate, replenishing the funds of the international financial institutions, and giving particular attention to the poorest countries. The liberalization of the IMF compensatory financing facility was not new, since the facility existed, but it was significant. One illustration of its significance is that drawings from it were more than double in 1976 alone than what they had been in the previous fourteen years combined.

Many writers have cited the Seventh Special Session as a success for United States diplomacy in that the United States, by taking the initiative, set the agenda for the international debate. Another interpretation is that the Seventh Special Session represented a point of synthesis of the dialectic. The confrontation had not ended, it had just moved on. Today, developing country references to special sessions rarely cite the resolution adopted at the end of the Seventh Special Sessions (it had the humdrum title "Development and International Economic Cooperation," something that hardly anyone remembers), but rather the NIEO resolutions adopted at the end of the Sixth Special Session (which everyone involved in the North-South debate remembers). The United States can take rhetorical initiatives in the UN, but it is not likely to be able to sustain substantive ones since that would require its sacrifice of privilege in the world system. Such sacrifice occurs from time to time, and the United States has been a leader in this field, as when it initiated the provision of foreign aid to countries not formerly colonies or possessions, but there is a political and self-interest limit to the number of times and ways in which this can be done.

The general system of preferences that went into effect in the United States at the beginning of 1976 was the result of UNCTAD pressure initiated in 1964. United States leadership in negotiating the first coffee agreement in 1962 was a response to Latin American pressure exerted over most of the previous decade. The adoption of Part IV of the GATT was the consequence of the pressure being exerted by UNCTAD to become the central forum for dealing with trade issues. The United States proposal for the IMF trust fund grew out of a desire not only to reduce the role of gold as a reserve asset in the international monetary system, but also to blunt the developing country drive for an SDR-aid link. The idea for a link between resource transfers to poor countries and the creation of international liquidity is not a new one, but it reached its first international confrontational peak at UNCTAD-3. The trust fund in the IMF is largely an indirect outgrowth of this pressure.

Confrontation can be mitigated, but it would be unrealistic to expect it to be eliminated. For example, during the Kennedy years of the Alliance for Progress, the United States was perceived in Latin America as a cooperative and interested neighbor. During those years, however, the confrontation between hemispheres did not cease on trade, investment, and aid issues. It was Eduardo Frei of Chile, the president of the country that had probably been treated more generously than any other under the Alliance, who wrote an article in *Foreign Affairs* titled "The Alliance that Lost Its Way."

Some confrontation of a general, or systemic, nature will seek to alter the ways in which decisions are made. Some pressure will be exerted to alter the weighted voting system in the IMF or the World Bank group; this already has occurred to a certain extent, when the OPEC countries were given greater voting shares at the expense of the developed countries. The formation of the Committee of 20 to negotiate reform of the international monetary system and the subsequent creation of the Interim Committee of the IMF were responses to developing country pressures against the use of the Group of 10 for these processes. This did not eliminate the Group of 10, or decision-making by the developed countries in even smaller groups, but it was a step in the direction the developing countries were seeking since they were included in these bodies. The voting system in the IFAD was another step in this direction.

Some pressure to alter decision-making processes is designed to make the UN itself the key decision-making body of the international economic system. This is a goal of the NIEO. Other pressures will be focused on specific substantive issues, such as the SDR-aid link, freer technology transfers, alteration of the patent system, and more commodity agreements.

Policy Implications

If one accepts that change requires some degree of confrontation, and not simply "reasoning together" or conciliating differences, then United States policy should expect the UN to be the focus of that confrontation process. Efforts to work out procedures for conciliation of the precise words of resolutions will occasionally work, as they did at the end of the Seventh Special Session (though, even then, the United States felt constrained to enter major reservations on the concept of the NIEO, manipulating terms of trade, commitments on resource transfers, the SDR-aid link, and decision-making in international financial institutions). Words, however, cannot eternally mask underlying substantive differences, and confrontation means that these differences exist. This does not argue against seeking to mitigate vitriolic confrontation or to formulate conciliation procedures, since an occasional donnybrook might be avoided or a particularly acrimonious debate tempered, but rather to warn against excessive expectations.

The confrontation is best expressed in sloganeering (the New International Economic Order) and in resolutions. Railing against the tyranny of votes is to deplore the very nature of the beast. A vote resolves nothing unless accepted by those against or to whom it is directed. More than any other nation, the United States tends to be upset by losing votes. Other developed countries, in varying degrees, are more prone to accept a vote or abstain on a resolution and only occasionally to vote no but in all such cases to make their reservations clear for the record. The vote as such need be given little weight; the essence of policy should be to understand what lies behind a vote since it reflects the thinking of spokesmen for a majority of the nations of the world and often of the world's population.

Developing-country votes are sometimes egregiously outrageous, as in the Zionism-racism case. UN economic resolutions sometimes have a real impact on events, as when they involve budgets or when action can take place without the consent of those who oppose the resolution. Demands by developing countries are not always reasonable, as indexing much of the world's trade would not be. These require a reaction, but most votes can be calmly accepted or rejected.

It makes little sense for the United States to consent to a proposal that it considers unwise in order to obtain some political good will. This is ephemeral. When a specific concession is obtained by developing countries, this is not the end of the process but instead a signal for the natural process to renew itself either to improve the details of that concession, as with the IMF compensatory finance facility, or to move on to a new area. Since no quid pro quos are given, there can be no end to the process of concession seeking until such time as individual developing countries are deemed equal enough to provide something tangible in return for concessions granted.

From time to time it is advocated that the weighting systems in the IMF, the World Bank group, and the regional development banks should be altered to give equal or majority votes to the developing countries. The developing countries believe this would be meaningful since these institutions dispose of resources and a resolution in them is likely to be carried out. However, this first reaction may be deceptive. If these institutions were transformed into aspirant-dominated bodies, they would cease to be what they are and new bodies would have to be created in their stead. Making the structure of the IMF more like that of the UN would likely be a Pyrrhic victory. It would transform the existing tacit division of lavor in an unsustainable way. The developed countries will not accept decisions deeply affecting their income and employment in bodies in which they provide the resources and undertake the obligations and others make the decisions and accept only the concessions.

The very word *confrontation* has a pejorative ring. Developing countries may feel that they are educating the populace of the richer countries about the true state of world privilege. The General Assembly and UNCTAD do serve this educational purpose. The United States has also used the UN for educational purposes when it has suited its objectives. The World Food Conference in Rome in November 1974 was a United States initiative to this end. With occasional exceptions, however, the General Assembly or a plenary involving all the nations of the UN is too large a body for a sustained debate on a complex issue. The Economic and Social Council theoretically could serve this purpose in the UN structure, but to date it has not.

There are global issues for which the UN is a natural forum for negotiation. The law of the sea is one of these; environmental control may be another. Inevitably, because these are universal themes with diverse interests, progress on these issues will be slow. But for most economic issues, the negotiations are likely to be more partial, involving either functional areas, such as trade, money, and aid, or not require near universality to reach decisions. In these cases, developing countries will seek to propose and confront in the UN, and the United States will negotiate elsewhere, if at all. The development of the UN into an attention-getting forum in the economic field has not been a deformation of the institution. Rather, given the nature of the array of other institutions, their control mechanisms, and the essential requirement that the less privileged must use some form of leverage to successfully obtain concessions from the more privileged, the UN is the result of a rational process.

There is tension between those who advocate radical organizational change, namely, the have-not countries (or more precisely, those countries between the very poor and the rich) and those prepared to accept incremental change, generally the developed countries. This organizational tension is also played out on a substantive level of real problems. The tensions can be mitigated by the United States by the degree of its responsiveness to institutional and substantive change, but they cannot be eliminated over the foreseeable future. This is not deplorable; it is the stuff from which change occurs.

"North-South" Negotiations

The developed nations, largely of the Northern Hemisphere, "the North," and the developing nations of the Southern Hemisphere, "the South," have confronted each other with growing frequency on economic problems. The developing countries share feelings of widespread dependence on the industrial world. Reactions to colonialism, to the racism and paternalism of industrial countries, and to the developing countries' lack of influence within the world economy all contribute to the claims the developing countries make in the United Nations and other bodies. They are pursuing both internal development and greater participation in international systems in a complex series of negotiations with industrialized countries.

The differences among developing nations, the variety of their relations with the developed world, and the diversity of the issues under negotiation make it difficult to put all third world policies in one framework. Moreover, developing nations do not seek all of their goals with equal determination. One common element in UN discussions of development, however, is opposition to dependency. Yet some measures that the developing countries have sought, such as the tariff preferences negotiated by the UN Conference on Trade and Development (UNCTAD) and the Lomé Convention between fifty-two developing countries and the European Economic Community, could well maintain rather than decrease third world dependence on the developed countries. The UN declarations of 1974 and 1975 calling for a New International Economic Order (NIEO)[1] further confuse categorization by advocating cooperation and interdependence as much as fundamental change in international economic systems.

The interdependence stressed as an objective of the NIEO implies that both developed and developing countries have the capacity to strike mutually beneficial bargains within a framework of economic interactions. Thus the NIEO does

[1] Guy F. Erb and Valeriana Kallab, eds., *Beyond Dependency: The Developing World Speaks Out* (Washington, D.C.: Overseas Development Council, 1976), Annex B, pp. 185–250.

not envisage a "decoupling" or separation of developing nations from the international economy, although such a concept has been considered within the third world.

Negotiations for International and Internal Change

The NIEO declarations treat nearly all aspects of the relationship between industrialized and developing states. But as NIEO embraced proposals for trade in manufactured and primary products, aid, debt, renegotiation, and technology, the developed nations began to emphasize meeting the basic human needs of the populations of the poor countries.

As developing nations press for major changes in the economic policies of developed nations and as industrialized countries emphasize the internal changes that "real" development requires, the two camps risk heightening the tension between them.[2] On one hand, the NIEO approach stresses negotiations among states in order to meet the needs of developing countries for access to markets in rich countries, greater stability in their earnings from primary commodities, official and private transfers of resources, technology transfers, and greater participation in decisions made within international economic systems. In contrast, the basic human needs strategy emphasizes the welfare of individuals and the domestic policies required for widespread economic and social development. The United States Congress and the executive branch have also stressed the protection of political rights and have linked United States bilateral and multilateral development policies to violations of the security of individuals by governments of developing countries.

Representatives of developing nations often make their claims on international systems on behalf of the impoverished masses in their countries, but in doing so third world governments are frequently calling for the elimination of international political and economic inequities that merely mirror domestic social and economic imbalances that few governments effectively address. Furthermore, governments of the developed countries face electorates that are reluctant to take from the poor in rich countries to give to the rich in poor countries. The attitudes underlying such views can constructively question development assistance programs. They can also strengthen those in developed countries who resist what they see as encroachments by developing nations on existing international power relationships and the living standards of industrial nations.

Negotiations within the UN system on NIEO proposals or basic human needs strategies may affect various third world countries in different ways. A decade ago, Alister McIntyre drew a distinction between *"structural dependence*—the dependence that arises because of the size and structure of economy and cannot be helped, and *functional dependence*—the dependence that arises as a result of

[2] Robert W. Tucker, *The Inequality of Nations* (New York: Basic Books, Inc., 1977).

the particular policies chosen and can, therefore, be avoided if alternative policies are pursued."[3] The small size and limited weight within the world economy of many developing countries indicate that they will continue to experience some form of "structural" dependence for some time to come, but even small nations, and certainly the larger developing countries, can affect the way in which their economies interact with the global economy through trade, investment, and technology transfers. Policies affecting external relations will not necessarily alter internal political-economic systems, however, and some developing countries claim that greater self-reliance and less dependence will occur only if economic and political measures within developing countries contribute to social justice, the effective utilization of national resources, an increase in popular participation in development decisions, and a reduction of the internal concentration of economic power.[4]

Yet the leaders of developing countries would probably not accept a link between the reduction of external dependence, on one hand, and internal economic and social change on the other. Since governments can more easily negotiate on issues that do not affect the status quo within their borders, they emphasize the internationally oriented NIEO proposals. Through trade and investment negotiations affecting economic relations between rich and poor nations, countries can alter their "functional" dependence on the developed world. If the achievement of international objectives and internal development are not linked, the dichotomy between the NIEO and basic human needs strategies will continue, leaving the status of many people in developing countries essentially unchanged and possibly weakening the support in the developed countries for policies that meet some of the NIEO demands.

From Confrontation to Negotiation

The changes sought by developing nations have been perceived by many in the industrial world as unacceptable intrusions upon the status quo. The central objectives of the NIEO proposals were the developing countries' desire to exert more influence on systems of world trade, finance, and technology and to increase the competitive strength of their investors, traders, and governments. Although a principal aim of the developing world was a change in the rules of the game, rather than of the game itself, even that objective appeared to affect adversely the interests of the industrialized countries. As a result, the latter only reluctantly entered into negotiations on some of the facets of the new order advocated by the developing world. Developed countries rejected many of the NIEO demands just as they had rebuffed previous attempts to modify their economic policies and the

[3] Norman Girvan, "The Development of Dependency Economics in the Caribbean and Latin America: Review and Comparison," *Social and Economic Studies* 22 (March 1973), pp. 4–12.
[4] Samuel L. Parmar, "Self-Reliant Development in an 'Interdependent' World," in Erb and Kallab, p. 6.

Bretton-Woods system. However, they could not deflect the increasingly confident developing countries from their intention to press the apparent advantage gained by an alliance with the Organization of Petroleum Exporting Countries (OPEC). The alliance with OPEC endures even though the declines in raw materials prices and the rapidly rising debt of developing countries disabused many of them of the notion that the oil price rise had caused an immediate and widespread alteration in world power relations.

"North-South" encounters have taken place in several international institutions: the UN General Assembly, the UN Conference on Trade and Development (UNCTAD), the Conference on International Economic Co-operation (CIEC), the International Labor Organization (ILO), the International Monetary Fund (IMF), the General Agreement on Tariffs and Trade (GATT), and a variety of other international settings. Some of these negotiations affect policy by producing resolutions and declarations that provide developing countries with the concepts and proposals to put before decision-makers in industrialized countries. The NIEO Declaration of 1974 was one of the more influential of such resolutions. The Sixth Special Session of the General Assembly, at which the NIEO was proposed, culminated a long period of North-South debates on economic reform. The declaration and the program of action contained many proposals made by developing countries during the 1960s. The NIEO Declaration was distinguished from its predecessors by a sense of self-confidence among the developing countries that they expressed by emphasizing collective self-reliance.

The developing countries complemented the NIEO Declaration both with the Charter of Economic Rights and Duties of States, agreed on in December 1974, and by meeting outside the framework of the UN to agree on the Dakar Declaration and Action Program on Raw Materials. The Dakar Declaration and later initiatives taken under the auspices of the nonaligned countries quickly became part of the UN deliberations, while the Solemn Declaration of OPEC member countries in April 1975 provided further support to the developing countries. These statements by developing countries set the framework for North-South negotiations, providing the basis for subsequent conferences between industrialized and developing countries.

To respond to third world initiatives and to reduce the likelihood of serious confrontations over international economic policies, the United States and other developed countries softened their opposition to the calls for a new international economic order and agreed to a Consensus Resolution of the Seventh Special Session of the General Assembly in September 1975. The United States shift from confrontation in 1974 to moderation in 1975 did not, however, diminish official skepticism about the ability of the UN to play more than just a rhetorical role in North-South issues. Significant resistance persisted in developed countries to "serious" negotiations within the UN, and particularly within the UNCTAD. This combined with the United States desire for an institutional mechanism in which to confront oil producers on energy prices led to the compromises that created the Conference on International Economic Co-operation (CIEC) in Paris, also known as the North-South dialogue. In forming CIEC in late 1975 the United States sought a forum for energy deliberations and the transfer of such NIEO issues as raw materials, debt, and development finance out of the UN. But the developing countries maintained a NIEO approach in CIEC, and the North-South dialogue did little to alter the concepts that had originated in the UN. When CIEC adjourned in June 1977, UNCTAD was specifically requested to negotiate on commodity policy, while most other issues were transmitted back to the General Assembly or to the World Bank and the International Monetary Fund.

Despite the inconclusive ending of CIEC, a reasonable chance remains that North-South negotiators can successfully address specific issues such as commodity policy, liberalization of trade in manufactured goods, and raw materials investment policies. This possibility owes much to the insistence by the OPEC and other third world countries that the developed countries deal adequately with the NIEO demands. By their example, their financial contributions to institutions such as the International Fund for Agricultural Development, and their commitment to the UNCTAD's common fund for international buffer stocks, members of OPEC have contributed fundamentally to bringing the developed and developing countries to the bargaining table. Whether the OPEC coalition with developing countries that do not produce oil can be maintained will be a critical North-South issue in the years ahead. Although the oil exporters have greatly influenced the North-South negotiations on a new international economic order, these nations have a large stake in the present international economic system because of their contacts with the corporations, banks, and international capital markets of the industrialized countries.

In addition to the commodity policy talks, which have become central to the NIEO debates, negotiations are under way on (1) the relationship between the European Communities and the Africa, Pacific, and Caribbean (ACP) signatories to the Lomé convention; (2) the contracts between host countries and corporations that affect raw materials development as well as production of and trade in manufactured goods; and (3) within the multilateral trade negotiations (MTN), the pattern of world industrial production of manufactured goods. International negotiations have also considered the law of the sea and the debt position of developing countries, including their relations to private banks in developed countries. All of these issues of course have important implications for the UN.

The UNCTAD Commodities Negotiations

Developing countries that export raw materials have traditionally stressed the problems they confront as a result of the slow growth that their exports have experienced because of competition from synthetics or other substitutes and from production of like products in developed countries. They also emphasize the often unfavorable relationship (or terms of trade) between the prices of raw materials and the prices of goods imported by raw materials exporters and the fluctuations that characterize the prices of and total earnings from primary commodities. Finally, they point to their incapacity to process the products that they mine or produce and the obstacles to trade they face with those goods that they do process.

The developing nations and the UNCTAD secretariat have advanced a comprehensive set of proposals to meet these issues in an "integrated commodity program." To stabilize commodities trade, the program proposes international agreements to govern trade in individual commodities, using buffer stocks when appropriate to help stabilize price fluctuations, and intergovernmental commitments to purchase and supply raw materials to increase the stability of markets. In addition, an international common fund to finance the buffer stocks for ten core commodities (cocoa, coffee, copper, cotton, hard fibers jute and manufactures, rubber, sugar, tea, and tin), chosen because of their importance for developing countries and their ability to be stored, is suggested. Finally, requests are included to improve compensatory financing available to offset shortfalls in anticipated earnings from the export of primary commodities and to stimulate increased processing of raw materials in producing countries through greater investment in such industries and through reduction of developed-country trade barriers to processed goods.

The nonaligned countries have announced their frustration with the lack of progress on commodity and debt issues and thus raised the possibility of a return to the confrontational tactics of 1973–74. For example, a common fund financed primarily by OPEC and other developing countries could be used to intervene in individual commodity markets without adequate participation by the consuming countries. As the early Tin Agreements and the cocoa negotiations of 1975 indicated, raw-material producers and consuming countries can negotiate individual commodity agreements without United States participation. The "threat" of United States withdrawal from a negotiation is therefore insufficient to prevent establishment of a commodity agreement that may include provisions objectionable to consuming governments. Moreover, producer countries have demonstrated an ability to work with each other. Their incapacity to take concerted action on the pricing of commodities does not necessarily indicate what some of them might attempt if developed and developing countries fail to agree on joint and viable commodity policies.

Developed countries have much more to gain by joining commodity agreements, especially given the anti-inflationary benefits that commodity price stabilization can bring to consuming countries, than by remaining aloof from agreements or initiating a "commodity war" in which the United States and other industrialized countries mobilize their considerable reserves of raw materials. From the point of view of the producing countries, participation in commodity agreements with consuming countries exposes their objectives to the possible veto of consuming countries, but it also offers the distinct advantage of ensuring the support of consuming countries for agreed policies of intervention in commodity markets. Without the participation of the consumers, the producers have little chance of successfully influencing markets for most commodities. Normally, power is divided equally within commodity agreement councils between producers and consumers, with the major members holding a decisive share of the votes within each group. This interdependent situation is evidently regarded as an improvement by producing countries that would otherwise be subject to the vagaries of the market with little prospect of effective measures to counter unfavorable price fluctuations.

Multilateral Negotiations on Trade in Manufactured Goods

The current round of multilateral trade negotiations (MTN) is associated with the General Agreement on Tariffs and Trade (GATT). Although the relationship of the GATT with the UN has been the most tenuous, its procedures and the basic agreement itself have been influenced by UN debates, particularly those held in UNCTAD. The present trade negotiations were launched by the "Tokyo Declaration" of 1973 and include several different approaches to tariff reduction and to the liberalization or surveillance of nontariff measures.

The interests of the developing countries in the trade negotiations are far from uniform. A few countries, such as Brazil, export both primary products and manufactured goods and thus may consider policies designed to maximize their gains in both the multilateral trade and the commodity negotiations. Others, like the Republic of Korea and Singapore, have concentrated on developing their industrial sectors, often utilizing foreign-based corporations, and have a considerable capacity to export manufactured goods. Some of these goods now benefit from preferential tariff systems that the developed countries accept after years of negotiations within UNCTAD. Still other countries, particularly those in Africa, are so dependent on the export of primary commodities that their interest in the multilateral trade negotiations is at best long-term. The African, Caribbean, and Pacific (ACP) signatories of the Lomé Convention are in a separate category because they have obtained duty-free treatment for nearly all of their exports to the Common Market. This gives them a margin of preferential advantage (particularly on tropical products) over developed and other developing countries offering products in the Common Market.

Developing countries therefore are generally seeking ways to participate more fully in tariff and nontariff liberalization while maintaining advantages they have obtained from tariff preferences. Consequently, their demands can be inconsistent. In UN resolutions they have stressed the maintenance of present margins of tariff preference, the advance implementation of concessions in favor of developing countries, the elimination or liberalization of quantitative restrictions and other nontariff barriers affecting exports by developing countries, differential treatment of developing countries in the provisions of the various codes for nontariff barriers to trade, and adherence by developed countries to the principle of "nonreciprocity." Their demands for tariff preferences, differential treatment on nontariff barriers, and nonreciprocity are particularly relevant to an assessment of the potential impact of trade negotiations on the developing countries. Tariff preferences are extended unilaterally by developed countries, but multilaterally negotiated tariff cuts are "bound"—that is, increases in tariff rates require compensation to affected trading partners. Preferential margins in contrast, can be altered or abolished at any time, leaving the recipient country dependent on decisions of a developed country.

Some developed countries, notably those in Europe, have improved their preferential schemes since they were first introduced by adding products and by simplifying or reducing the impact of limitations or restrictions. Although the gains from these schemes tend to concentrate on the major developing-country exporters of manufactures, some such gains have accrued to smaller exporters as a result of limitations placed on the benefits that single countries can obtain from exports of particular items.

Many developing countries, therefore, feel that tariff preferences should be safeguarded as much as possible. They argue that tariff preferences are immediately available without reciprocal concessions, whereas potential benefits from negotiated tariff reductions will be available only at some future time.

The dilemma of the tariff preference issue is that developing countries tend to overcommit themselves to the preferences while developed countries have not yet indicated that their offers in the MTN will be substantial enough to demonstrate convincingly the advantages that all nations could receive from multilateral trade liberalization. If significant multilateral tariff cuts are agreed on, it should be possible to reconcile the short-run interests of developing countries in tariff preferences with their long-term interests in a world trading system that ensures them access to the markets of developed countries. The initial ten-year period of tariff preferences, expiring in the early 1980s for most schemes, will almost certainly be prolonged for another decade, and developing countries can expect a transition period of some fifteen years during which preferential margins will gradually decrease as multilateral tariff cuts are introduced.

The MTN now includes talks on codes of conduct for trade practices such as subsidies and countervailing duties, quality standards, rules for purchases by governments, and import safeguards. Comparable to their demands for tariff preferences, developing countries have requested special allowances in such codes to help them overcome nontariff obstacles to their exports. Differential measures might include special tariff-cutting procedures applied to developing countries and revisions in the GATT itself.

The Tokyo Declaration accepts the introduction of differential measures in favor of developing countries. Nevertheless, the need to provide developing countries with special and differential treatment to ensure their support for the outcome of the negotiations is a new development for negotiators accustomed to a "key-country" or trilateral approach to international economic policy. Trade disputes have already arisen between new exporters and importing countries on the use of such measures as subsidies and standards. Without guidelines for trade policies that commit all parties to the effective surveillance of nontariff measures, such disputes are likely to increase in number and seriousness and greatly complicate economic relations between developed countries and nations such as Brazil, Mexico, and India. These nations can export products facing barriers that trade policy codes will govern. From the point of view of developed countries, then, excluding the developing countries from decision-making on the management of codes for international commerce is potentially disadvantageous. For developing nations, however, there is the danger that differential practices could engender discriminatory practices analogous to the divergences that now exist in the various preference schemes; in other words, such special measures could place developing countries in a situation where they remain subject to unilateral decisions by "donor" countries.

Developing countries have protective motives for trade barriers at least as strong, and often stronger, than those in developed countries. They defend nonreciprocity by arguing that they will spend most of any increased export earnings in the markets of developed countries for the imports on which they rely heavily. Also, it is difficult for them to commit themselves to long-term concessions that would inhibit their ability to impose import restrictions to protect their fragile balance of payments. In contrast, United States insistence on the need for reciprocal concessions from developing countries is based on the view that some of them, particularly those with a considerable capacity to export manufactured goods, can make trade concessions that would in fact rationalize their own structures of import protection and benefit their own economies. While it may be possible to convince developing countries that concessions, including the acceptance of obligations under trade policy codes, are in their interest, there will be problems of "burden sharing" within the group of developing countries. Despite their relatively advanced levels of development and their position as a dominant supplier of the products in question, those countries selected for contribution may well ask why they should be singled out from other developing countries.

During 1976 and 1977, while progress was slow on tariff and nontariff liberalization, developing nations did not feel that a prior commitment to reciprocity would be worthwhile, although several indicated a willingness to make concessions when the negotiations concluded. At that point, a lack of appropriate reciprocity from developing countries could limit their participation in the final decisions on the liberalization of trade. In other words, they would have allowed a commitment to nonreciprocity—which had its origin in UNCTAD deliberations—to detract from potential long-term gains from the trade negotiations.

The Lomé Convention

Negotiations between the members of the European Economic Community and forty-six ACP countries established the Lomé Convention after a process quite different from other North-South negotiations.[5] A unified group of developing countries, numbering fifty-two in 1977, sought and obtained a set of uniform trade and financial measures from a group of industrialized nations. This contrasts with most bargaining over contributions to international financial institutions, or the UNCTAD preference negotiations, which resulted in developed countries' implementing a wide variety of national schemes with many different sorts of restrictions.

The Lomé Convention has been described as the first step toward a new international economic order, but the relevance of the Lomé Convention to the evolution of new economic systems and the NIEO proposals lies primarily in the fact that it was jointly negotiated between developing and developed countries. It is an example of both a successful North-South negotiation and an alternative regional and "vertical" model to the global framework of North-South cooperation sought within the UN system. The negotiations leading up to that convention exemplify a North-South bargaining process that achieved its objectives. The convention contains concrete development policies, although it fell short of the demands of ACP countries. However, when analyzed as an alternative to the UN model, one must admit that the Lomé Convention perpetuates former relationships between colonized and colonizing countries. The administration of Lomé policies remains firmly in the hands of the Commission of the European Communities.

The ACP countries had to first negotiate among themselves before bargaining with the Common Market. These preliminary negotiations forged stronger links between French- and English-speaking African countries, and between the African group as a whole and the Caribbean and Pacific participants. These relations among the ACP countries may nevertheless have strengthened their tendency to adopt defensive reactions to global proposals, like tariff preferences or new commodity programs, that potentially dilute the effects of the Lomé Convention.

The ACP countries, in their approach to international economic negotiations, appear reluctant to trade hard earned gains, however small, for multilateral measures of uncertain impact and problematical implementation. Perhaps because of their great need for external financial support and their dependence on relatively unstable earnings from a few commodities, African nations within the ACP group have generally sought immediate benefits such as aid transfers, compensatory finance, and European tariff preferences. They also want guarantees that their interests as emerging exporters of such commodities as tea and coffee will be safeguarded in international agreements.

Although the Lomé Convention expires in 1980, the ACP countries will probably seek to renegotiate and improve its main components rather than to globalize its measures. In one sense, then, the Lomé Convention could impede global North-South initiatives. Commodity agreements between all producers and con-

---

[5] Commission of the European Communities, "ACP-EEC Convention of Lomé," *Official Journal of the European Communities* 19 (January 30, 1976).

sumers are never easy to achieve, and negotiations on such instruments can become more complicated if a significant number of the producing nations have an incentive to maintain their ties to the Common Market.

Negotiations between Countries and Companies

Countries endowed with raw materials and other nations with significant foreign investments have frequently renegotiated contracts with foreign private investors.[6] This process has proceeded furthest in the petroleum industry, but hard rock mining and other raw materials companies as well as manufacturing companies came under increasing pressure from host countries during the 1960s and 1970s. Some commentators in developed countries now claim that investment in exploring and developing minerals in the third world has virtually ceased as a result of escalated demands by host countries.

There has been a slow and often difficult movement away from the types of concessions and leases that governed mineral production and trade during the colonial and immediate postcolonial period. Traditional concessions, entitling the concessionaire to exploit one or more natural resources, were first supplanted by more modern concessions and then by production sharing, service, and work contracts. Royalties were once the main instrument used to calculate payments made to governments, but income taxes increased in importance by the 1950s, and other changes were introduced later to link mineral extraction and other parts of the host country's economy.

Traditional concessions have given way to more complex agreements because in many instances producing countries have desired to increase government participation in the ownership of mining operations and to expand the government's management role. Modern concessions thus include equity sharing arrangements of various types and government attempts to exercise some management decisions. In some cases, after nationalization has given complete control to governments, management contracts that govern day-to-day operations have been signed with foreign firms. Royalties fixed per ton have been replaced by complex mineral arrangements, including stipulations on such issues as loan-to-equity ratios, plant capacity, employment and training requirements, and other conditions intended to increase the contribution of mineral investments to the economic and social development of the host country.

Aside from oil producers, host countries in the developing world remain heavily dependent on direct and portfolio investors for the capital necessary to develop raw materials projects. By increasing demands on foreign companies, host countries may improve their returns, but they can also worsen the climate for substantial new investments there and in other countries that are considered

---

[6] Guy F. Erb, "Issues Affecting Trade and Investment in Non-Fuel Minerals," *Journal of International Law* (Case Western Reserve University) 8 (Spring 1976): 429–51.

likely to make similar changes. Thus governments controlling raw materials face a choice between policies that aim at maximizing the return from specific projects but perhaps discourage investments in new projects and policies, including enhanced investment security, that offer adequate returns to the companies with the necessary access to capital, technology, and markets.

In addition to unilateral contractual, tax, or investment law actions, some producing countries have tried to increase their participation in raw-material development by joining producer associations. The UN Charter of Economic Rights and Duties of States strongly emphasizes the right of raw materials producers to form such associations: although difficult to implement, they are considered self-reliant measures by developing countries. These associations, with the exception of OPEC, do not yet have a cartel's ability to raise and hold prices, but they can increase the bargaining strength of their members by exchanging information and by making joint decisions. Their attempts at concerted price action, while less successful than OPEC's, have nevertheless aroused concern in consuming countries. Producer associations are only one of the measures available to exporters of primary products to increase their influence over the marketing and production of raw materials. Producing countries need to improve their marketing capabilities, upgrade their products to stem competition from substitutes, and make investments in the infrastructure as well as in the expansion of raw material processing to increase their export capacity.

Developing countries rich in resources are becoming more involved in the production of their petroleum, minerals, and other primary products. They also want to exert greater influence over the marketing of their products. Thus they now challenge the reliance of developed countries on their corporations' ability to supply adequate amounts of inexpensive raw materials. Producer associations might well succeed in raising prices of their exports during a business upturn even if they lack the ability to counter price declines during recessions. Consumers may respond to such price increases by switching individually or collectively to different sources or to substitutes, or governments of consuming countries may intervene through negotiation or threats of economic retaliation. Such actions are unlikely, however, to deter producing countries whose primary objective is to maximize earnings from raw materials production and trade. Indeed, the commercial objectives of the producing countries are not very different from those of private producing companies.

Conditions placed by host countries on the employment and training of local personnel, technology transfer, and the distribution of profits obtained from raw materials projects represent an increase in influence that the host countries have achieved outside the framework of the UN. UN agencies can aid the producers of raw materials through technical assistance and training, but they have not usually been able to sustain a direct involvement in the negotiations between producing countries and the firms of the industrial world. UN declarations and resolutions, however, have supported the gradual increase in the bargaining power of developing countries.

The UN and a New North-South Relationship

As an organization that includes both industrialized and developing nations, the UN must seek an effective role in fostering and managing international economic interdependence. Its first responsibility, therefore, is to improve its capacity to serve its member nations as a forum for negotiation. The closing phase of the CIEC illustrated that merely changing the venue of international discussions alters neither the North-South debate, the issues considered by developing and developed countries, nor the cast of characters. Moreover, the decision at CIEC to provide guidelines to other bodies has provided the World Bank, IMF, UNCTAD, the GATT, and other UN agencies with a mandate for negotiations.

Within the international financial institutions and the IMF, negotiations on policy concerns build on considerable experience. For other institutions, such as UNCTAD, the transition to an effective negotiating body poses more problems. Although UNCTAD has successfully concluded negotiations on tariff preferences and some commodity agreements, developed nations still consider it committed to the third world. It is to an extent trapped in its traditional role as originator and disseminator of proposals to improve the circumstances of developing nations and as the de facto secretariat of the Group of 77. For a restructured UNCTAD to take on more operational functions and to mediate between the two sides, it would have to become more independent of the Group of 77.

While moving toward support for international negotiations, the UN must heed the potential for conflict between policies concerning the claims of developing countries on industrialized nations at the state-to-state level and policies emphasizing the welfare of individuals. Historically, in the absence of measures that try to achieve an equitable distribution of the benefits, the higher income groups in any society have tended to receive the largest share of the resultant gains from an international trade or investment policy. This tendency, when coupled with the opposition of developing nations to policies that appear to affect their national sovereignty, may lead to resistance to development strategies directed toward meeting the basic human needs of their peoples. That response is understandable in the context of national attitudes formed by a recent emergence from colonialism, but unfortunately it can help erode the support in developed countries for policies responsive to third world concerns. The concept that the United States should not aid rich people in poor nations at the expense of poor people at home strikes a resonant chord in America and presumably in other developed nations as well. Critics of development assistance programs and opponents of adaptation to the economic changes can find a pretext for their positions in the developing countries' reluctance to allow international negotiations to focus on basic human needs.

The UN system must therefore devise measures that enhance the likelihood that NIEO policies and flows of external resources would be accompanied by measures that reach the poorest people within developing nations. Yet, attempting to direct the results of changes in international economic policies to poor people is perhaps the most intractable of the many problems that confront those concerned with development. Although the two types of measures are connected, it is difficult to determine how to link changes in relations between developed and developing nations with the satisfaction of the needs of the majority of individuals within a nation. A development strategy oriented to basic human needs would draw most heavily on domestic resources, but in most developing nations the standards of living are so low that external resources would greatly facilitate progress. Therefore, even a significant change in the domestic distribution of income, thus far an accomplishment of only a few countries, would appreciably lessen neither the need for adequate rates of growth nor the consequent dependence on external resources.

In UN debates, representatives of developing countries often advocate changes in international economic systems in order to eradicate poverty in the developing world. In contrast, representatives of industrialized countries frequently stress the inequalities in the distribution of wealth and income that exist in many developing nations. In fact, the record of all national and international policymakers in transferring the fruits of policy changes to poor people is far from satisfactory. Two changes are required. First, the developed countries must design trade, aid, investment, and technology policies that will increase the stability and the amount of resources transferred to the developing world; second, private and official institutions in the developing countries must channel additional resources to their poor. Both rich and poor nations are somewhat skeptical about each other's intentions and capabilities, but the UN could mediate and oversee these efforts. Both sides could search for some common ground within a UN framework as they design the international development strategy for the Third Development Decade. If the challenges posed by explicitly linking the NIEO to human needs and development were complemented by an effective restructuring of the UN system, then the organization could gain a sense of purpose comparable to that which prevailed at its formation.

The Transnational Corporations

SEYMOUR J. RUBIN

The industrialized and developing nations agree that a code of conduct dealing with transnational corporations (TNCs) is desirable. Indeed, the United Nations Commission on Transnational Corporations, at its first session in March 1975, decided to assign priority to the drafting of such a code, and much of its attention since then has been directed toward that end. The priority was assigned despite the controversy about the nature, the content, and the very purpose of such a code. Wide divergence developed at the first session on the "areas of concern" expressed on the one hand by the Group of 77 (the developing nations) and on the other by certain industrialized nations.[1] It is still hotly debated whether a code should be voluntary ("an instrument of moral persuasion"[2]) or mandatory ("obligatory and contain[ing] penalties for nonobservance"[3]), whether it should cover entities such as state-trading companies, and whether it should include reference to governmental treatment of TNCs as well as the obligations of the TNCs themselves. Nevertheless, it has been agreed that among the various tasks the commission "would undertake in the next few years, the priority would be assigned to the formulation of a code of conduct."[4]

Prior to drafting a regulatory measure, it would be desirable to decide exactly what is to be regulated. ECOSOC Resolution 1913 (LVII) of December 5, 1974, which established the commission, thus prescribed defining the transnational corporation as one of the four primary tasks of the commission. Though logical, this task has proved impracticable as the work of the commission has proceeded. Although various criteria for a definition were put forward in the second and third sessions (1976 and 1977) of the commission, no real progress in that direction

---

[1] Seymour J. Rubin, "Reflections Concerning the United Nations Commission on Transnational Corporations," *American Journal of International Law* 70 (January 1976), p. 73.

[2] United Nations, Economic and Social Council, Commission on Transnational Corporations, 1st Session, *Report on the First Session of the UN Commission on Transnational Corporations* (E/C.10/6), March 1975, par. 144.

[3] Ibid., par. 45.

[4] Ibid., par. 9.

was made, and the report of the third session states that little time was given to this issue. The commission has seemed content to postpone the question of a definition, while insisting that such a definition be broad enough to cover most entities involved in internationalized production of goods or services—that is, entities with some sort of centralized direction, with operations in more than one country, and of sufficient size to affect international economic affairs. A principal point of dispute is the insistence of the socialist nations, as well as some others, that state trading enterprises are not TNCs, at least for the purposes of the work of the commission. Market economy nations, however, hold the contrary opinion.

There is also some doubt about including as TNCs the corporations that do not own or control overseas production or service facilities. Corporations like Lockheed would probably be included in most definitions likely to occur to the commission, though they may technically be sellers either of technology or of goods or services, rather than producers in foreign nations. Conceivably, a definition useful for an agreement dealing with illicit practices, for example, might differ from one dealing with problems of transfer pricing.

The inability to arrive at a definition, however, has not retarded the search for a suitable code. On a procedural rather than a substantive basis, the commission has made considerable progress. The Lima (1976) session of the commission set up an intergovernmental working group to formulate an annotated outline of a code. The outline was to be considered in the third (April-May 1977) session of the commission "with a view to finalizing a draft code of conduct to be considered" at the May 1978 session of the commission.[5] Although the working group did produce an annotated outline of a code in the early days of May 1977, partially by working while the commission itself was in session, the difficulties of producing even this outline cast some doubt on the prospects of preparing a draft code, as distinguished from an outline, in time for the 1978 meeting of the commission. The production of a mere outline, annotated in nonnormative terms and guarded by a disclaimer that governments would in no way be bound by its terms, does not in itself seem to have been a difficult task. But to produce acceptable annotations, even with these limitations of nature and effect, took much longer than had been anticipated, rekindled the confrontational atmosphere of the first session of the commission, and emphasized the difficulty of advancing from a mere listing of issues to conclusory agreements resolving them.

The UN Commission on TNCs faces several issues in its attempt to move from outline to code. First, and most basic, is a preliminary inquiry: Are TNCs sufficiently important, in view of their effects on international economic or political relations, to warrant the great effort involved in attempting to reach an international agreement dealing with their conduct? Then, assuming both that the TNCs are important and that some sort of international arrangements governing their conduct are desirable, what should be the content and the form of such interna-

---

[5] United Nations, Economic and Social Council, Commission on Transnational Corporations, 2nd Session, *Report on the Second Session of the UN Commission on Transnational Corporations* (E/C.10/16), March 1976, par. 14.

tional arrangements? Finally, assuming that some type of code is desirable, is the United Nations, given its flaws, the forum in which to seek that code?

The Importance of the TNC and of a "Code of Conduct"

There can be no doubt that TNCs are a major factor in world production of goods and services and that intraenterprise trade is enormous and growing. By the mid-1970s, the output of the TNCs was estimated at some $450 billion, or about 15 percent of the gross world product. It is estimated that by the year 2000 this figure will rise to nearly 50 percent. Moreover, a large share of world trade takes place among the components of TNCs. Indeed, a principal defense of the American-based TNC against the charge that it "exports jobs" (by establishing production facilities abroad) is that many exports and export-related jobs in the United States are a direct consequence of the existence of those TNCs: subsidiaries buy more, and more regularly, than do independent customers.

It has indeed been suggested that intraenterprise trade is large enough to render obsolete traditional concepts of comparative advantage. Furthermore, some commentators have felt that the spread of the TNC and the growth of its power threaten the sovereignty of the states. This conclusion has been accepted with equanimity by Arnold J. Toynbee and others who saw this as a hopeful indication that man might destroy the concept of national sovereignty before it destroyed him. But this is a minority view; the more widespread opinion seems not only to guard but to revere sovereignty, a conclusion attested to by many UN resolutions. However, all are seemingly agreed that, in a real sense, the TNC is a factor that diminishes the freedom of action traditionally associated with national sovereignty.

In part, these conclusions result from a fascination with sheer size and from its confusion with effective power. (One may recall that the largest of dinosaurs had the smallest of brains, was a vegetarian, posed little threat to other species, and became extinct early in the evolutionary cycle.) It is not self-evident that a large corporation has more effective power than a small nation. To draw the familiar comparison between the gross sales of the giant TNCs (most of which may well be domestic sales) and the gross national product of some of the smaller UN member states, and to discover that the first exceeds the second, is not very meaningful. Gross sales do not represent value added, although the gross national product does.

Nonetheless, size itself can be intimidating, and the TNC that is both important to the economy of a nation and has a certain mobility may gravely affect the policies of nations. These two prerequisites, importance and mobility, are not characteristic of all TNCs. Companies engaged in the extractive industries, like those selling in a national market, are tied by the nature of their businesses to the place where they operate. Industrial enterprises have a large fixed investment in plant and equipment and sometimes in a trained labor force. They often depend on an existing infrastructure and on proximity to raw materials or markets. These factors often make it difficult for them to shift their activities, even if governments displease them.

Despite these limitations, the size and the considerable flexibility and facilities of an international structure do give rise to justifiable concern. Among numerous possibilities, the TNCs might set up production where wages are low and unions are weak, thereby placing workers in other nations at a disadvantage. Transfer pricing within the enterprise might deprive a government of its appropriate share of tax revenues. Shifting of currencies, or the use of "leads" and "lags" in intra-enterprise adjustment of accounts, might accelerate the fall of weak currencies and the rise of strong ones. Finally, the perceived optimum benefit to a global TNC might not coincide with the best interest of either home or host nations.

At the same time, it seems clear that the TNCs do contribute to much of the world's economic development. Their resources of capital, technology, entrepreneurial skills, and worldwide organization make some form of accommodation essential. Though some mainly see the TNC as the source of an undesirable intrusion of alien "sociocultural" concepts, inappropriate consumerism, and a "dependencia" of which "poverty is the product," most in developing as well as industrialized nations find the TNC generally beneficial. Many see some sort of international arrangement, either regulatory or supervisory, as a way of maximizing benefits and minimizing costs. Such an agreement would provide "rules of the game," as the director of the UN Centre on TNCs, has put it.[6] It is to the formulation of such mutually desirable rules that the work of the UN Commission on TNCs has largely been addressed.

The Content and Form of a Code

Over the years, a number of proposals for some form of international supervision or regulation have been proposed. The Group of Eminent Persons, in its report which stimulated the birth of the commission and the centre, suggested a "General Agreement on Multinational Corporations." Testimony from bankers, industrialists, and reformers—from developed as well as developing nations—has been nearly unanimous that some such international agreement is desirable. As Robert Stobaugh testified before the Joint Economic Committee in 1970, "the managers of most multinational enterprises would likely heartily subscribe to [the] suggestion of international agreements. . . . In this way, they would be assured of equitable treatment."[7] Certainly the developing nations have pressed strongly inside and outside the UN Commission on TNCs for a code of conduct. Thus there seems to exist a consensus on the desirability of a code.

Such a wide concurrence of views among those often found on opposing sides is not entirely reassuring. It may in fact suggest that the phrase "a code of conduct" does not mean the same thing to all who advocate it. The long and difficult

---

[6] *Proceedings of the American Society of International Law*, 70th Annual Meeting (April 1976), p. 25.

[7] U.S., Congress, Joint Economic Committee, *Hearings on a Foreign Economic Policy for the 1970s*, 91st Congress, 2d sess., 1970.

history of attempts to find acceptable formulas for a code supports this suspicion.

Attempts to achieve general agreements in the field of foreign direct investment—an area greatly overlapping if not identical with that of a code for the activities of TNCs—have not been notably successful. At least when capital exporting and capital importing nations or industrialized and developing nations are involved, difficulties have prevented agreement. (Clearly, none of these categories is an exclusive one: the United States is both a major capital exporter and a major capital importer; Canada, a developed nation by generally accepted standards, has been very much concerned about the effect of TNCs on its economy and politics, which is also the main preoccupation of the developing nations; Mexico and Brazil, leading members of the Group of 77, are themselves increasingly home countries of TNCs.) The only "code" that has had reasonable success is the group of documents produced by the Organization for Economic Cooperation and Development (OECD) in June 1976. The OECD, however, is an association solely of "developed" nations, and since the issues that divide industrialized and developing nations in the UN were not relevant to the OECD exercise, its "guidelines" can hardly be taken as a reason to be optimistic about the efforts of the United Nations to draft a code. In addition, previous attempts to draft a code that would satisfy both developed and developing nations have foundered between the Scylla of meaningless generalizations and the Charybdis of unacceptable precision. One attempt, the Havana Charter for an International Trade Organization drafted in 1948, was rejected on all sides and was the first of several attempts to founder.

The problem is both content and form. As for content, the developing nations are likely to insist on an emphasis on permanent sovereignty over natural resources and on a reference to numerous General Assembly resolutions involving the "New International Economic Order," whose implications give rise to grave doubts on the side of the investing nations. The investing nations are likely to insist on guarantees—for example, "prompt, adequate and effective compensation" in the case of an expropriation of property or rights, a formulation that violates beliefs firmly held by the other side. So long as broad statements of principle are debated, the issue seems unlikely to be resolved by consensus, without which any solution would be of little value. It has been suggested that a multilateral treaty dealing with TNCs ought to be negotiated, which would be "capable of accomplishing for the world economy what modern corporation laws have accomplished for national economies," and that the aim ought to be "a code of law to govern . . . activities in accordance with agreed principles, which should protect the interest of both the corporation and the host countries."[8] But desirability should not be confused with attainability.

To some extent, the difficulty results from a certain blurring of definitional lines. It is unlikely that there is any "typical" TNC or, indeed, any typical devel-

---

[8] Eugene V. D. Rostow "The Need for International Arrangements," *Global Companies,* ed. George Ball (Englewood Cliffs, New Jersey: Prentice Hall,), pp. 157, 170.

oping nation. The developing nations form a spectrum from the tiniest and least developed to the huge and rather highly developed. An ability to deal with the TNCs is not notably absent in countries like Mexico, Brazil, or Singapore, but similar expertise may well be absent in others. Above all, there is the question of whether one is to deal with the conduct of *the* TNCs or with their duty to serve the cause of a transfer of resources from developed to developing nations—a concept that however meritorious has different aspects for privately owned corporations and for governments.

Added to these issues of content is the question of form. The OECD guidelines are firmly and explicitly stated to be "voluntary," while the developing nations in the UN commission have insisted on a mandatory code. However, whether voluntary and mandatory codes are in practice as explicitly distinct as the words suggest is doubtful. A "voluntary" code, accompanied by stated procedures for reviewing its effectiveness and by requirements of disclosure that, once set forth, become the norm, is not notably different from a "mandatory" code. But the insistence on a binding form of agreement, presumably reflected in treaty commitments to principles that are themselves subject to varying interpretations, particularly disturbs those to be regulated. This is especially true when there is equal insistence on the preeminence of national laws and of national procedures and a disclaimer of any right to protection by the home government of the TNC. Consequently, at least in the UN forum, the content and the form of a "code," a concept that seems to command wide support, are issues for which solutions are not readily apparent.

The United Nations Forum

The years of constant consultation, even among nations of roughly comparable stages of development and of ideology, that preceded attainment of the OECD guidelines show that the substantive issues at hand would present problems wherever debated. Nor have regional organizations been able easily to overcome less significant questions. Thus the attempt to attain a uniformed "Companies Law," or corporation law, for the European Economic Community is now in its eleventh year of discussion, though it has the limited objective of facilitating business activities in nations bound together by the Rome Treaty.[9] In the UN, chasms appear where in the Common Market there would be mere cracks in the paving. It might thus be concluded that the UN forum is inherently unlikely to produce any useful result.

This impression is reinforced by the apparent differences in the "annotated outline of a code of conduct" which emerged in the session of April-May 1977. Despite the clearly less confrontational rhetoric of the third commission session and the growing recognition, in practice if not in UN resolutions, of the power of

[9] Pieter Sanders, "The European Company," *Georgia Journal of International and Comparative Law* 6 (Spring 1976): 367.

TNCs and their investments to alleviate difficult balance of payment problems, the issues of principle seem no closer to agreement now than previously. Indeed, as the actual drafting of code provisions comes closer, the continuing conflict of views becomes sharper.

Thus one may plausibly argue that the UN, with its North-South division, its tendency to politicize issues, its often exaggerated statements of position, and its incredibly inefficient work methods, is a forum to be avoided. Such a conclusion, however, would probably be a mistake. Of course it is a cliché so say that the fault lies not in the UN but in the will of its members, but there are legitimate reasons why members distrust the UN, at least as an effective instrument of determining essentially economic policy. But it provides at least a forum for the discussion of different views, the education of both sides, and the negotiation of compromises essential to the operation of an interdependent world economy. In debating questions of the activities of TNCs, the UN addresses as well the more fundamental issues of the interrelations between North and South. The dialogue does not proceed with maximum efficiency, and indeed it seems to many weary representatives that maximum inefficiency is the objective. But issues of substantial importance are debated, with at least some prospect for a de facto international arrangement benefiting both TNCs and governments.

Debate in the UN forum has not merely illustrated these points, but has moved participants to a sort of tacit understanding of the importance of these matters. For example, no formal resolution has been made whether a code should be addressed not merely to TNCs, as contended by the developing nations, but also to governments, whose attitudes will obviously greatly affect the conduct of the TNCs. Yet discussion has made clear that, however phrased, governmental actions are implicated. The developing nations rightly insist that TNCs should not be the instruments of governmental policy (as, for example, in the United States's use of the Trading with the Enemy Act to prohibit foreign subsidiaries of American corporations from trading with Cuba, although such trade may be encouraged by the countries in which these subsidiaries are incorporated). This is obviously an admonition more relevantly addressed to governments than to TNCs. It is equally clear that TNCs are subject to the mandates of at least two governments, home and host, and that code principles must recognize this fact. Whether admonitory language with respect to "investment climate" is used or not, it is apparent that such a climate affects the conduct of TNCs.

The commission seems to be moving toward a better understanding of the realities that possibly underlie what may be a set of mutually acceptable arrangements, which might indeed be called "rules of the game" even if they do not resemble the popular conception of a "code" neatly printed and bound. It is a step forward to recognize that there are major differences not only between TNCs but also between members of the "developing nations." It seems generally accepted that a composite might emerge that would include the following: a treaty or a unanimous resolution regarding a consultative organization (not a great matter, in view of the present existence of both the commission and the centre); some reasonably firm commitments in specific areas (such as standards for transfer pricing); and progress in harmonizing national legislation in other areas, such as restrictive business practices. Just as there is no single TNC that is representative of all, no developing nation that is typical, and indeed no home nation that does not face problems, so there is not likely to be a single, neatly packaged panacea. As this becomes the evident conclusion from studies, research, and discussions, the likelihood grows of solutions that are workable though untidy.

Finally, the UN has the advantage of more or less squarely recognizing that the TNCs and their relations to home and host nations alike are part of the larger problem of organizing the world economy in a way that will give reasonable satisfaction—perhaps one should say more or less equal dissatisfaction—to all. Interdependence is a term much overworked, especially in its facile use in the rhetoric of the American Bicentennial, but it does suggest that relations between the nations are, as Maitland said of the law, a "seamless web" of which the TNC is an integral part. In this sense, the UN forum is *the* appropriate arena for the analysis of TNC issues in the context of global economic relations and for the process of thesis, contradiction, and eventual synthesis. The procedural handicaps of intelligent discussion in the UN are formidable, but it remains the organization in which all are represented, in which even confrontation has its utility in defining important issues affecting a viable world order, and from which a basic modus vivendi may emerge.

Despite justifiable doubts, the effort is worth making. For the United States, with its major stake in relations with the developing nations and in a peaceful and equitable world order, it is indeed vital that the effort be vigorously pursued.

The Law of the Sea

JOHN TEMPLE SWING

Shortly after the most recent session of the Third United Nations Conference on the Law of the Sea that concluded on July 15, 1977, the United States ambassador, Elliot L. Richardson, held a news conference to disavow portions of the Informal Composite Negotiating Text that had emerged following the session. He stated that last minute changes made in the text at the instance of one of the three principal conference committee chairmen rendered the text fundamentally unacceptable to the United States. He found the situation so serious that he recommended that the president undertake a review to determine whether it was any longer in the United States's interest to continue to participate in the negotiations that had been under way under UN auspices since late 1973. The charge raises troublesome questions both about the conference and its importance to the United States and the UN system as a whole.

To evaluate the significance of the problem, it is necessary to understand something of the law of the sea, its evolution over time, and the problems that it has posed for solution, if not by the United Nations conference, then by other means. For all practical purposes, the modern law of the sea dates from the early 1600s when "freedom of the seas" as expounded by the Dutchman, Hugo Grotius, won out over the arguments of the territorialists who defended claims such as those made by Spain and Portugal to the Gulf of Mexico and indeed the entire Atlantic Ocean. Following a century of worldwide exploration and the beginnings of ocean commerce far beyond the coasts, the doctrine was well suited to the times. Through the slow but steady growth of customary international law, it came to be universally recognized by all countries that sailed the seemingly boundless oceans or fished for the seemingly inexhaustible fish stocks that swam beneath its surfaces.

As freedom of the seas developed over the next two centuries, two important qualifications came to be recognized. While the high seas were free to all, except pirates, to use or go where they wished, a three-mile band around each nation's coastline became the territorial sea of the coastal state and subject to its will, except for the right of passage accorded to vessels of other states (so long as that passage remained "innocent" and not "prejudicial to the peace, good order or security" of the coastal state). Second, during the nineteenth century the common sense doctrine of reasonable use developed: the seas might be "free" to all but the rights of others exercising that freedom must be reasonably respected.

Had the rate of increase in ocean usage continued to be slow and steady, all might have been well. The inexorable process of customary law might have continued to serve in the twentieth century as it had in the previous two. Instead, the growth curve of ocean usage began to rise sharply, much like (and indeed perhaps reflecting) the sharp upturn in the world population growth curve. Two statistics, both dealing with traditional ocean uses, well demonstrate the problem. In the third quarter of the twentieth century alone the total world fish catch rose from 16 million to 69 million tons, while registered merchant tonnage in the same period rose from 76 million to 306 million tons. The nature of the problem is perhaps even better exemplified by the increase in size of the world's tanker fleet. Following World War II no tankers exceeded 25,000 deadweight tons. By 1974, there were 508 tankers in service that weighed more than 200,000 deadweight tons, two that weighed more than 500,000, and one on the way at over one million tons.

The twentieth century brought more than a sharp increase in traditional ocean uses, which would have provided challenge enough. Two nonliving resources of the oceans were also to become a lively issue. By all estimates the more important of these was oil, discovered during World War II on the continental shelf in the Gulf of Mexico. The continental shelf is the shallow portion of the continental margin (the underwater prolongation of the continental land mass) that, further out, slopes down to the deep ocean bottom, which is of a different geological structure. At the base of this "slope" in many parts of the world is found a third part of the margin called the "rise" composed of sedimentary deposits of continental origin that overlies the geographical intersection of the slope and the deep ocean bed, gradually tapering down and blending into the latter in some cases hundreds of miles out from the coastline.

The second resource, small "burnt baked potato" like objects called manganese nodules, is found scattered in belts over wide portions of the deep ocean bed itself. Rich in copper, cobalt, and nickel as well as manganese, a commercial interest in the nodules was evinced for the first time in the 1960s, although their existence had been known for a century. One estimate has set the value of the minerals contained in the nodules to be in excess of $3 trillion in present terms.

The impact of these minerals and of the increase in traditional ocean usage generally was first reflected in the law of the sea in 1945, when President Truman proclaimed that the United States had the exclusive right to explore and exploit the mineral resources (read oil) found in its continental shelf, including those portions that extended, as in the Gulf of Mexico, far beyond the three mile territorial sea. It was the first time since the sixteenth century that a major power had asserted an exclusive claim in an area of ocean space that had previously been assumed to be part of the high seas and open to all users or takers.

The lead of the United States was soon followed by three countries on the west coast of South America, Chile, Ecuador, and Peru, with the assertion of their jurisdiction over fisheries out to two hundred miles. These unilateral claims and others that followed ran clearly in the face of the traditional customary law of the sea, and in 1958 the first law of the sea conference was convened under UN auspices to attempt to clarify by treaty what customary international law no longer had time to achieve—new rules that would be generally acceptable by all.

The 1958 conference developed conventions in four distinct areas: one on fisheries; a second on rights and duties in the territorial sea setting its maximum limit at twelve miles; a third codifying rights and duties on the high seas; and a fourth on the continental shelf. One provision of the latter proved to be of particular importance. It provided that the coastal state had the sovereign right to "the seabed and subsoil of the submarine areas adjacent to the coast but outside of the territorial sea, to a depth of 200 meters or, beyond that limit, *to where the depth of the superjacent waters admits of the exploitation of the natural resources of the said areas."* (Emphasis added.)

Since virtually all of the world's recoverable underwater oil and gas resources are believed to be contained in the continental shelf and rise, this clause provided the basis for present resource recovery claims of a handful of countries whose margins extend hundreds of miles beyond their coastlines, including India, Australia, Canada, the USSR, and the United States. Two years later a second conference, by a margin of one vote, failed to agree on the breadth of the territorial sea within twelve miles. This was of particular importance to the major maritime and naval powers since over 116 international straits, including Gibraltar, Malacca, and Hormuz at the mouth of the Persian Gulf, would become territorial seas if all states moved from three to twelve miles. No longer would they be part of the high seas free as a matter of right to all comers as in the past.

If 1945 marked the beginning of the nation-state claims outward into ocean space, 1967 was a milestone of a different sort. In that year, Arvid Pardo from Malta proposed to the UN that a stop be imposed on the seaward claims of coastal states and that the resources of the seabed "beyond the limits of present national jurisdiction" be declared the "common heritage of mankind." to be held in trust by a new international authority. It would manage the resources and provide the residual net proceeds for development of the poorer countries of the world.

The "common heritage" principle was adopted by the UN General Assembly in 1970 by a vote of 108 to 0 with only 14 abstentions, largely from the Soviet bloc. The United States voted in favor. The need to establish the new international agency contemplated in the "common heritage" resolution led directly to the empanelling in late 1973 of the Third United Nations Conference on the Law of the Sea. The conference was also charged to try again where the two earlier conferences had failed—to set an agreed breadth for the territorial sea. It was in addition called upon to define the rights and duties of all states in all areas of the oceans and to ocean resources.

Before attempting to evaluate what has happened at the conference, it is well to remember its dual lineage, resulting in effect in two separate negotiations wrapped up into one, both proceeding simultaneously. The first, dealing with the traditional maritime issues and with the regulation of scientific research and the marine environment, has been largely jurisdictional in nature. Here the task of the conference has been to set the outer limits of coastal state claims into ocean space and to allocate national versus international rights and duties in a series of bands moving away from the shoreline. The other half of the negotiations has been organic in nature: to create an entirely new institution for the deep seabed where none had existed before. Taken together the two negotiations add up to a charge that is comprehensive in nature, nothing less than the development for the first time of a written constitution for the oceans.

The work of the conference has been complicated by the constant pull, evident on both sides of the negotiations, between the political realities of the 1970s on the one hand and underlying geographical reality on the other. Politically the relatively few advanced industrial countries of the North have been pitted against the far more numerous developing countries, primarily of the South, which have organized themselves into a loose but effective coalition known as the Group of 77, although it now numbers over 100 countries. The rhetoric of the North-South debate has been most evident in that part of the negotiation dealing with the creation of the new regime for the deep seabed that will control access to its resources.

Geographic reality, on the other hand, no respector of politics, divides the conference in a very different way. There are some 120 coastal states, some 48 of which have continental margins more than 200 miles in breadth; 30 landlocked states; and 20 geographically disadvantaged states, which because of the close proximity of their neighbors can never have fully developed jurisdictional zones off their coastline. These states, under leadership as diverse as Poland on the one hand and Singapore on the other, have been forced by geographical reality increasingly to band together in the face of the growing tendency at the conference to favor coastal state rights.

The fact that developing coastal states from the Group of 77, particularly the Latin Americans, have pushed the hardest for the extension of these rights is not without irony. Thirty-five percent of all ocean space will be preempted if, as now appears likely, there will be a worldwide 200 mile coastal economic zone. Yet the realities of geography will award one-third of the new area (including an estimated 50 percent of world underwater oil reserves) to just ten states, seven of which, Australia, Canada, Japan, New Zealand, Norway, the USSR, and the United States are developed, and only three of which, Brazil, India, and Mexico, are not.

In this situation what progress, then, has been made by the conference since 1973, what problems have been encountered along the way, and finally, what is the significance of both for the UN system and for the United States?

Let us look first at the jurisdictional side of the conference and the work of two of the three principal conference working groups, Committees II and III, that have dealt with the traditional maritime issues, science, and the environment. Over the past four years the conference has met at least once each year for sessions lasting approximately eight weeks each, and considerable progress has been made toward developing textual provisions that are acceptable in varying degrees to most states at the conference. There is now general agreement on a series of three bands or jurisdictional areas, in each of which the rights of the coastal state in relation to other states in the international system have been differently weighed.

The first band will be a *territorial sea* with an agreed breadth of twelve miles, subject to "innocent passage" (now better defined than in the 1958 convention on the territorial sea), but concurrently providing for "unimpeded transit" through, over, and under the international straits that would otherwise be overlapped by the twelve mile territorial seas of adjacent states.

The second band involves the *exclusive economic zone* 188 miles beyond the territorial sea, thus covering a distance of 200 miles from the shore. Here, also, the allocation of rights and duties of the coastal state as against other states is largely complete, with most of the resource rights over fisheries and nonliving resources on the continental shelf going still to the coastal state. One of the more difficult issues involving the zone was substantially settled during the latter days of the session just concluded. The United States and the maritime powers in general had argued that the waters of the economic zone must be clearly designated as "high seas" for all purposes except for resource and other rights granted expressly by the text to coastal states. The coastal state group, particularly the Latin Americans, argued that the waters should not be "high seas" except for limited rights expressly granted to all nations, such as the right to navigate for peaceful purposes within the zone. By implication, unspecified and residual rights would ultimately belong to the coastal state and not to the international community.

Thanks to the effort of a small, informal working group of key countries, this matter was resolved by providing in the economic zone articles for the freedoms of navigation and overflight "and other internationally lawful uses of the sea related to these freedoms, such as those associated with the operation of ships, aircraft and submarine cables and pipelines, and compatible with other provisions of the present convention"[1] and by the statement in the introductory article to the section governing the high seas beyond 200 miles, to the effect that "the provisions of this Part apply to all parts of the sea that are not included in the exclusive economic zone . . . in the territorial sea or in the internal waters of a State. . . . This article does not entail any abridgement of the freedoms enjoyed by all States in the exclusive economic zone in accordance with article 58."[2]

With the settlement of this issue in a manner generally acceptable both to

[1] United Nations, Third Conference on the Law of the Sea, Sixth Session, *Informal Composite Negotiating Text* (A/CONF. 62/WP 10), July 15, 1977, Article 58, p. 42.
[2] Ibid., Article 86, p. 56.

maritime and coastal states, only a small handful of issues remain: definition of the outer edge of the continental margin (at what point does the "rise" end and the abyssal plain begin?); the extent to which coastal states will have to share revenues from resources developed on their continental margin lying beyond 200 miles; and finally, rights of landlocked and geographically disadvantaged states, particularly to living resources found in the economic zones of their coastal state neighbors. Draft articles governing access to and from the sea and freedom of transit, negotiated at the previous session of the conference now appear in the Informal Composite Negotiating Text. With the possible exception of the right of landlocked and geographically disadvantaged states to living resources, settlement of these issues could be quickly achieved without extensive further negotiation and undoubtedly would be if issues in other parts of the conference appeared to be on the verge of solution.

The third band or area encompassing the waters beyond 200 miles clearly remains "high seas" for all purposes, with coastal states having no greater rights than any other state in the international system. Here again, the text provisions already developed have almost universal support and require no further negotiation.

While all of the issues noted above have been negotiated in the second committee, the third committee has worked on the preparation of two specialized texts affecting each of the three jurisdictional zones or bands. These texts cover preservation of the marine environment and the conduct of scientific research. As to the former, a text has been developed that strikes a generally acceptable balance between the interest of the coastal state in protecting its marine environment, particularly against vessel-source pollution, and the concerns of the maritime states that favor uniform international regulations as an essential protection against a welter of varying national regulations that could interfere with reasonable freedom of navigation necessary to the transport of goods in these days of increased interdependence. The text generally relies on international standard setting in the territorial sea and exclusive economic zone, but enforcement powers here are shared by the flag state with coastal states In addition, the latter are permitted to adopt national standards more stringent than those set internationally to govern vessel discharges in the territorial sea. Coastal states can also adopt special regulations for vessel-source pollution in areas of special hazard, such as the Arctic zone.

For marine science, the developing trend at the conference has not been encouraging. Early during the conference, in an effort to avoid the need for coastal state consent for research to be undertaken in the 200 mile economic zone, the United States agreed to a substantial list of obligations to be assumed by a researching state including advance notification, the sharing of results, and the like. As the text evolved, however, it provided first for coastal consent for research "related to resources of the economic zone" but not for research of a "fundamental nature"; and in a later version for all research, although consent was not normally to be withheld unless the specific project "bears substantially upon the exploration and exploitation of living and non-living resources." The

Informal Composite Negotiating Text just issued provides that the coastal state shall "in normal circumstances" grant their consent but may in their discretion withhold it if the project "is of direct significance for the exploration and exploitation of natural resources, whether living or non-living."[3]

It is ironic that the United States, having agreed initially to a substantial list of obligations so as to avoid coastal state consent, now finds itself facing a text that requires both the obligations and coastal state consent. Yet there are saving graces that likely make the text preferable to no text at all. First, there is at least some limitation on the discretionary denial of consent, as already noted. Second, there is a tacit consent provision that research can proceed after six months if no response is received from the coastal state within four months. Finally, the most recent version of the text does preserve compulsory dispute settlement for scientific research issues that arguably would apply to an abuse of discretion by the coastal state. Absent any text at all, given the trend in recent years, marine scientists would likely soon find themselves having to ask for consent for all research, regardless of its nature, conducted within two hundred miles of the coastline.

A separate word should be said here about dispute settlement. Under the guidance of the president of the conference, Shirley Amerasinghe, and somewhat to the surprise of most participants at the conference, substantial progress has been made during each of the recent sessions, accompanied by a growing commitment among conference participants, which few had anticipated, toward development of a comprehensive system for the peaceful settlement of disputes, in most cases leading to a decision binding on the parties. The text establishes a new Law of the Sea Tribunal having jurisdiction over virtually all substantive aspects of the treaty. But it also preserves to treaty signatories some choice as to the forum in which litigation against them must be conducted: the Law of the Sea Tribunal, the International Court of Justice, special arbitral procedures for functional areas such as fisheries or navigation, special nonbinding conciliation procedures, and, finally, general arbitration. If a party bringing an action does not agree to litigate in the forum of the defendant's choice, then the issue must be submitted to binding arbitration.

At the session just ended two important steps were taken. First, it was agreed that a special panel, to be chosen from members of the Law of the Sea Tribunal, would hear disputes arising from the deep seabed regime. At an earlier time, many states had argued for the creation of a separate deep seabed tribunal for such issues. Second, despite strong pressure from members of the coastal state group, dispute settlement was retained both for scientific research, as already noted, and for fisheries. The latter provision is of importance both to distant water fishing states and to the landlocked and geographically disadvantaged states group since it provides at least some mechanism for the challenge of arbitrary acts by the coastal state in establishing the optimal sustainable yield of

[3] Ibid., Article 247, 130.

a given stock and settling its own harvesting capacity for that stock and consequently determining what surplus amount, if any, will be available to other states.

If, as described above, reasonable progress has been made on the jurisdictional side of the negotiations, what about the organic negotiation to construct a deep seabed regime, that has been the province of the first committee? At issue is the control of the mineral resources of the deep seabed—the area of the "common heritage" of mankind—and it is here that the conference from the outset has been seriously split. The United States and the other advanced industrial countries, having the technical capability for deep-seabed mining, have insisted that guaranteed, secure access is essential to protect the large capital investments that will be needed for full scale production. The Group of 77 on the other hand has argued for a monopolistic seabed authority, in which it would have the dominant voice, having total control both over marketing and production. This would protect the economies of those developing countries that depend on their own land-based mining of the same minerals found in the nodules, nickel and copper being the most important.

At early sessions of the conference, little progress was made at finding an acceptable middle ground between these two widely opposing views. Then a small group of countries consisting of the United States, land-based producers, and moderate landlocked countries from the Group of 77, in the spring of 1976 in New York, did propose a framework for compromise. The essence of the compromise, largely adopted in the text issued at the end of that session, was found in a proposal for a parallel system of exploitation whereby one-half of the mining sites on the deep seabed would accrue to the developed world, leaving the balance of the sites to be developed by the enterprise arm of the new International Sea Bed Authority. To protect the land-based producers from possible loss, the United States agreed, with reluctance, to an interim production limit tied to the annual growth of the nickel market over a twenty-year period.

At the second New York session that summer, the provisions of this compromise were largely rejected by the Group of 77, which continued to argue that the system of exploitation must be unitary, wholly in the hands of a seabed authority that they controlled. Toward the end of that session, Secretary of State Kissinger attempted to break the deadlock by offering to see to the financing of the enterprise arm of the authority so that it could begin to exploit the authority's share of the mine sites simultaneously with the developed world. He also suggested that the entire parallel system be subject to review after twenty-five years. While of interest to the developing world, the proposals came too late in the session to act as a catalyst for compromise.

The year 1977, however, began with a ray of hope. First, the naming of Elliot L. Richardson to lead the United States delegation was viewed as a good omen both at home and abroad. Second, intersessional negotiations conducted in Geneva in February and March, under the chairmanship of Jens Evensen of Norway, tended to be both purposeful and pragmatic, and began the job of fleshing out the proposal for an interim parallel regime, subject to review, with financing for the enterprise to be provided or at least guaranteed both by the developed and developing countries on a basis proportionate to the United Nations scale of assessments.

By and large, progress toward development of a generally successful compromise text continued during much of the recent session that commenced in May. In the process, several barriers that might have proved insuperable at an earlier point were overcome. Among the most important of these were the change or elimination of draft text provisions that could have been construed to give the International Sea Bed Authority discretionary control over (and thereby possible withholding of) reasonably assured access on the private side of the parallel system. The second important hurdle was a text that balanced the voting powers of the executive council of the International Sea Bed Authority in such a way as to provide reasonable assurance to the developed world that it would not be subject to arbitrary decisions imposed by the far more numerous Group of 77.

Not all issues, however, were being resolved in a manner satisfactory to the advanced industrial world, or the United States in particular. In the area of production controls, the trend during the recent session has been toward successive further limitations on seabed production, first to 75 percent and later to 66 2/3 percent of the estimated growth segment of the world nickel market over the next twenty years, thereby tilting the entire resource policy so as to restrict rather than encourage the production of deep seabed minerals, at the expense of consumers both large and small throughout the world. In addition, given the painfully slow process of developing compromise texts based on negotiations involving nearly 150 countries, there simply was not enough time for the negotiating group chaired by Jens Evensen to work its way through all the major outstanding issues.

When the sixth session of the conference opened in New York in May, the plan had been to develop a consolidated text by the end of the sixth week and a draft treaty by the end of the session in which most of the major outstanding issues would be resolved. A shorter follow-up session was then envisaged to negotiate preliminary and final articles, including provisions for entry into force, and to make final adjustments that might be necessary to produce a treaty to be voted on and initialed by two-thirds of the countries participating. While such a result might have been possible in Committees II and III and dispute settlement, Committee I again proved to be the stumbling block. Production of the consolidated text was successively delayed and only finally emerged five days after the end of the session.

Insofar as the conference was concerned, this delay set the stage for a most unhappy turn of events. For reasons not quite clear to anyone, in the text issued following the end of the session, the chairman of Committee I Paul Engo of the Camaroon, chose to tamper with the delicate balance struck in the Evensen group text between the positions of the developed and developing worlds. In changing the article providing for the review of the system of exploitation after twenty years, he went even further than the agreed position of the Group of 77 when he provided for the automatic conversion of the parallel system to a unitary one in the event that the review conference should be unable to reach agreement. On other issues that had not been the subject of the Evensen negotiations, he inserted provisions that were not the product of negotiation and that were wholly unacceptable to the developed world. These included provisions for the mandatory transfer of technology as well as the imposition of financial requirements on contractors on the private side of the parallel system so burdensome as to throw into question the likelihood of any development at all. Equally serious, the International Sea Bed Authority was given broad discretion to regulate production "as appropriate," a provision made even worse by the elimination of a key phrase that Evensen had devised to balance voting power in the executive council of the authority.

While committee chairmen, along with the president of the conference, had the right to make changes in the texts for their committees, it represented folly at this late stage for Engo to upset the negotiated compromise that was evolving in the Committee I negotiations. In one stroke, he once again rendered the Committee I text unacceptable to one of the two sides in the negotiations, in this case the developed world including the United States. It was this that led the United States to question the viability of the negotiating process, raising doubts as to continued United States participation.

Against the background sketched above, what observations, then, can be made about the conference, its processes, and its importance to the UN system and to the United States? To begin with its processes, the undertaking by any stretch of the imagination was enormous. Not only were the major issues in and of themselves complex, but by one estimate there were at least 100 of them on the agenda. In addition, the conference has been the largest ever. Over 2,000 delegates representing 143 jurisdictional entities, many of them relatively new countries with no prior experience in dealing with ocean issues. and each with one equal vote, convened in Caracas for the first substantive session in July 1974. As might be guessed, the sheer size of the conference has plagued its deliberations from the outset. On one hand, it is nearly impossible to negotiate anything in a group with as many as 150 participants, each of whom has the right to be heard. On the other hand, when smaller groups, formal or informal, meet to attempt to negotiate solutions, the results are almost immediately suspect by other countries for no better reason than that they did not participate in the small group negotiations. It was this factor, perhaps as much as any other, that caused the deadlock that ensued during the entire second New York session during the summer of 1976, aiding the more radical leadership of the Group of 77 in its attempt to discredit the compromise proposed during the spring session by the small negotiating group in which the United States and land-based producers from the Group of 77 had participated.

Various procedural devices were attempted to overcome this problem. In the second committee the chairman appointed small formal working groups, limited in number usually to no more than thirty countries, to address a specific problem area but provided that other countries could observe from an outer tier, as it were, and participate if they thought it necessary. This solution worked little better than sessions at which all countries were equally represented at the outset. All too often they simply provided forums for the reiteration of national positions which might serve well for home consumption but which, particularly at later stages of the conference, did little to advance the negotiations.

How then has it been possible to achieve any progress at all? The answer lies in a combination of factors. First, the countries most concerned with a given issue in dispute are the most likely to strive for compromise. If one can be achieved, it is likely that other countries not deeply involved will acquiesce. Thus, it was possible for a small group of a dozen or so countries, including several that had emerged as natural leaders at the conference, to evolve a compromise on the "high seas" status of the economic zone that in earlier formal sessions of the second committee had divided almost equally the one hundred countries that spoke on the question.

This result would not have been possible, however, without the impact of a second factor—the perception that the conference, particularly in the first committee, was now making sufficient progress that issues must be resolved "now or never." Thus, it can be argued that the pressure of time is essential to move countries from rhetoric to serious negotiation, regardless of the forum. A third factor, and perhaps the most important of all, has been the role of fair arbiter, the neutral draftsman who, having listened to the debate, can prepare text provisions that move the opposing sides more closely together. He often works through successive drafts, finally producing a draft that, while fully pleasing no one, can nonetheless grudgingly be accepted by all. Jens Evensen of Norway played such a role in Geneva in 1975 developing texts on the environment and exclusive economic zone and, more recently, in the Committee I negotiations to the extent that they were conducted under his aegis. The success in achieving a viable dispute settlement text is due to the similar role played by the president.

Similar authority in a formal sense was accorded near the outset of the conference to the committee chairmen in preparing informal negotiating texts. While progress was enhanced thereby, as in the instance of the first single negotiating text prepared by the chairman of the second committee, much depends on the standing and integrity of the fair arbiter, as the recent near disaster in the first committee well illustrates.

One other problem deserves particular note, since it is central to the concern of the United States as it faces other multinational negotiations in a North-South context in which it can easily be outvoted by a preponderence of developing countries. What is to be done about the one country, one vote principle when islands like the Seychelles, for example, have the same vote as, say, the USSR? The mechanism adopted by the law of the sea conference to circumvent the problem has been to proceed as long as possible by consensus, rather than by voting. Thus, during the past four years, not a single issue has been voted up or down, nor is one likely to be until an entire treaty package has emerged containing elements that make the whole of sufficient interest to two-thirds of the participants to assure their support against all challenges. One adverse effect of proceeding by consensus, however, has been to leave the casual observer with the impression that, since nothing has yet been voted on, nothing has been accomplished at the conference, a complaint frequently heard in the halls of Congress and the press.

What then is the significance of the conference to the UN system and to the United States? For the UN the answer is clear: the effort to achieve a comprehensive law of the sea treaty is of major importance. If successful, it will do much to restore the credibility of the organization as one capable of producing concrete results rather than idle rhetoric or paper resolutions of little significance. If successful, a new international organization will have been created under UN auspices that has important operating authority as opposed to rule-making or advisory powers. If an International Sea Bed Authority is devised in which both the developed and developing worlds can work together and in which a meaningful role is provided for multinational companies such as those participating in Western mining consortia, it will be an important precedent in other areas of the North-South debate. Finally, in a more general sense, a successful treaty would be an important milestone in the world's slow progress away from the principle of "might makes right" and toward an international rule of law.

To the United States, the law of the sea treaty is important both on its merits and because of its value as a precedent in assessing the worth of international negotiations generally. It should immediately be observed that even if the Committee I negotiations are put back on the track at the session beginning in March 1978, the emerging treaty will by no means be a perfect one. Fisheries experts will point out that regional fishing management schemes, for example, would have made more sense than the almost total coastal state control provided in the present draft. Oceanographers will wring their hands over the burden of coastal state consent for marine scientific research. United States environmentalists would have preferred to see the United States retain the right to set design, manning, construction, and equipment standards for vessels in transit in the United States territorial sea, something that is denied in the present draft. Representatives of United States mining companies were critical of the emerging compromise in Committee I even before Paul Engo tampered with it. Others, too, will undoubtedly find cause to complain that the treaty has not given them everything they would have liked.

What, then, is right about the treaty that appears to be emerging? First, the effort to achieve a comprehensive treaty must be seen in the context of steadily increasing nationalism in the world's oceans. The number and content of unilateral claims have increased dramatically even since the conference itself opened four years ago. Thus, rather than ask whether the treaty is perfect, the better question may be, Is it likely to be preferable to no treaty at all? In this context the answer almost surely is affirmative. The preservation of even minimum international rights, as for fisheries, or the minimal safeguards provided to pure scientific research, are likely to be preferable to no international safeguards at all. In the absence of a treaty, the coastal state is all too likely ultimately to do as it pleases, within or even beyond its 200 mile zone, without international recourse except to the extent provided by the International Court of Justice. Even that court is likely to find increasingly for the coastal state as customary international law itself adjusts to a world of increased national control unilaterally imposed on the oceans.

It would be a mistake, however, to view the treaty solely as "better than nothing," valid as that view may be. The present draft does contain many positive aspects. Dispute settlement is one, and the articles protecting salmon even beyond 200 miles is another. But perhaps most important to the United States is the protection of the freedom of navigation on and below the surface and of overflight and related uses that remain virtually inviolate throughout the treaty as a matter of cardinal importance to United States security and general maritime interests.

As is true of the UN the United States has an overriding concern in maintaining a peaceful and stable world. This concern surely will be better served by the rule of law that the treaty would represent than by the disorder and idiosyncratic developments that will ensue if no treaty can be achieved.

Does the United States really have the option, then, of withdrawing from the negotiations, as Ambassador Richardson has suggested? While the answer is clearly yes, the wisdom of doing so may well be doubted. Were the United States to withdraw, one immediate result would be the adoption of legislation licensing United States-led mining consortia to mine manganese nodules in the "common heritage" area and providing some form of protection from the international ramifications that might ensue. Indeed, the Congress may so act, even if the United States does continue in the negotiations, although the form of legislation in that case is more likely to acknowledge the existence of the international negotiations and to make for provision for conforming to the treaty, if one is ultimately adopted.

Timing, here, is of the utmost importance. The threat of United States legislation, like the sword of Damocles, can have a salutary effect of keeping up pressure on the negotiations. The actual passage of legislation, however, even of the more moderate type, is another matter. Passage of the United States 200 mile fisheries bill hurt the United States at the conference, making it more difficult to argue for the maintenance of other international rights in other countries' 200 mile zones, but that legislation at least anticipated what was already evolving internationally in any case. United States mining legislation of whatever variety would fly directly in the face of the "common heritage" principle and, by destroying any vestige of the cooperative spirit essential to the success of the negotiations, would likely result in their collapse. Were this to occur even the mining companies could be the losers, since in the long run they are likely to be better off operating with rather than without international sanction, the protection of United States legislation or even the U.S. Navy to the contrary.

The law of the sea negotiating process has been inherently a messy one, painfully slow, and frequently frustrating to its participants and to foreign offices around the world, not just to the United States Congress. Yet progress has been made, and the opportunity in the spring of 1978 to undo the last minute damage done to the Committee I text and to negotiate the few remaining outstanding issues does exist. If a majority of the Congress or at best the president can resist the temptation to serve short-term political considerations by satisfying the United States mining-company lobby at the expense of longer term national interests, the international negotiations have at least a reasonable chance for success. If a generally acceptable comprehensive treaty can be achieved, marking the beginning of an era of constitutional growth for four-fifths of the world's surface, the effort surely will have been worthwhile for the UN, the United States, and indeed, for all countries of the world, rich and poor alike.

The Politics of the
New International Economic Order

C. CLYDE FERGUSON, JR.

Amid bitterness, recrimination, and confrontation, the New International Economic Order burst upon the international political scene in April 1974 when the Sixth Special Session of the United Nations General Assembly adopted a Declaration and a Program of Action on the Establishment of a New International Economic Order (NIEO).[1] Hardly an area of global economic concern escaped recommendations for radical reform. Bitterness at the negotiating tactics adopted by the third world persisted long after the session's conclusion. The United States representative stated: "We are prepared to participate in examining specific issues in appropriate fora and we are prepared to discuss our differences with others of contrary views. But, we utterly reject the notion that just solutions flow from a negotiating process which consists of demands to take it or leave it."[2]

The United States accused the third world of conduct approaching bad faith. In voting against a third world resolution to implement the provisions of the NIEO resolution in the Economic and Social Council, the United States representative declared:

We are not willing to lend our support to the creation of the kind of New International Economic Order envisaged by the Program of Action adopted by the Sixth Special Session. The position of my Government on this matter is also influenced by the manner in which the Declaration and Program of Action were adopted in New York. My Government believes it was not accorded the usual prerogatives generally accorded to Member States of the United Nations. We believe that our views were not given appropriate weight in the processes of consultation and negotiations, particularly on the

[1] UNGA Res. 3201 (S-VI) and 3202 (S-VI), May 1, 1974.
[2] Statement, C. Clyde Ferguson, Jr., head, United States Delegation to the 31st session of ECOSOC, New Delhi, February 28, 1975.

Program of Action. There were occasions upon which we were even denied the opportunity to be heard. There were occasions upon which previously made commitments to my Government were peremptorily withdrawn without explanation.[3]

For more than a year after the Sixth Special Session, United States representatives to international economic conferences were following instructions to abstain or vote against any decision or resolution that referred to the New International Economic Order with the initialism NIEO. These reactions on the part of the United States to the economic demands of the third world more than amply demonstrate that the NIEO involves far more than international economics.

There is little question that the global economic order for the quarter-century after World War II was shaped to accord with the interests of the industrialized West in general and the United States in particular. *Pax Americana* was not limited to political issues but necessarily comprehended the economic order.

The call for a new global economic order marks the end of that old order. The global economy during the period of *Pax Americana* was remarkable for the stimulation of explosive growth in productive capacity, the establishment of a regime of relatively free trade, and, for most of the period, the maintenance of a stable international monetary system. But the system was flawed—particularly in regard to the newly independent countries that joined the system late, mainly in the 1960s. Persistence of the colonial economic structure could be seen in patterns of international trade, commerce, finance, and transportation.

What is at issue, then, in the NIEO is nothing less than an attempt to create a new world order after a new model. And the question of the nature of the new world order is preeminently a political question. Hence the politics of the NIEO becomes central to the matter of the world order of the next quarter-century.

The World of Worlds

So far the leading actors in the global economic-political confrontation have been identified as the United States and the "third world." Such a bifurcation is much too simplistic to be useful in examining the politics of the NIEO. The World of Worlds is far more complex and fragile than the popular image of monolithic blocs colliding with enormous force and in the process releasing very high temperature rhetoric. There is, however, a basic political reality represented by the worlds of international politics.

The simplest model of the world of international politics is in fact bipolar in an almost literal sense. Employing the criterion of the stage of economic development, it is a fact that most developed national economies lie north of the equator while most less developed economies are in the Southern Hemisphere.

---

[3] Statement, C. Clyde Ferguson, Jr., head, United States Delegation to the summer session of ECOSOC, Geneva, August 1, 1975.

Of course, if the equator were moved a thousand miles northward the equaspheric model would appear to gain a few more degrees of validity. There are, however, objections to the model. Australia, New Zealand, and South Africa are "honorary" members of the Northern Hemisphere. This extension of honorary membership suggests that "North" and "South" are defined by reference to factors other than global geography. Japan, for example, is classified as a Western country on economic issues but Asian in regard to political issues. Nonetheless, North-South is a useful concept in examining the political confrontation over the global economy.

A more common terminology is that of the worlds—the first world and the third world. The first world in UN parlance consists of "Western Europe and others." The others are North America (Canada and the United States but not Mexico), Australia, New Zealand, and Japan. All other countries are third world —except the USSR and Eastern Europe, which constitute the second world. China, incidentally, and with perhaps some justification, insists it is a world unto itself, and in any event the first and second worlds are populated solely by the two superpowers.

In the politics of the NIEO, it is the third world that commands attention. The third world is not, however, a monolithic entity, despite the impression created by its admittedly monolithic voting tactic exhibited in the UN and its subsidiary bodies. Economically the most glaring discongruity of interest is between the "resourch rich" and those nations described as the poorest of the poor, a condition generated by their lack of marketable resources. In addition, there is a lack of commonality of interest between the middle class economic powers, such as Brazil, and the preindustrial, agricultural poor. Finally, there are inherent diverse economic interests on the part of the Africans and the Arabs and cultural conflicts whose roots lie in the history of African slavery.

If the third world is not monolithic, the same may be said for the first world. There are industrialized countries that have exhibited a sensitivity and responsiveness to third world demands in international organizations. Sweden, the Netherlands, and Canada have consistently exhibited a flexibility in their reception of third world demands that has not been characteristic of the attitude of the Federal Republic of Germany and the United States. Harold Wilson, the former prime minister of the United Kingdom, at the Kingston Commonwealth Meeting in May 1975, stated: "I want to make it clear . . . that the British Government fully accepts that the relationship, the balance between the rich and the poor countries of the world is wrong and must be remedied. . . . The wealth of the world must be redistributed in favor of the poverty-stricken and the starving." A prime illustration of such "inequalities" and "injustices" is the UN finding that the developing countries, which constitute 70 percent of the world's population, account for only 30 percent of the world income.

The political tension between the third world and the industrialized world perhaps reached its peak at the General Assembly in 1973. Not only did developing countries increasingly insist that industrialized countries had an obligation to provide assistance and other relief, but also that they—the developing countries—had the right to receive it in response to those demands. For the first time in twenty-five years there was an insistence on making the kind of comprehensive review of all trade and development issues on a scale that had not been done since the close of World War II. If developed countries had tended to prefer the continuation of the monetary and trade practices marked by the period of *Pax Americana*, with only periodic updating and modification, the newly independent countries insisted that they be given the opportunity radically to alter most of the existing procedures that they had no part in establishing. The richer donor countries urged that the transfer of resources had to be voluntary and administered mainly through programs of technical assistance and private capital formation. The response of the third world came out of a meeting in Algiers in 1973. The poorer countries demanded that the world economic system be changed through the redrafting of global financial and trading policies so that transfers of resources would flow automatically from the rich to the poor.

If the frustration, the disappointment, the bitterness, and indeed the hatred exhibited in Algiers was the mother of the Sixth Special Session, it is equally clear that the oil crisis was the father. Late 1973 saw the use of the oil weapon by the Organization of Petroleum Exporting Countries (OPEC), although admittedly it was not exercised by all of its members. In response, Secretary Kissinger conceived of the necessity of organizing Western consumer nations to confront the producers on the issue of oil prices and the global economy. But his initiative was not the only one. France had called for an energy conference, but its initiative differed in two significant respects from that of the United States. First, its conference was to be global. Secondly, it was to be under the auspices of the UN. Both of these elements were missing from the Kissinger initiative.

It is certainly clear that the third world, and principally Algeria, saw in these twin initiatives a grave risk to the third world. Politically, there was the risk that out of either or both such conferences there could emerge a condemnation of a part of the third world for triggering the then global economic crisis. Also there was the risk, principally in the Kissinger initiative, that the OPEC countries might be split from the rest of the third world. With the growth of wealth in the OPEC and the resource-rich members of the third world, there was an easily perceived fault line in the supposedly monolithic third world alignment. The adverse interests of the rich oil producers and the poor of the rest of the third world and the threat of third world disunity were perceived by President Boumédienne of Algeria. His response was an urgent call for a special session of the General Assembly to meet in the spring of 1974 to address the problems of raw materials and the global economy. In political terms, it is clear that President Boumedienne sought to preempt the field covered by the Kissinger and French initiatives in order to avoid the risks of a fracture in the less developed third world alignment. These political initiatives revealed that there was indeed a fourth world—the resource poor, those economically crippled members of the third world whose interests were radically different from those who had the fortune to be endowed with natural resources, particularly fossil fuels.

The reaction of the United States to the call for the Sixth Special Session is noteworthy. For example, when informed of Boumédienne's call for the special session, Secretary Kissinger is reported to have said: "Well, I suppose we'll have to humor them along." Similarly, Ambassador Scali, the United States permanent representative to the UN, stated that the United States would "listen constructively" to proposals of the third world and would determine their inherent justice.

The actual proceedings and result of the Sixth Special Session demonstrated how wrong Secretary Kissinger and Ambassador Scali were in appraising the nature of the demands from the third world. The first miscalculation by the United States was that the essential issue for discussion in the Sixth Special Session was that of official foreign assistance in helping the fourth world meet the international payments crisis occasioned by the tripling and quadrupling of oil prices. Given the history and assumptions on which *Pax Americana* rested, this miscalculation is understandable.

Foreign assistance, although it came late as a component of United States foreign policy, was an essential underpinning for the era of *Pax Americana*. The benchmark, of course, in United States foreign assistance derived from Secretary Marshall's speech at Harvard in 1948. He said, "The role of this country should consist of friendly aid in the drafting of a European program and of later support of such a program as far as it may be practical for us to do so. The program should be a joint one, agreed to by a number if not all European nations." The Economic Cooperation Act of 1948 stated its purpose was "to promote world peace and a national interest by providing assistance to maintain conditions abroad consistent with the needs of the United States." The major goals of the program were to establish monetary stability and promotion of free trade principally through reducing trade barriers.

It was inevitable that the methods of increasing production would remain primarily the responsibility of each country. Material assistance from the United States strengthened these efforts and particularly those directed to the improvement of capital investment. Approximately 85 percent of the European reconstruction was financed by savings in European countries themselves. Two further aspects of this program deserve mention. First, part of the investment resources were directed to the economic development of the then overseas territories. Second, part of the American participation was in the form of technical assistance given to encourage production.

Given the fact that there had been a steady decline of the percentage of the GNP devoted to official assistance and given the assumptions that underlay United States foreign assistance programs, it is understandable that the United States thought the principle focus of the Sixth Special Session would somehow revolve around the need to modify the strategy for the so-called Development Decades: a modification, however, limited to the issue of official emergency aid to those countries most seriously affected by the oil-price crisis. The political advantages to the United States and to the West of a General Assembly so limited are all too apparent. This miscalculation certainly contributed to the inadequate preparation of the United States position for the Sixth Special Session.

On the eve of the Sixth Special Session of the General Assembly in 1974 there was little doubt among any of the delegations, first world and third world alike, that a serious problem had been created by the quadrupling of oil prices. Moreover, there was general agreement that a disproportionate burden fell on those least able to afford new hard currency outlays. In fact, the UN had compiled an official list of "the poorest of the poor." The Programme of Action adopted by the Sixth Special Session called for the creation of a special UN fund for the benefit of those most seriously affected by general economic dislocations.

The formal position of the United States was that the Special Fund was unnecessary. It duplicated both the World Bank family and the UN's own institutions. The United States pointed out, for example, that a substantial part of the resources of the Special Fund would be, in the usual UN practice, devoted to nonproductive overhead. Moreover, the United States objected to the fact that the Special Fund had as its charter, not only the authorization to assist the most seriously affected in emergency conditions, but also the authorization to undertake the task of assisting in long-range development. In this regard, the United States pointed to the duplication between the Special Fund and the United Nations Development Program and possibly also, the UN Childrens' Fund (UNICEF).

The real basis for objections from the West, and particularly from the United States, was much more fundamental. One of the insistent demands of the third world was to participate on a basis of sovereign equality in all of those international institutions that affected them. In fact, borrowing from a decision of the United States Supreme Court, the third world adopted the view that in all international organizations, decisions should be taken on the basis of one nation, one vote. Of course, in the World Bank family, the voting is not by units of sovereignty—one nation, one vote—but of money. The United States as a major contributor to the World Bank family was in the position of exercising the predominant influence. Both as a matter of principle and as a matter of relations with Congress, the position of the United States was that it could not abandon the responsibility for oversight of its contributions to others, many of whom would be in the donee rather than the donor class of countries.

While the United States participated as a board member of the Special Fund and also in its creation and drafting of its working rules, it nonetheless steadfastly refused to make a pledge to the fund. Finally, in December 1974, it withdrew from the fund. The Federal Republic of Germany followed.

The domain of global finance is not the only area in which the third world insists the rules be rewritten. Modern technology in the industrialization and agricultural development of the third world is essential. Obviously, however, the third world is poor in technological resources. The principal source of technological know-how is the first world.

The main concern, therefore, of the third world is to have technology transferred from the developed to the developing countries. Accordingly, third world nations have called on developed countries to support international action to eliminate and effectively control restrictive business practices that directly limit the transfer of existing technology to developing countries. By seeking action at national, regional, and international levels to achieve a reorientation in the activities of transnational corporations, the third world has awakened latent fears of a world government. The third world has particularly sought to establish rules to control practices of transnational firms thought adversely to affect the economies and the ideology of third world countries. To this end, a secretariat was established within the UN to begin work on drafting a code of conduct for transnational corporations.

The specter this proposal raised was that for the first time the UN itself would assert its power directly to control a citizen or an institution of a sovereign state. The prospect that out of the deep-sea mining proposal in the law of the sea the UN might develop the power to tax directly or, at least, to have the advantage of an independent income and the power to act directly against a citizen or entity of a member state awakens fears of an effective world level government. The successful transition in the American experience from the Articles of Confederation to the Constitution is not lost on those who fear global level governance.

Confronting the Third World

The Sixth Special Session of the General Assembly was an unmitigated debacle for the United States and the first world. The causes lay not only in miscalculations of the intentions of the third world, despite the clear signal emanating from Algiers, but also in certain Western attitudes about the role of the third world in global economics. Of more consequence to the United States was a final exposure of a major flaw in the international economic policymaking process in Washington.

The disarray of the United States delegation to the special session was a mirror image of the disarray in Washington arising from the unreconciled positions of the Departments of State and Treasury. Moreover, an American initiative responsive to the acute needs of those countries most seriously affected by the oil prices was not launched until the waning hours of the last morning of the session. Having calculated that the essential thrust of the session would be directed toward official emergency aid transfers, the United States initiative launched late in the session was an imaginative response designed to assist those countries that had been most seriously affected by the increase in petroleum prices. The initiative, however, reposed in the pockets of the American delegation from the very first days of the session. The secretary of the treasury had ordered the indefinite withholding of its introduction. Secretary of State Kissinger, after having heard from President Boumédienne in Algeria of the importance the third world attached to the session, dispatched instructions to the United States delegation to launch the initiative. Within twelve hours, countermanding instructions were delivered, not from the secretary of state, but again from the secretary of the treasury.

In the instructions to proceed with the initiative there were indications that the secretary of state was aware of the Treasury opposition and, apparently, was of the opinion that that opposition could be handled at the cabinet level. (In fact, the United States was unable to secure a hearing on its proposal in the various working committees of the Sixth Special Session.) The second countermand was dispatched to the delegation to assure that the United States initiative did not go forward. This performance, most embarrassing in a diplomatic context, was a reflection of the problem of economic policy process in the then administration in Washington.

It is apparent that the problem of the economic policymaking process arose out of structural characteristics of the foreign policy and economic institutions of government. That structural problem is the result of one undeniable attribute of the society: there is no hard, clearly ascertainable line between that which is "domestic" and that which is "foreign" in policies on economic issues. This is to say much more than domestic political prejudices, biases, and interests have a profound influence on the substance and execution of economic foreign policy. This truism can be easily grasped by reflecting on the range of issues raised by international demands for the adoption of generalized tariff preference schemes. On January 1, 1976, the United States adopted a preference system covering some 2,724 tariff items. There is hardly a domestic constituency unaffected by one or more of the items covered by the scheme. An even clearer illustration of the lack of compartmentalization into "domestic" and "foreign" in economic policy can be seen in the complex of issues that must be resolved and managed in American global food policy.

Since economic issues cannot be compartmentalized into neatly labeled categories of foreign and domestic, it follows that the State Department and its secretary are not vested with exclusive subject matter jurisdiction over international economic policy. The Departments of the Treasury, of Agriculture, of Commerce, of Defense, and even of Transportation and Interior all have legitimate interests in American economic policy as it is reflected in the international sphere. Sources of their interests lie not only in their acquired domestic constituencies but also from responsibilities imposed by law, executive direction, political necessity, and past conventional behavior. Indeed, if the thesis asserted is true—there is no hard line between domestic and foreign policy—it would follow that the Treasury, Agriculture, Commerce, and other departments clearly must have a voice in formulating that policy. It is suggested that the United States does not have a developed institutional process by which it can speak with a single voice as to its position on issues of international economic concern.

Preparations for the 1975 Seventh Special Session of the General Assembly differed markedly from the preparations for the sixth. First, unlike preparations for the Sixth Special Session, high level attention of the secretary of state was engaged from the onset. Again, unlike the Sixth Special Session, the Congress of the United States directly concerned itself with the administration's preparations. Second, a deliberate, well-conceived United States diplomatic effort was undertaken to convey to the third world the parameters of the United States's international economic position. The United States's representative at the meeting of the Committee on Natural Resources in April 1975 was able to assert a clear, unified United States position on the question of expropriation, nationalization, and compensation. Similarly, in the Economic and Social Council (ECOSOC) session of 1975, the United States, for the first time, was able to state with precision its position on the role of the General Assembly in the process of reforming the international economic order. Substantive positions of the United States on the major issues of international economic policy in response to the demands of the third world were set forth in the secretary of state's speeches in April 1975 and in July 1975.

In April 1975, the secretary of state announced a dramatic change in United States economic policy. For reasons derived from economic ideology, the United States had previously opposed intervention in international commodity markets. Although this opposition took the form of specific objections, as was the case in the Cocoa Agreement and the old Coffee Agreement, it was nonetheless clear that the basis of American opposition and objections was simply that of economic ideology. Intervention in the marketplace could be justified only in emergency conditions. In April 1975, however, the secretary of state announced that the United States would consider international commodity agreements on a "case-by-case basis." In addition, the secretary announced that the United States would abandon its opposition to linked discussion of commodity issues and international negotiations on energy. The significance of these changes was reflected in the secretary's July 1975 speech in Milwaukee clearly recognizing some merit in certain third world economic demands and expressly committing the United States to a position of flexibility and openness. The culmination of this diplomatic effort was the secretary's speech to the Seventh Special Session in September 1975, delivered by Ambassador Moynihan.

By the conclusion of the Seventh Special Session in September 1975, it was apparent that United States economic policy had been drastically changed, through clarification, in four critical respects. The first was that the United States recognized the need to respond to the problem of stabilization of export earnings from sales of commodities by the less developed countries. Second, the United States recognized the principle of permanent sovereignty over natural resources but would insist that upon nationalization or expropriation compensation would have to be paid according to accepted standards of international rather than domestic law. Third, the United States would put aside the essentially semantic or theological debate as to whether the international community was about the creation of a "new international economic order" or the reform of the "global economic order." Lastly, there was the dramatic reversal of prior policy in that the United States would no longer pose objections to third world demands that international discussions of energy be linked to discussions of commodities and raw materials. This latter reversal of policy on a question of procedure made possible the reconvening of the Paris Talks on International Cooperation, commonly called the North-South dialogues.

Another problem, however, remained. The third world is heavily dependent on exports of primary commodities for earnings from which development is financed. The critical problems in the international trade in commodities are excessive price fluctuations from year to year or season to season, declining price trends of many key commodities, and the erosion in the purchasing power of developing coun-tires. These issues render rational planning and steady economic development virtually impossible to sustain. This is acutely so in those third world countries dependent upon the vagaries of a pricing pattern of a single commodity.

The third world solution has been to call for an integrated program for com-modities (IPC). The IPC envisages a comprehensive and effective integrated pro-gram based on a common fund for financing stocks and on complementary mea-sures relating to price stabilization, processing of raw materials in the developing countries, rationalization of the marketing and distribution system, and assured access to first world markets. The scope of IPC covers a range of eighteen com-modities that, in 1972, were estimated to have accounted for about 75 percent of agricultural and mineral exports of developing countries (excluding petroleum). The UN Conference on Trade and Development (UNCTAD-IV) meeting in Nai-robi identified these commodities as bananas, bauxite, cocoa, coffee, copper, cotton, hard fibers, iron ore, jute, manganese, meat, phosphates, rubber, sugar, tea, tropical hard timbers, tin, and vegetable oils. During the special session in 1975, the third world was led to believe that the United States would address the problem of commodity trade and would do so in a new spirit of cooperation and flexibility. On January 16, 1976, however, after the end of the regular Gen-eral Assembly session, an assistant secretary of the treasury suggested that a case-by-case approach to commodity agreements was illegitimate—in the sense that, in the absence of an emergency, commodity agreements were unjustified inter-ventions in the free market system asserted to exist in international commodity trade. Speaking for the Treasury, the assistant secretary ruled out any retreat from the position that international commodity agreements were economically suspect and only in rare circumstances such as the Tin Agreement (where most producers are American entities) could the United States envisage its participa-tion in such arrangements.

This, then, was the legacy of the prior administration to the incoming Carter administration in foreign economic policy process. The Carter administration has recognized the problem. But its institutional structures created in response to the problem appear to have encountered difficulties. The administration, as of Sep-tember 1977, has created a committee of six to reconcile conflicting economic policy views.

A second fundamental issue exposed by the economic demands of the third world upon the first world is that of the role of the UN itself. Secretary of State Kissinger's long, complex, innovative, and imaginative set of proposals put before the Seventh Special Session was generally well received as reflecting a new attitude and a new sensitivity on the part of the United States. Examination of that speech, however, reveals one factor with disturbing implications. The role of the UN in the process of formulating or reformulating or reforming the global economic order was not discussed or even mentioned.

The attitude of the United States toward the General Assembly and those subsidiary organs concerned with economic affairs has long tended to force United States economic policy in the UN into a negative posture. This negativism in the economic field long predates the confrontations that marked and marred the regular 1975 session of the General Assembly.

The final fundamental issue exposed by the third and first world confrontation on the nature of the global economic order is that of emotion and the politics of international economics. For purposes of analysis, it is useful to separate the "emotional" dimension of the confrontation from the "political" dimension despite the fact that the two dimensions are clearly symbiotic.

There is no demand that evokes as much anger and even rage among many first world foreign policy establishments as the third world demand for reparations for past ravages of colonialism and neocolonialism, racism, and segregation. The permanent representative of the United States to the UN in 1975 described this third world position as a demand that the West plead guilty before the plea bargaining begins. There is indeed truth in this characterization. While the offense charged against the West is of the nature of a misdemeanor rather than an international felony, the rhetoric accompanying this "nonnegotiable" demand is cast in terms of "rape and pillage" of the third world—felonies in any legal lexicon.

The demand for reparations is emotionally based and, in origin, is not unrelated to the "reparation" phase of the Civil Rights Movement in the United States of the late 1960s.

Most senior members of the newer third world governments have direct, personal, and mostly bitter memories of the era of colonialism. They directly experienced the insults of racial discrimination. Some still have vivid memories of the signs—"No Natives, No Dogs." They do indeed want the first world to admit that colonialism was characterized by aspects of economic exploitation and in most instances also by racism. These conclusions are not mere surmise or conjecture, but are rather the essence of hundreds of reported conversations on this issue with senior third world officials around the world. Essentially this demand boils down to a plea to the West to at least "admit you did it and say you are sorry." This is the emotional dimension of this demand.

There is, however, a political demand for an internationally sanctioned redistribution of global wealth. No more intractable issue arose in the intensive formal exchanges by the United States with the Group of 77 in Geneva in July 1975 than that of global redistribution not only of income but also of capital. The third world position is that redistribution has to commence with present income and from present capital. It was the position of the United States that in the shaping of the interdependent global economy, new patterns of wealth distribution could be negotiated, but only out of the wealth produced in the future through cooperative efforts. These positions were, and appear to remain, irreconcilable.

The third world position can most easily be seen in the matter of "permanent sovereignty." The issue upon which the United States and the third world are at an impasse is whether, upon expropriation of a foreign capital invesment, compensation shall be paid in accordance with "domestic law" of the expropriating state or in accordance with the recognized principles of international law. The issue is fundamental since it is clear that valuation formulas, if resorted to under "domestic law," could eventuate in the expropriated enterprise becoming indebted to the nationalizing state upon seizure. Such a result is nothing more than an enforced redistribution of capital wealth.

The United States representative to the UN Committee on National Resources in April 1975, after setting forth the traditional view of the United States regarding the imperatives of international law, added:

> The United States believes that these recent formulations of the principle of permanent sovereignty over natural resources are simply bad policy—regardless of the legalities of the issue. The major mechanism for the transfer of real resources to the developing world has been investment from private sources—not official aid. It requires no sophisticated analysis to demonstrate that these transfers are discouraged when nations adhere to formulations which of themselves create additional risks of uncompensated loss of investments.[4]

Whether the United States conception of international law is the essence of rectitude will not be determined by votes in the UN, but by the course of events outside the UN. It still remains true, however, that foreign capital investment in third world countries present a convenient target for commencement of the process of forced redistribution of a portion of the capital wealth of the world.

The Environment of the Worlds

In opening the ministerial level talks in the North-South Dialogue in Paris, in June 1977, UN Secretary General Kurt Waldheim stated: "Let's not forget that this North-South conference began with what we call the energy crisis." While the United States had changed its position to accept the linkage of oil discussions with those of commodities, the dialogue remained centered on a new energy order. And, in the end, it was energy that was the cause of the virtual failure of the talks. But, in the nonoil sector, the industrial powers had finally been able to agree to two proposals thought responsive to the third world. First, the creation of a special aid fund of $1 billion for the poorest of the poor, those who, in UN terms, were "the most seriously affected." Second, and ideologically perhaps more important than the $1 billion special fund, was the final acceptance of a

---

[4] Statement, C. Clyde Ferguson, Jr., head, United States Delegation to the fourth meeting of the UN Committee on Natural Resources, Tokyo, April 1, 1975.

major demand of the third world in the commodity area for a common fund to finance commodity stocks and to stabilize prices and markets. These first world responses, however, were rejected out of hand by the third world. The third world spokesman Manuel Perez-Guerrero stated: "The proposals are far below our hopes." The collapse of the North-South Dialogue in mid-1977 again suggests that factors other than technical economic reordering of the world order is at stake. There are underlying political forces that impede economic accommodations.

In examining the political environment in which economic accommodations must be made, it is apparent that there are five clusters of issues that now affect the relations between the first and third worlds. A first cluster of issues relates to perceptions of the worlds and the attitudes held by those in the first and the third world as to each other. It is here that the question of race becomes acute. For the most part the third world is nonwhite. Of the major leaders of the third world only Yugoslavia can be unquestionably classified as Caucasian. Of course, there are members of the third world in Latin America who, for various reasons, identify with the nonwhite component. Increasingly, the third world has identified racism as an attribute of the present economic system. In this connection the irrelevance of the second world (the Soviet bloc) becomes apparent. That second world is white: on occasion the Chinese have pointed this out in very blunt terms.

It is not so much the allegation of the presence of a racial element in the economic order that carries the message of perceptions and atttitudes as it is the allegation that the colonialist system and mentality has persisted into the present economic system. Colonialism is often used as a code word to describe an attribute of colonialism—racism. Until very recently there has been little public discussion of this aspect of the confrontation between the first and the third worlds. Experienced diplomats, however, have often remarked on the obvious presence of racial tensions in discussions with the third world, particularly on such issues as participation in decision-making on the basis of sovereign equality, participation in the decision-making process of financial institutions by donee countries, and the apparent global correlation between race and poverty.

A second cluster of issues relates to political and economic ideology. The first world is marked by its adherence to the market concept of economic organization. Some, such as the United States and the Federal Republic of Germany, are much more explicit than others in setting forth this ideological basis for their economic positions. Nonetheless, in the West, whether socialist or nonsocialist, there is a discernible tilt toward the market as the most efficient allocator of resources and the most efficient mechanism for tranfers of resources from the first world to the third world. Here again the irrelevance of the second world (the Soviet bloc) is patent. Many in the West have taken umbrage at the fact that the demands of the third world are for the most part made on the first world rather than being made equally on the second world. Rather than being a sign of partiality, one could just as easily interpret this phenomenon as an opportunity on the part of the first world to capitalize on the third world.

A third cluster of issues shaping the political environment relates to attitudes and conceptions of the role of the UN in general and the General Assembly in particular in shaping the economic world order. A bias against a UN role in economic matters can be detected in United States policy. It is clear, for example, that at San Francisco the Economic and Social Council was considered to be an analogue to the Security Council. Over the past twenty-five years, however, the Economic and Social Council has been denied a significant role in the formulation of global economic policy. This can be seen most clearly in the relationship between the Economic and Social Council and the World Bank family. While the council was conceived as the overseer of the World Bank, its function has atrophied to that of merely receiving a report annually from the president of the World Bank. Moreover, the isolation of the Economic and Social Council from major global economic matters has ensured that these issues will not be raised in the General Assembly.

Prior to 1975, the United States had not made a general policy pronouncement of the United States position on the role and function of the General Assembly in economic matters. There is, nonetheless, considerable evidence that United States policy was to limit the scope of the General Assembly's concern with economic matters and the concern of its subsidiary organs. An examination of United States positions in the Economic and Social Council, in the UN Conference on Trade and Development, and in the UN Industrial Development Organization clearly reveals a distaste for the prospect that the General Assembly might seize itself of vital economic questions of international concerns. In some instances, the rationale for this position was that the particular economic issues raised in the General Assembly were vested in some other international institution such as the World Bank or the General Agreement on Tariffs and Trade (GATT) and hence the General Assembly could not consider such matters at all. On other occasions, it was asserted that the particular matter at issue was within the exclusive jurisdiction of a specialized agency of the United Nations and that that particular agency could not be subjected to directives issued by the General Assembly.

On several issues it has been asserted that the "political character" of the General Assembly disqualified it from considering certain economic issues presumed to be devoid of political considerations. In July 1975, however, the United States addressed the precise issue of the role and function of the General Assembly in economic affairs of international concern. The explicit statement of the United States policy on the issue of the role of the General Assembly was accepted, even welcomed, by the third world. Its impact, however, was obscured by the pretense that the United States had not, in fact, changed its position from that which most delegations knew to have been the center of gravity of United States policy since the early 1950s. In diplomacy, as in law, there appears to be an accepted convention that any pronouncement of a new rule or policy must never be characterized as new or changed. The pretense must always be that what is now said was ever thus. Despite the employment of that patent fiction,

United States policy pronouncements were perceived both as a change in policy and a significant indication of intent to deal seriously and responsibly with the express concerns of the third world.

There remains, however, the ghost of a portent that the United States might well disengage from the UN by first disengaging from the General Assembly. The Carter administration and the new United States ambassador to the UN have apparently abandoned the thesis of disengagement. The extent of American disaffection from the United Nations has not, however, substantially changed with the advent of the Carter administration. In a canvas of the range of possible retaliatory measures against the UN, it appears that the least drastic measure is considered to be precisely that of nonparticipation in the proceedings of the General Assembly. It is not an overstatement to assert that if such a disengagement eventuates, the probability of an escalation from rhetorical to direct economic confrontation is indeed very high. Avoidance of such a consequence should be of the highest priority in American foreign policy. Vital national interests are at stake, principally and primarily that of access to raw materials of the third world.

The fourth complex of issues relates to the structure of the economic decision-making process in Washington. It has been demonstrated that in the departmental organization of the United States government it is a fact that several if not all departments of the United States government have a vital stake in foreign economic policy. Those interests cannot be ignored in the formulation of policy, whether or not responsibility for execution is left to the Department of State or the Department of the Treasury or the Department of Agriculture. The options for structural reorganization appear to come to two: the effective formulation of policy by the cabinet or by the National Security Council. While in the traditional parliamentary democracies of Western Europe, it appears that this structural problem is precisely the kind of problem resolved at the cabinet level, and it also appears that even Secretary of State Kissinger, while he still wore two hats as secretary of state and chairman of the National Security Council, thought that conflicts between Treasury and State on economic issues could be resolved at the cabinet level.

The development of the cabinet as a decision-making instrumentality in the more recent history of the United States has not been felicitous. There is little evidence in the last twenty-five years that the cabinet has performed the function of finally formulating a unified policy on issues that transcend traditional cabinet level jurisdictional lines. That leaves the National Security Council as the only existing institution with the structural potentiality for addressing the problem of transdepartmental concerns. The new organization of the National Security Council into "clusters," at least one of which involves North-South problems, is some indication that the structural problem of the policymaking process is being deliberately addressed. Nonetheless, in a vital respect, the absence of the Department of the Treasury and the Department of Agriculture from formal membership on the National Security Council cannot be characterized as other than a jurisdictional defect. A response to the problem of the policymaking process would appear to necessitate either formal representation on the National Security Council by other departments of the government vitally affected by a particular issue or alternatively the organization of a cluster that would primarily address the problem of a unified United States foreign economic policy. Neither of these two options appears to have commended itself to the new administration.

Finally, a fifth cluster of issues relates to the substance of United States policy. The successes of OPEC against powerful Western economies and a group of multinational companies that lead to substantial increases in revenues of OPEC have inspired many developing countries—even though ironically most of the developing world was worst hit by the oil price rises—to look at cartels for economic salvation.

Experts doubt whether cartels of the nature of OPEC would be possible in any other product dominated by the third world—copper, bauxite, tea, sugar, manganese, and, as sometimes mentioned, bananas. The key conditions that led to OPEC's successes were unique, control of exports, a high degree of political and regional unity, absence of immediate prospects of substitution, and the ability to hold back production (which cannot be done with cocoa or sugar) as well as the capacity, in the case of petroleum, to store in the ground itself.

Nonetheless, producers' associations have mushroomed in the last two years in bananas, copper, cocoa, tea, tin, phosphates, and, of course, coffee. Malaysia, even now, is leading an attempt to establish such associations for rubber and vegetable oils. One of the outcomes of the Group of 77 organization was its adoption of the producer association as a technique for increasing the bargaining leverage of the producers as against consumers. The prime objective of the producers' cartel would be to increase the world price of the subject commodity.

The first of the problems of policy is identification of the real costs to the American economy, and indeed the costs to the American society, of responding to cartel demands. There has been considerable discussion of real costs to the American standard of living in responding to obligations undertaken to provide food to the third world. The ratios of grain fed to animals per pound of meat or per egg or per gallon of milk produced have more than amply demonstrated that response to the obligation to assist the rest of the world in feeding itself might well require a reduction in the American standard of living in such mundane matters as the frequency of meat servings or the quantum of alcoholic consumption. But the problem of real costs is much more complicated than it appears to be on the surface. For example, an examination of the economics of bauxite production would indicate that it is within the power of the American consumer to deny the cartel the purported power to fix aluminum prices. It appears to be a relatively simple matter to impose classic rules of economics on the producers' association by reducing demand for bauxite by abandoning aluminum foil in the American kitchen and throwaway beer cans before American television screens.

In classical economic theory, since there are readily available substitutes, one would suppose that the reduction of demand would effectively remove the price fixing power from the Bauxite Producer's Association.

There is a question, however, whether the use of aluminum by American consumers might not exhibit the characteristics of inelastic demand just as much as petroleum: that is, at no conceivable price would a consumer oriented consumptive society in the United States give up aluminum foil or the throwaway beer can. The range of choices for each of the major commodities raises substantially the same question of real costs and the nature of the consumptive demand for the underlying commodities.

A second aspect of "real costs" raises the issue of domestic political support for an accommodating response to the third world. One need not cite voluminous statistics to indicate that the popularity of official aid transfers in any sum likely to be significant is nil. It is possible, however, to garner domestic political support for outlays that appear to have a humanitarian base such as the alleviation of starvation in the Saheel or assistance in disaster situations in a country such as Bangladesh. If domestic political support is a constraint, and that constraint is not a limitation when dealing with the humanitarian response, it suggests that an American policy based on and focused on helping the poorest of the poor is one that would receive the most support in the present political environment.

Few conclusions can be drawn from this canvas of the politics of the New International Economic Order. But among those that might command general acceptability are the following: First, making substantive responses to the third world will require reexamination and, perhaps, reformulation of attitudes toward it. Some of the presently held attitudes clearly are the result of racist considerations that only complicate the tasks of arranging accommodations. Second, a pure free market does not exist in international commodity trade. Guidelines for appropriate market intervention can be negotiated with the third world, as has been the case of the successive coffee agreements. Third, essential to an accommodation with the third world is a recognition of the General Assembly as a policymaking organ in the sphere of international economic intercourse. Fourth, the United States must devise institutional processes for effective formulation and execution of global economic policy. Finally, any economic policy formulation must take account of the real costs to American society of responses to the most insistent of third world demands.

Nuclear Diplomacy

ABRAHAM BARGMAN

A new sense of international insecurity pervades nuclear diplomacy. Nuclear programs have proliferated, circumventing the Non-Proliferation Treaty (NPT), and the development of more efficient instruments of mass destruction has undermined other arms control measures. Eminent authorities even question the conventional wisdom that a nuclear war between the superpowers is improbable, while others debate the economic potential of nuclear power and draw contradictory conclusions from identical statistics on the availability of uranium and alternative fuels. Indeed, the international control of atomic energy entails problems of international economics and finance as much as problems of power politics.

Although its military and economic predominance is seriously challenged, the United States still prevails in each branch of nuclear activity. United States command of the nuclear export market has diminished in the last few years from 85 to 50 percent, but it remains undeniably influential as a supplier to other countries heavily engaged in nuclear commerce. Furthermore, the United States still provides the nuclear umbrella embracing the non-Communist world, while the United States's most vital national interest in nuclear deterrence remains ineluctably linked with the world community's supreme interest in preventing a nuclear war among the great powers. The United States thus retains a material basis for leadership in the movement for international control of atomic energy.

This essay identifies and analyzes two impediments to such leadership. The first is the legacy of foreign perceptions of the United States as an inconsistent and self-serving participant in international nuclear affairs. The United States is responsible for virtually all institutional innovations for control of the peaceful uses of nuclear energy, but it has appeared either unable or unwilling to sacrifice commercial and political advantages for the sake of fundamental structural change. The second impediment to United States leadership is the more recent American antagonism toward the changed UN. American officials reared on the primacy of order and stability have found it easiest to ignore whenever possible the majority's rhetoric of a militant movement in the new UN. Such a response has even been logical when considering the technical issues of nuclear disarmament or when the majority opposes one's arms control policy. It is unnecessary, however, when a change of policy is responsive to the opposition.

Two recent developments, however, provide opportunities to overcome these impediments. The Carter administration seems to assert unapologetically its leadership in a new movement to control nuclear energy and reduce armaments, and the UN has decided almost simultaneously to convene a special session of the General Assembly on disarmament. If the United States would rely more on the UN as it pursues nuclear policies more responsive to some of the criticism it has received, it could thereby build political bridges to the nonaligned countries and help overcome the resistance of the great powers.

President Carter is undoubtedly correct in assuming that the time is right for a comprehensive nuclear arms control initiative despite recent adverse technological and political tendencies. To retard proliferation, to reduce the nuclear arsenals of the superpowers, and to bring research and development of new weapons under some control are objectives with a broad appeal at home as well as abroad. To be effective, however, the new administration must consciously seek to counter the legacy of skepticism nourished by the uncertain support of previous administrations for the international control of nuclear energy and by a widely perceived American preference for duopolistic arms control diplomacy.

Impediments to Leadership

President Carter has brought to Washington new ideas and new officials committed to the optimistic proposition that one can still distinguish between the peaceful and nonpeaceful uses of nuclear energy. However appealing it may be to turn back the clock to a prenuclear era, the projection that nuclear power may supply more than half the world's total energy by the year 2000 defines the realistic limits within which international control of nuclear energy must be achieved. Perhaps the most impressive changes in Washington are, first, the close link between American cooperation in diffusing nuclear technology and, second, the president's stand on international nuclear proliferation controls and the conjunction of international and national policies. The executive branch is attempting to delay domestic construction of the ingenious breeder reactor and simultaneously to propose to other nations an International Nuclear Fuel Cycle Evaluation Program that encourages the use of uranium derivatives of little use for military purposes.

Successful nuclear diplomacy always depends on the active personal leadership of the president, but the record shows that leadership has been inconsistent. Carter's immediate predecessors deferred policymaking to parochial and commercial interests, thereby leaving political objectives and commercial policies uncoordinated. Eisenhower, however, provided an initial idealistic impetus, but opponents of international nuclear controls were often able to undercut his good intentions because he never personally controlled the actual negotiations.

A president personally interested in details of nuclear policy is more likely to use the world platform of the UN than one who readily entrusts the matter to experts. He will do so both because it is likely that public interest in the UN can send political signals to officials at home and because consent at the UN is particularly useful when placing one's personal as well as the nation's power behind idealistic solutions. It is therefore noteworthy that President Carter so coveted UN consent for his nonproliferation campaign that, shortly after assuming office, he assembled the UN delegations by his own invitation because the General Assembly was not in session. At this gathering on March 17, 1977, he announced his intention to maintain the distinction in international controls between the peaceful and military uses of the atom and to end the practice of reaching partial nuclear arms control agreements merely to demonstrate good will rather than to curb the arms race. He also accepted the principle that the United States as a dominant nuclear power should make more than its proportional share of the sacrifices.

But President Carter will doubtless find it difficult to persuade the world that his new policy is a reliable, long-term commitment, particularly if his proposals contain significant international institutional elements, for inconsistency in this regard has characterized United States nuclear diplomacy. Often one group of officials has proposed international institutions while others have carried out contradictory national policies or held back the kind of material support that might ensure success. The Baruch Plan and the Atoms for Peace Plan are cases in point.

The United Nations Charter must have appeared fundamentally inadequate to American scientists working on the atomic bomb during World War II. Their views were belatedly reflected, however, in the Acheson-Lilienthal Report on the International Control of Atomic Energy, which warned that a nuclear arms race was inevitable so long as "intrinsically dangerous activities may be carried on by nations [because] no degree of ingenuity or technical competence could possibly hope to cope with them."[1] This premise led in turn to the unprecedented proposal to the UN for the creation of an International Atomic Development Authority with worldwide jurisdiction over the entire nuclear fuel cycle. However, the supranational aspects of such widespread authority to own, manage or license, and control all nuclear facilities in the world impelled the USSR to counter with its own more traditional, nationalistic solution for the prior and unverifiable prohibition of nuclear weapons, which defused the proposal.

---

[1] Lawrence D. Weiler and Anne P. Simons, *The United States and the United Nations* (New York: Manhattan Publishing Co., 1967), p. 440.

As the years have passed, however, the imaginative United States plan lost some of its aura of political generosity. Its UN endorsement despite Soviet objections, for example, has been attributed not to the plan's merits but to bloc voting, and some now perceive it as a moral shield behind which the United States exploited its nuclear superiority. The United States did not couple with its proposal for internationalizing the peaceful uses of the atom any unilateral measures befitting a nation holding a significant military advantage. On the contrary, domestic and international policies were not integrated as Congress simultaneously took steps to maintain the American nuclear monopoly. Nor was it altogether the fault of Congress, although the world is well aware that it is one systemic impediment to international solutions.

President Truman himself practiced this double barrel approach, backing proposals for international control not by renouncing but by exploiting the bargaining chips found in existing advantages. This inability or unwillingness of the chief executive to advocate international controls exclusively, if only temporarily, also accounts for Truman's failure in 1950 to follow the advice of Oppenheimer and Rabi to declare the United States's intention not to build the H-bomb. The potential contribution to international control of such unilateral restraint by the dominant power made these scientists regard such a declaration as a worthwhile, calculated risk. But self-restraint requires a much deeper and broader domestic consensus than do isolated proposals for new international institutions.

The history of United States relations with the International Atomic Energy Agency (IAEA) has also aroused skepticism about United States intentions. An autonomous part of the UN system, the IAEA was designed to disseminate nuclear technology and to control its peaceful uses. Initiated by President Eisenhower's Atoms for Peace plan in 1953, the agency was finally established in 1957, and in 1977 some sixty inspectors carry out on-site verification of the peaceful uses of atomic energy. The United States has aided the agency by developing, among other things, tamper-resistant instrumentation for its inspection operations, but American officials tend to belittle the IAEA safeguards system as little more than a burglar alarm. IAEA secretariat officials resent such criticism, which they say tends to undermine confidence in the only functioning international nuclear control agency and also express concern lest the proposed multinational fuel centers, for example, fall outside the IAEA's operational responsibility. The failure of the United States to fulfill the pledge made by President Johnson in 1967 to open up all United States peaceful nuclear reactors to IAEA inspection has also fostered charges of unreliable leadership.

The United States's choice to avoid exclusive reliance on the IAEA is probably due to the new American policy of encouraging suppliers to assume more responsibility in preventing the export of dual purpose nuclear facilities such as reprocessing plants. This policy is generated by the fear that IAEA safeguards might be used to excuse policies that, despite on-site inspection, would indirectly undermine the nonproliferation principle. The United States has also questioned the utility of universal international organizations in imposing sanctions and has displayed little or no confidence in the UN in this area. Hence the United States itself called the London Suppliers Conference, following the Indian nuclear test explosion in 1974, to organize both prophylactic and punitive measures.

However, the United States has failed to mobilize broad support for approaching nonproliferation through ad hoc conferences, and it may have also undermined confidence in the IAEA and the UN. For instance, periodic secret meetings of nations supplying nuclear materials have sought to complement the NPT by extending IAEA safeguards to nonsignatory states that import nuclear facilities, and the conferences have generally raised the salience of the issues for bureaucrats in government and industry and for other elites, but among others they have incited fears that yet another caste system is being added to the hierarchy of nonproliferation controls.

Also, the United States is attempting to convince the world that the development and testing of peaceful nuclear explosives could undermine the nonproliferation controls. Other countries, such as Brazil and India, reject this advice, however, and insist on their right to engage in activity that the NPT has partially legitimized. Nonnuclear states are also encouraging the IAEA to investigate questions of feasibility, cost, and verification of peaceful nuclear explosions in the spirit of Article V of the NPT.

Ironically, the United States contributed to the eagerness of the developing countries that it now opposes by its own Plowshares Program designed to develop and encourage the use of nuclear explosives for peaceful purposes. Countries desiring to maintain the possibility of developing nuclear weapons would have doubtless perceived in so-called peaceful explosives a perfect rationalization for such development, but the Plowshares Program in the period 1957-70 must have nonetheless aroused their expectations. Consequently, the advanced developing countries now suspect that the United States wishes to retard the dissemination of nuclear technology to frustrate their movement to close the development gap. This perception of unilateral and self-serving behavior on the part of the United States hampers its leadership on behalf of nonproliferation or other elements of the international control of atomic energy.

A characteristic of American disarmament diplomacy has also nourished foreign skepticism. Just as the United States insists that each branch of its strategic nuclear deterrent have an independent overkill capacity, it tends to seek too much insurance and too many advantages in disarmament negotiations. For example, its general and complete disarmament plan of 1962 would have provided security by simultaneously instituting an advantageous ratio of nuclear reductions, an International Disarmament Organization with unprecedented rights to carry out surprise inspections, and a new international security enforcement organization with a monopoly of nuclear force. Although each of these stipulations required of the USSR asymmetrical military, political, or ideological sacrifices, the United States was not prepared to engage in intersystem bargaining which would have allowed for a balancing of short- and long-term sacrifices. It is also noteworthy that the plan implicitly rejected the UN system as if what was not politically feasible through the UN would be acceptable through new supranational institutions. The UN Secretariat perceived the American approach as a means of stonewalling serious negotiations and as a broad hint of the United States's desire to bypass the world organization.

Actually, there is nothing at all unusual in the American behavior recalled here. International policy must inevitably be Janus-faced and proceed sporadically. The conflicts between commerce and strategy, between domestic and foreign demands, and between theoretical necessity and political acceptability in Congress prevent even a strong president from restructuring international affairs. Still the history of arms control negotiations demonstrates how even American initiatives with qualified support at home can soften Soviet opposition to international institutions with independent executive functions. During the decade of the 1950s, for example, the USSR changed its original negative attitude toward the IAEA and finally accepted the proposal for an international control organization comprising 170 ground control posts for the on-site verification of a comprehensive nuclear test ban. Had such American initiatives in international conferences been consistently supported by appropriate unilateral measures and reasonable risk-taking, American arms control diplomacy might have been truly successful. In any case, the knowledgeable representatives of such countries as Mexico and Sweden still seem to expect that meaningful initiatives can more easily come from the United States than from the USSR.

In the changed international system, however, the United States will find it more difficult to influence the policies of its adversaries as well as of its allies by unilateral measures. There is still, nonetheless, a definite place for such measures as the delay in the construction of the breeder reactor or the voluntary acceptance of IAEA inspection of its peaceful nuclear activity. Such measures help create a more hopeful atmosphere than would otherwise exist. Another contribution to this end would be United States participation in an international body in which nonnuclear states would be adequately represented for the purpose of studying the feasibility of controlled peaceful nuclear explosions under IAEA auspices. These measures have no special magic that could solve the stubborn problems of the international control of atomic energy, but they may help forge the consensus at home and abroad that is an indispensable condition for real progress.

The United States must also learn that by minimizing the role of universal international organizations it angers an increasingly significant group of participants in international relations, the developing or nonaligned nations, without at all approaching its nuclear arms control objectives. A small group cannot decide the issue of nuclear energy, and the adverse political consequences of any attempt by the United States to focus its leadership in that direction could undermine new opportunities for progress. American officials should realize that they can accomplish little of lasting value in this difficult field outside of organizations like the IAEA and the UN that can mobilize consciousness and consent for United States leadership. Such support for its new nuclear control policies would prove helpful when forward-looking policies arouse the ire of allies as well as adversaries.

Options at the UN

Immediately after World War II, the majority at the UN looked to the United States for their security and for economic reconstruction. The UN thus became a useful part of the American concept of world order, a concept expressed by the slogan "peace through strength." Within this context, the United States repeatedly sought UN endorsements of its nuclear disarmament plans. Because of the nascent cold war, these endorsements served mainly to mobilize support at home and abroad for the United States's new role as leader of the free world. The United States did not need at that time many officials working on disarmament. Moreover, Americans could be certain both of UN support and of Soviet rejection. The UN's function was thus ideological rather than traditionally diplomatic.

The situation changed, however, when the superpowers cautiously began experimenting with détente around the time of the first summit meeting in July 1955 and the conciliatory Soviet disarmament plan that led to American rejection of nuclear disarmament as the goal of international negotiations. Arms control, which proposed the buildup and stabilization of nuclear deterrence, emphasized step-by-step negotiations outside the UN, and arms control negotiators claimed that UN endorsement of proposals impeded businesslike negotiations. The General Assembly, eager to help relax tensions, endorsed the shift in emphasis from elaborating a single plan of general disarmament to negotiating partial nuclear measures.

In the eyes of American officials, therefore, the ideological function of the UN has become progressively less useful. Nevertheless, the General Assembly has continued to debate so many disarmament isssues that its Political Committee has little time left for other questions. The Geneva Conference of the Committee on Disarmament has been adopted by the UN as its own organ for negotiation with a consequent growth in membership from eighteen to thirty-one as the UN itself has increased in size to almost 150 members. But UN deliberations would influence the great powers only if UN approval, as in the case of the NPT, were indispensable because of the treaty's universal obligations. In all other situations the major powers, as well as most other UN members, have participated in the annual deliberations without much interest or purpose.

For twenty years the two superpowers have advanced toward their present unique relationship in SALT as well as in numerous other bilateral working groups on issues ranging from a comprehensive nuclear test ban to the demilitarization of the Indian Ocean. Many agreements have resulted from this process, but they have not prevented the acceleration of the arms race. This paradoxical state of affairs posed no problem for the superpowers so long as they both preferred a nuclear stalemate to either an unregulated arms race or the actual reduction of nuclear weapons, but the Carter administration has indicated a desire to make nuclear arms reduction an immediate objective of Soviet-American talks. This seems to be appropriate because the previous trend has become a conservative element in international relations at a time when radical international ideas and movements are reverberating in the halls of the UN.

In the twenty-year interval in which bilateral arms control negotiations have dominated diplomacy outside the UN, the movement of the nonaligned countries has become the dominant force in the UN. Militant members have redefined international peace and security as a struggle against dominant powers, and the conservative concept of world order is being replaced by talk of a new order based on the principle of distributive justice. Such a changed UN has increasingly alienated the United States to the point of its threatening to ignore the majority and even to withdraw from the International Labor Organization.

In the new conflict between the United States and the nonaligned countries, disarmament is secondary to the issues of decolonization, white minority rule in southern Africa, and economic development. In 1976, however, the Conference of Non-aligned States proposed a special session of the General Assembly to consider disarmament. It is scheduled to convene in 1978, indicating that the increasingly influential movement of the nonaligned countries is ready, after a long period of acquiescence, to subject the disarmament policies of the superpowers to public and critical scrutiny. The special session may criticize significant acts of omission in the superpowers' arms control negotiations as well as dangerous acts of commission in their endless nuclear arms race, but the special session is more important because of the expectation that with it negotiations begin a new phase whose first goal is nuclear disarmament.

Under the pretext of expanding the role of the UN, the leaders of nonaligned countries or of neutral states like Sweden will evidently seek to hold the superpowers accountable in a field that the latter have jealously guarded from "mischievous" UN interference. In developing a suitable strategy for the special session and for the changed UN in general, the United States must therefore consider some of the less obvious characteristics of the nuclear arms control process.

Negotiations have been more successful in generating political side effects than in actually controlling the development and deployment of military hardware. This is especially true of the relationship between arms control and Soviet-American détente. Expediency and political rather than military needs have motivated the timing and scope of proposals and agreements. In the context of the changed UN and disarmament, the United States should be able to improve relations with the nonaligned and neutral countries by joining in common proposals and by engaging in actions responsive to previous criticism of, for example, the discriminatory features of the nonproliferation controls. The

United States might profitably study the unsuccessful proposals submitted by the nonaligned countries to the NPT Review Conference of 1975, and by accepting as many of the specific proposals as the government will support, the United States would generate a spirit of reconciliation and thereby reduce North-South tensions. Apart from its stated purpose of stopping or reversing the arms race, disarmament is thus a useful political issue; by engaging the nonaligned countries in a disarmament dialogue at the UN, the United States will transmit a political message of even broader significance.

Also characteristic of arms control negotiations is the interaction between proposals to the UN and negotiations within the United States government. The distinction between hawks and doves probably oversimplifies the bureaucratic conflict over arms control and disarmament measures, but it helps to distinguish the faction that understands both the ideological uses of UN disarmament negotiations and the limitations of a further reliance on arms control as such from the faction that dismisses UN deliberations because the powerful states can easily ignore the resulting resolutions. The opposition of bureaucratic, congressional, and business interests wishing to perpetuate past policies and attitudes is not easily overcome.

Within this context the interaction between domestic and international policymaking may be considered. The developments at the UN in recent years have shown that not even the traditional realists can ignore the importance of international movements. The possibility that UN deliberations and decisions might conceivably support the dovish faction in Washington is especially noteworthy at a time when President Carter has already pledged to the UN that the United States would make a strong and positive contribution to the upcoming special session on disarmament. An awareness of the effect of UN disarmament deliberations and negotiations on bureaucratic disputes might help the Carter administration fully exploit the opportunities in the special session.

The main work of the special session will be to draft a declaration of principles and a program of action to give a new impetus to multilateral negotiations. The United States may have the option of remaining uncommitted, reacting to suggestions in broad terms and seeking consensus rather than sharpening the issues. By pursuing such a strategy, the United States would simply continue the policies of limiting damage that it has employed at recent regular sessions of the General Assembly. It would also be abandoning a potential leadership role.

The other option requires a willingness to anticipate the principles supported by the nonaligned countries and to take responsive measures in advance. For example, the majority is likely to insist that the nuclear powers accelerate the dissemination to developing countries of equipment, materials, and scientific information for the peaceful uses of nuclear energy, and will no doubt demand a commitment in principle to the transfer of military resources to official development assistance. In response to both cases, the United States can either define its objectives minimally and remain flexible regarding the wording of the declaration of principles and the program of action, or it can take action prior to the special session and implement these principles in advance. The second option is preferable for establishing a new image of leadership.

The nonaligned movement also contends that the nuclear powers must lead the disarmament process by making more than proportional arms reductions. The United States has already enunciated this principle but has not acted accordingly. A dramatic instance of forebearance, however, such as the refusal of the Carter administration to build the B-1 bomber would not only affect relations with the USSR but would also contribute to improving the United States's image in the nonaligned movement.

Finally, and most importantly, the United States should anticipate as part of the nonproliferation package the principle that the nuclear powers must pledge not to use or threaten to use nuclear weapons against nonnuclear states. This principle has always been difficult for the United States to accept because of its forward nuclear deterrence strategy designed to protect its allies. Congress has nevertheless accepted and ratified the principle in relation to the Latin American Nuclear-Free Zone. Similar though less extensive undertakings, ranging from regions to individual countries, are also conceivable. The option of leadership thus appears to require the Carter administration not only to consider simply the principle of prohibiting the use of nuclear weapons against nonnuclear states but also to take advance measures to implement it.

The special session will no doubt recognize the need of the superpowers to continue SALT negotiations, since their expertise and special responsibility is irreplaceable for the maintenance of international nuclear security. Participation in SALT, however, has never precluded the use of disarmament issues in broader ideological struggles. It is therefore noteworthy that the preparatory committee for the special session has decided to invite nongovernmental organizations and research institutes to participate. Traditional notions of international organization and law are therefore unlikely to help one understand the new amalgam of sovereign states, international movements, and nongovernmental organizations. This new type of international organization seems to generate ideological objectives and to invite methods designed to raise consciousness and mobilize consent.

Most American officials retain negative attitudes toward the UN and dismiss any attempt to consider it a useful mechanism for creating a new nuclear disarmament movement among sovereign states and nongovernmental organizations. Nuclear arms control is still viewed by them as the primary, if not exclusive, responsibility of the superpowers, most effectively carried out through businesslike diplomacy. According to this view, the superpowers have parallel interests that should lead them to avoid open conflicts at the UN. UN deliberations are never an end in themselves but rather part of a decision-making process linking domestic politics with international diplomacy. At the very least, an American initiative at the UN together with more concrete measures would provide a constructive impulse to which both allies and adversaries would have to respond openly, exposing any attempt to gain unilateral advantage to a small but attentive public.

On the other hand, the current tempo of the nuclear arms race clearly shows that the limited and often perverse achievements of bilateralism are responsible for the loss of faith in nonproliferation controls and in the likelihood of nuclear arms reduction. The universal assumption seems to be that the arms race will tend to become worldwide. Twenty years ago, however, quite different hopes and expectations launched the bilateral step-by-step approach to nuclear arms control that the United States sponsored, and now the new American leadership, aware of the limitations that current military and political tendencies impose on its security objectives, clearly faces an opportunity to redefine the principles and priorities of arms control negotiations. Raising the issue of nuclear disarmament to the level of an ideological challenge to all participants in the Special Session on Disarmament will provide a much needed humanistic impulse to national decision-making on this supreme question. As Henry Noel Brailsford wrote during World War I in support of a league of nations, "By mechanism alone, we shall never unite the world, yet without mechanism its best impulses, its instincts of fraternity, and its craving for peace may be squandered and frustrated."[2]

---

[2] Henry Noel Brailsford, *A League of Nations* (London: Headley Bros., 1917), p. 317.

The Arms Trade

EDWARD C. LUCK

In recent years, the international traffic in conventional weapons has grown both in quantity and quality, unchecked by any multilateral control measures. Despite the far-reaching security, political, and economic implications of this growing problem, the United Nations has reflected the will of most of its member states and has failed to give it serious and sustained attention. Yet the UN should not be singled out for blame for the inability of the world community so far to attain effective limitations. None of the major military powers have given a high priority to conventional arms control by limiting either their own conventional arsenals or the arms they export to the third world. Likewise, the recipient countries have generally resisted any attempts to restrict or regulate their arms imports from the developed arms-manufacturing countries.

This essay summarizes recent trends in the arms trade, reviews past multilateral efforts to publicize or control arms transfers, analyzes the factors accounting for the lack of progress in developing multilateral control measures, and recommends certain modifications in United States policy and international mechanisms to deal more effectively with this issue. One of its basic premises is that, while there has been little concrete progress in arms limitations, there have been several encouraging signs that the international community is beginning to recognize the dangers of an unrestrained arms trade. Thus, it is time to review the prospects for effective international controls, particularly since the General Assembly will hold a Special Session on Disarmament in May and June of 1978.

The volume of global arms transactions has increased rapidly during the past decade to an annual level of about $20 billion. The United States, the leading arms merchant, has accounted for about one-half of this total. United States arms sales alone have grown from under $1.5 billion in FY 1970 to an average of more than $10 billion in each year between FY 1974 and FY 1976. Although inflation may account for some of the growth, the volume of trade has nevertheless substantially expanded.

The geographical distribution of arms transfers has also shifted considerably. About one-third of all arms transfers went to developed countries and two-thirds to the developing world between 1966 and 1970. By the period 1971-75 the disparity had widened, with 25 percent going to developed and 75 percent to developing countries. In 1966 East Asia was the leading recipient region, with 39 percent of the total, while the Middle East accounted for only 7 percent. By 1975, the Middle East proportion had risen to 33 percent and the East Asian percentage had fallen to 19 percent. Africa, traditionally an area of low arms imports, doubled its share from 5 percent in 1966 to 10 percent in 1975.

These trends reflect not only the rise and fall of regional tensions but also the influx of oil money into the Middle East. The OPEC countries received only 5 percent of global arms transfers in 1966, but they accounted for one-fourth of all imports in 1975. Almost two-thirds of United States arms sales in recent years have been to just three countries—Iran, Saudi Arabia, and Israel.

Not surprisingly, the developing countries as a whole are not only receiving more arms, but also they are spending increasing sums on military activities in general. The developing countries' share of world military expenditures increased from 15 percent to 22 percent between 1966 and 1975. Unlike the developed countries, they have devoted a steadily increasing percentage of their gross national product to military outlays. As a result they are now spending a greater proportion of their GNPs for military purposes than are the developed nations. This growing diversion of scarce resources is bound to retard the pace of economic development that third world spokesmen have widely enunciated as their highest priority.

More disturbing than the quantitative growth has been the increasing sophistication and destructive power of the weapons transferred to volatile regions of the world. While the arms-manufacturing countries once supplied primarily second-hand or obsolete weapons to developing nations, they have more recently transferred many of their most advanced conventional weapons to the third world. For instance, the United States has agreed to sell F-14, F-15, and F-16 fighters, Lance surface-to-surface missiles, and Spruance class destroyers to the tense Middle East. In many cases, the supplier country must also provide large numbers of advisers, instructors, and maintenance personnel to support the transfer of highly complex weapons systems. This may increase the danger of directly involving the great powers in local conflicts or domestic crises.

An unrestrained arms competition in the third world would clearly favor the larger and wealthier countries and leave the poorer states unable to compete effectively either economically or militarily. A new class of states, such as Iran and Brazil, is emerging with the military and economic capacity to influence events well beyond its members' borders. As their military power grows and their horizons expand, they may increasingly behave like regional superpowers, perhaps policing affairs throughout a region.

The introduction of new kinds or large numbers of weapons into an already troubled region may exacerbate local rivalries and fuel regional arms races. As one country begins to build up its arsenal, its neighbors may perceive a growing threat and may react either by seeking new arms from another supplier or even by launching a preemptive attack. Unfortunately, it is difficult for an outside power to evaluate accurately or to manipulate effectively the security concerns of regional rivals. It is still more difficult to achieve a stable regional equilibrium by increasing the quantity or quality of armaments flowing into an area. The best way to reinforce regional security is through multilateral understandings among local countries and major arms suppliers, rather than unilateral attempts to gain a favorable short-term military advantage.

As the great powers become more directly involved in a region through the transfer of arms and related personnel, local disputes may become polarized and assume at least a symbolic importance in the global East-West struggle. There is always a danger that such a local conflict could escalate into an East-West military confrontation, particularly if one of the local client states suffers a serious defeat and calls on its more powerful benefactor for military assistance.

Arms transfer relationships between particular suppliers and their recipients tend to become self-perpetuating unless there are political upheavals within either country. Once these ties are firmly established, it is difficult to sever or even to diminish them without causing major political problems. Thus, officials of the supplier country may expect to gain influence over the recipient country through arms transfers, but they may soon begin to question who gains influence over whom. As recent events in Egypt, Sudan, and Ethiopia illustrate, any apparent influence gained through arms transfers can be quite transitory. On the other hand, the recipient nation may come to resent the presence and activities of the advisers and technicians from the supplying country and even consider this a new form of colonialism. In many cases, both the suppliers and recipients appear to be immersed in their own competitions for influence and security. While increasing arms transfers may seem an attractive alternative in the short term, it may prove costly or dangerous in the long run.

Past Attempts to Develop Multilateral Controls

The limitation of conventional weapons has been on the UN agenda almost since the organization was founded. A UN Commission for Conventional Armaments was established in 1947, but after five unproductive years its functions were merged with the newly created UN Disarmament Commission in 1952. A principal obstacle to progress in the Commission for Conventional Armaments was Soviet insistence that limits on conventional forces could not be considered without first limiting nuclear weapons. Even during these early years of the UN, nuclear arms control was generally assigned a higher priority and received far more attention than did limitations on conventional forces.

Although unable to come to grips with the general issue of conventional arms transfers, the UN has shown more interest in regional arms embargoes, particularly in areas of high tension or armed conflict. During the 1948 Palestine conflict, the Security Council passed a resolution calling for restraints on the import or export of war materials in the Middle East. During the Korean war, the UN adopted a stronger arms embargo.

In 1951 a General Assembly resolution imposed a strategic embargo, which included arms, ammunition, and implements of war, against the People's Republic of China and North Korea. In response to the Suez crisis, the UN in 1956 again called for an arms embargo in the Middle East. The First Emergency Special Session of the General Assembly approved a cease-fire resolution, introduced by the United States, that recommended a halt in the shipment of military goods to the conflict area.

These efforts were paralleled by agreements among the major suppliers to control their arms shipments to the Middle East. In May 1950 the three principal suppliers (the United States, the United Kingdom, and France) announced the Tripartite Declaration, conceding the need of the countries of the region for adequate arms for international security and self-defense but opposing "the development of an arms race between the Arab states and Israel." In order to implement the general policy of this declaration, the three major suppliers established a Near Eastern Arms Coordinating Committee to oversee the maintenance of a rough military balance in the Middle East.

These efforts were generally successful until Egypt began to receive large quantities of Soviet arms via Czechoslovakia in late 1955. The emergence of the USSR as an alternative source of arms eroded the Western monopoly that had allowed the policy of restraint to operate fairly effectively. The prospects for effective regional arms control faded once the Middle East conflict became embroiled in the East-West competition. In 1956 and 1957 the USSR made general proposals about limiting arms transfers to the Middle East, but the Western powers did not take the initiatives seriously in the charged political atmosphere of the time and among prevalent doubts about Soviet sincerity and intentions. Similarly, President Johnson's proposal following the 1967 Arab-Israeli conflict to register and limit arms shipments to the Middle East received little support in the General Assembly. The draft resolution was not even put to a vote.

Arms control analysts have long been perceiving Latin America as a promising area for regional arms limitations. Unlike the Middle East, it has not generally been at the center of the East-West competition, it has not been the scene of major international military conflict for many years, and military preparations by local countries have remained at a relatively low level. Paradoxically, however, the very conditions that seem to make the region fertile ground for arms control efforts at the same time appear to lessen the urgency of progress on arms limitations there. The 1967 Treaty for the Prohibition of Nuclear Weapons in Latin America (Treaty of Tlatelolco) established the area as the first nuclear-weapon-free zone. But there has been little progress toward a formal treaty on conventional arms, though limitations on conventional forces and military expenditures have received considerable attention within the Organization of American States (OAS).

Proposals by Costa Rica (in 1958) and Chile (in 1959) to study arms limitations in Latin America were considered but not acted upon by the OAS. At the Punta del Este Summit of 1967, the regional heads of state declared "their intention to limit military expenditures in proportion to the actual demands of national security." Finally, in December 1974 the Declaration of Ayacucho expressed the intention of eight local states to create "conditions which will make possible the effective limitation of armaments and put an end to their acquisition for purposes of war." However, further discussions by six of the eight countries have not yielded significant progress toward a substantive agreement.

In addition to regional efforts, largely outside of the UN, the General Assembly and the Security Council have passed a series of resolutions calling for arms embargoes against politically unpopular states. As the influence of third world countries increased in the UN in the early 1960s, the primary targets for arms embargoes became those states with racial or colonial policies unacceptable to most of the world community. Considerations of regional military stability and conflict prevention were also cited, but they appeared to be less important than the political factors.

Since 1962, the General Assembly and the Security Council have adopted a series of resolutions calling for an arms embargo against South Africa. Although most member states have observed the embargo, numerous violations have enabled South Africa to maintain a powerful fighting force. Moreover, the imposition of the embargo may have spurred South Africa's efforts to develop an indigenous arms manufacturing capability in order to be independent of foreign sources at least for small arms and ammunition. The first of numerous resolutions urging an arms embargo against Portugal was also passed in 1962, since its armed forces were repressing independence movements in its African territories. Southern Rhodesia has also been the target of several UN resolutions imposing economic sanctions as well as a ban on arms shipments.

A number of general proposals to limit conventional arms transfers have been put forth in the Eighteen-Nation Committee on Disarmament (ENDC) and in its successor, the Conference of the Committee on Disarmament (CCD) in Geneva, an active multilateral negotiating forum technically autonomous but in reality closely related to the UN. The United States has been the principal proponent of such measures, beginning with proposals by President Johnson to the ENDC in 1966 and 1968 calling for regional limitations on arms transfers. Similar speeches stressing the regional approach and exhorting the CCD to pay greater attention to conventional arms control have been made by United States representatives in most of the succeeding years. In 1970 Sweden, Mexico, and Yugoslavia proposed a comprehensive disarmament program that emphasized the role of regional conferences to consider limitations on conventional forces.

None of these proposals, however, have generated much enthusiasm among most of the CCD members. The USSR has been notably quiet and unsupportive on the issue, while third world comments have been generally negative. Some third world spokesmen in the CCD have suggested that limitations on arms transfers represent an attempt by the great military powers to "disarm the unarmed." According to his view, disarmament should begin instead with the countries possessing the largest arsenals and should assign the highest priority to reductions in nuclear weapons.

Besides these uniformly unsuccessful efforts to develop direct multilateral controls on arms transfers, there have been several proposals in the General Assembly regarding indirect measures, such as the registration and publication of international arms transactions. In 1965, Malta offered a draft resolution in the First Committee calling for an examination of the arms trade by the ENDC that would lead to the submission of proposals for a UN system to publicize arms sales and transfers. The resolution was defeated by one vote, as the United States and thirty-eight other countries abstained. Several third world states voted in favor of the resolution, but the combined opposition of the socialist bloc and many less developed countries ensured its defeat. A joint resolution sponsored by Denmark, Iceland, Malta, and Norway in 1968 called on the secretary general to determine the views of member states on the registration of all arms imports and exports and the periodic publication of information on these transfers. The proposal aroused such vigorous opposition from less developed countries that it was never brought to a vote.

These efforts to register and publish information on arms transfers recall the indirect approach of the League of Nations, which published an annual *Statistical Yearbook of the Trade in Arms and Ammunition* during the interwar period. Indeed, in 1970 Secretary-General U Thant suggested that the UN revive the yearbook concept and publish information on conventional weapons. This indirect approach was apparently based on five general assumptions: (1) more extensive and reliable information on arms shipments to particular regions would lessen the doubts and uncertainties that underlie local arms races; (2) the publication of trends in the arms trade would draw international attention to areas of growing tension; (3) greater information would incite public opposition to the arms trade and increase pressure on governments to exercise restraint; (4) the publication of this information would embarrass states with high levels of arms imports or exports and cause them to reconsider their arms policies; and (5) greater information would strengthen governmental awareness of and control over private arms merchants.

Yet there is no certainty that registration and publication would have a significant effect on the fundamental political, security, and economic motivations of the arms trade. Public opinion and moral suasion are unlikely to affect fundamentally the policies of many of the governments actively engaged in selling or receiving arms. Moreover, the experience of the League of Nations certainly does not provide a promising precedent.

Whether or not these proposals would actually curb the arms trade, they have aroused considerable opposition from a number of less developed countries that resist even indirect control measures. Some countries have claimed that it would be discriminatory to place constraints on the arms trade without any controls over the production and deployment of arms by the industrialized states. Others have contended that such measures would compel nonaligned states to enter into military alliances with arms-manufacturing countries. It was further argued that controls over arms transfers might be used to disarm national liberation movements.

An Analysis of Past Failures

Many interrelated reasons explain the UN's unimpressive record in dealing either directly or indirectly with the international arms trade. Some of these stem from the inherent complexities of the problem, with its broad political, security, and economic implications. Other explanations concern the divergent interests and perceptions of major groupings of member states. Finally, there is the question of the appropriateness and effectiveness of the UN as a mechanism for forwarding disarmament. The UN is severely tested by issues such as the arms trade that affect the fundamental security concerns of all its members but whose impact varies greatly from region to region.

Limitations on the development, manufacture, procurement, export, deployment, or use of conventional weapons directly influence a nation's capability to defend itself or to use force in support of foreign policy objectives. Although nuclear weapons may serve as a deterrent, wars are presently fought solely with conventional weapons. For most countries, conventional forces are the only means of defense. A severe restriction on conventional arms imports might even threaten the ability of the current government in some nations to maintain internal control. Moreover, almost all countries, except a few highly industrialized nations, must depend on arms imports for most of their defense needs. It is therefore not surprising that most countries have approached conventional arms control, particularly limits on the arms trade, with considerable caution.

Eighty percent of world military expenditures are devoted to conventional forces. Any serious proposals for major reductions in armed forces or military outlays would have to include conventional arms. Since limits on conventional forces are central to the problem of disarmament, however, their achievement will be especially difficult. The problem is compounded by the fact that nuclear arms control is almost always assigned a much higher priority than conventional limitations. This ranking is reflected in the proportion of UN debates devoted to the two topics, in the quantity of governmental and private research on the subjects, in the nature of arms control agreements concluded thus far, and in the extent of public interest in these areas.

In the past, proposals in the CCD and General Assembly to limit arms transfers have not received sufficient support from any of the three basic political groupings. Most nonaligned states have been negative or even hostile to these proposals. The socialist countries have been indifferent or opposed to these measures, contending that nuclear arms control should take precedence. Most Western nations have been lukewarm in their support. Although the United States has been the chief proponent, its support has sometimes wavered, as in its abstention on the 1965 Maltese resolution concerning the registration of arms transfers. No widely representative multilateral forum can be expected to endorse limitations on the arms trade until these groups change their political attitudes. To succeed, future efforts must gain the support of key third world states and take advantage of existing differences of opinion on this issue among the nonaligned countries, soften Soviet opposition and avoid the appearance of being Western initiatives, and strengthen and unify Western support.

While the arms trade is a global phenomenon, security and political conditions vary greatly from region to region. There are major differences in the nature of local rivalries, the quality and quantity of armaments, and the extent to which the great powers are involved in regional affairs. Few universal standards could apply equally to all areas, and this limits the potential effectiveness of global negotiating forums such as the General Assembly and the CCD. Recognizing this factor, past United States proposals stressed the regional approach.

A major complaint of third world spokesmen has been that limits on arms transfers would be discriminatory. They contend that it would be unfair to limit their arms supply without adopting constraints on the capability of the great powers to develop, manufacture, and deploy their own conventional and nuclear weapons. The United States and the USSR have shown little interest in negotiating reductions in their vast conventional arsenals. Thus, some perceive efforts by the great powers to impose restraints on arms transfers as paternalistic at best and at worst as attempts to maintain military dominance over the nonaligned countries.

These arguments are similar to those advanced by a number of nonnuclear states in criticizing the Treaty on Non-Proliferation of Nuclear Weapons. Article VI of the treaty, whereby the parties undertook "to pursue negotiations in good faith on effective measures relating to cessation of the nuclear arms race at an early date and to nuclear disarmament, and on a treaty on general and complete disarmament under strict and effective international control," was designed to meet many of these objections by nonnuclear countries. Though many observers feel that the nuclear powers have not fulfilled their obligations under Article VI, it does illustrate the widely perceived linkage between arms control progress among the great powers and in the third world. A similar trade-off may be a prerequisite to substantial progress in curbing the horizontal proliferation of advanced conventional weapons.

Although many states may perceive the Non-Proliferation Treaty as inequitable, over a hundred countries have nevertheless become parties to it. The crucial issue is not whether the treaty is fair, but whether, on balance, it contributes to the security of all the parties. In assessing the fairness of an agreement to limit arms transfers, the sacrifices of supplier states should also be recognized. Arms-exporting countries believe they obtain important economic, foreign policy, and national security benefits from the arms trade. Finally, in light of the recent arms acquisitions by many developing countries, the argument that restraints on arms transfers would "disarm the unarmed" has largely lost its credibility.

As a whole, the supplier countries have displayed only marginally greater interest than the recipient states in arms trade limitations. Attempts at unilateral restraint are met with the familiar objection that "if we do not sell arms, other countries will." The suppliers have become locked into a competition for arms sales on the assumption that they, as well as the recipients, derive significant benefits from these transactions. In addition it is widely believed that arms transfers increase the supplier's influence over the foreign and domestic policies of the recipient country. Arms sales are thus perceived as an important tool in the East-West competition for influence in the third world. Yet the historical record, as already noted, does not entirely support this proposition. There are very real limits to the leverage which a major power can exercise over the policies of a friendly nonaligned country. The principal third world recipients of United States arms have demonstrated a remarkable independence on high priority issues, such as human rights, oil prices, economic development, trade, the law of the sea, the Middle East, southern Africa, and even disarmament. This independence is reflected in their voting patterns in the UN and other multilateral institutions.

Arms sales clearly benefit the arms manufacturing companies, but proponents cite major benefits for the national economies of the suppliers as well. Arms exports aid the balance of payments and provide additional jobs in defense industries. In some cases, foreign sales may keep production lines open and lower per-unit costs of weapons systems also being procured for the armed forces of the supplier country. There can be little doubt that arms transfers have a positive effect on the balance of payments and employment, although similar benefits could be achieved by selling more nonmilitary products in foreign markets. Indeed, in the long run it makes more economic sense to encourage less developed countries to purchase goods and services that would more directly contribute to their economic growth. This would lead to an increasing demand for products from the developed states.

Supplier governments frequently see arms transfers as a means of furthering their overseas security interests without committing their own forces. According to this view, a well-armed client state is more able to protect itself and hence is less likely to require direct military intervention by the supplier state. Moreover, large sales of advanced weapons to already powerful states like Iran are justified by enabling these well-armed states to act as regional policemen and thereby contribute to stability. The independence displayed by most arms recipients, however, does not guarantee that they will use their newfound military strength in a manner consistent with the foreign policy and national security objectives of the supplier. In addition, there is always a danger that arms shipments to one country will be offset by equal or greater acquisitions by neighboring nations, sparking a regional arms race and lessening the security of the region.

The two primary arms producers among the socialist states, the USSR and China, have shown little enthusiasm for limitations on the arms trade. Presumably they share many of the foreign policy, national security, and economic interests in the arms trade that motivate the Western arms suppliers. In addition, their ideology of global struggle with the capitalist world makes it especially difficult for them to accept agreements that would appear to limit their potential assistance to "national liberation movements." They may not always perceive regional stability to be in either their national or ideological interests. Since their overall economic aid programs have been relatively small and they have been cautious about committing their own forces to conflicts far from home, arms transfers have been an important means of demonstrating material support for third world clients.

Besides the East-West competition, the USSR and China have been engaged in an intense rivalry for influence among the nonaligned countries. Neither could sign an agreement with Western suppliers to limit arms transfers without incurring ideological attacks from the other. Yet Chinese opposition has not prevented the USSR from actively supporting international efforts to discourage nuclear proliferation.

The USSR is the second largest arms exporter, with about 29 percent of the market over the past decade, while China is fifth with only 3 percent of the total. As a developing country, China cannot manufacture many kinds of advanced weapons either for its own use or for export. Indeed, China may conceivably become a large arms importer during the next decade. Thus it has neither signed any major international arms control agreements, except for Protocol II of the Latin-American Nuclear Free Zone Treaty, nor participated in the CCD and has openly disdained current incremental approaches to arms control. It would be far more critical, however, to gain Soviet rather than Chinese participation in limitations on the arms trade.

The USSR has tended to concentrate its non-Warsaw Pact arms exports on a relatively few key third world countries, clearly intending to influence their political orientation. Many advisers and technicians usually accompany the transfer of Soviet arms. Moreover, these recipient states also have frequently been the principal targets of Soviet economic assistance. Despite the large investments of men and material, however, the USSR has obtained no greater influence in the third world through arms transfers than the United States. The USSR has experienced major failures in China, Indonesia, and Egypt, and it may be losing influence in India, Somalia, and Sudan. These failures may have the sobering effect on Soviet arms sales policy of similar recent experiences on the United States outlook.

The USSR has adopted a pragmatic and often flexible approach to arms control negotiations, unimpeded by ideological constraints as long as progress has been perceived to be in the Soviet national interest. The crucial question is whether Moscow perceives the risks and liabilities of an unrestricted arms trade as outweighing the potential benefits. In the case of nuclear proliferation, the Soviet response has been unambiguous, but so far the USSR has not demonstrated equal concern about conventional proliferation.

France and Great Britain are the third and fourth largest arms suppliers. While their combined arms exports total only about 8 percent of the world volume, their transfers have a wide geographical distribution and include advanced aircraft, naval vessels, armored vehicles, missiles, and electronic equipment. Their participation in a limitation agreement would be important, if not crucial, to its success. Both countries are capable of considerably expanding their arms production if there is increased foreign demand.

In recent years, Great Britain has generally supported United States initiatives in the CCD concerning controls over the arms trade. But France, which does not participate in the CCD, has taken a more skeptical, though not entirely negative, approach in the General Assembly. Economic considerations may be particularly prominent in shaping French and British policies. It is frequently pointed out that, as medium powers, their armed forces are not large enough to support efficiently the output of a diversified armaments industry, so foreign markets are necessary to achieve economies of scale and to lower per-unit costs. Balance of payments and employment levels are also factors. In addition, arms sales may be seen as one means of carrying out foreign policies independent of the United States position.

Recent Events and Prospects for the Future

Several encouraging signs of growing international interest in controlling the arms trade suggest that it may be worth reconsidering the possibilities for developing multilateral limitations despite the failure of past efforts. The United States, for a long time the leading arms merchant, is apparently renewing its efforts to promote multilateral restraints. Congress, frustrated by its lack of control over increasing arms sales, passed several pieces of legislation from 1974 to 1976 expanding its oversight, calling for greater unilateral restraint, and urging the development of international control measures.

President Carter also appears to be giving a high priority to controls on the arms trade. In his first major foreign policy speech, delivered at the UN in March 1977, he stated, "There must be a wider effort to reduce the flow of weapons to all the troubled spots of this globe. Accordingly, we will try to reach broader agreements among producer and consumer nations to limit the export of conventional arms, and we ourselves will take the initiative on our own because the United States has become one of the major arms suppliers of the world." In May 1977, President Carter announced a new "policy of arms restraint" that focused on the shipment of advanced weapons to the third world and also urged "multilateral cooperation." The policy statement calls for discussions with other arms suppliers, including the USSR, and for efforts to encourage regional agreements among countries purchasing arms.

The USSR and the United States have also established an intergovernmental working group on arms transfers, which may indicate a growing Soviet willingness to consider international control measures. The Carter administration has also begun high-level consultations with the French, British, and West German governments on this issue. Although it is too early to determine whether these efforts will be successful, it is clear that they represent a broad effort to translate unilateral United States restraint into multilateral cooperation among the principal supplier states.

As the debate at the thirty-first session of the General Assembly demonstrated, opinions within the third world differ sharply on the arms trade. In a strongly worded speech, Singapore warned, "The massive flow of arms to the third world confronts it with a new danger. It is, first of all, a drain on their economies; but even more important is the fact that it creates a new form of dependence on the great Powers which can exploit the third world's dependence on them for arms to manipulate them, to engineer conflicts between them, and to use them as their proxies in their competition for influence and dominance."

During the thirty-first session, Japan introduced a resolution inviting member states to submit their views about conventional arms transfers, requesting the secretary-general "to make a factual study of the international transfer of conventional arms" for submission to the next session, and calling for the inclusion of an agenda item on arms transfers at the next session. The resolution was cosponsored by seventeen states, including twelve developing countries. After some discussion of modifications in the text, however, India successfully moved to adjourn debate on the item. Although the motion to adjourn passed by a comfortable margin, wide differences among the developing countries on the motion demonstrated the divisions within the third world on this issue.

The General Assembly voted to upgrade the Disarmament Affairs Group in the UN Secretariat, renaming it the UN Centre for Disarmament. It has been charged with publishing an annual yearbook and triannual bulletin reporting on recent developments in disarmament and military affairs. If allowed to develop without political constraints, these publications could become useful sources of information on the arms trade. At its thirty-first session the General Assembly also agreed to hold a special session devoted to disarmament in May and June 1978. The special session is primarily the result of an initiative by the nonaligned countries. Therefore, a principal theme will likely be the relationship between disarmament and economic development, and no doubt there will be more interest expressed in limiting the arsenals of the major powers than in controlling the arms trade. Yet the session will provide an excellent opportunity for pointing out that more rapid economic development will require military reductions in both the developing and developed world. After all, military outlays on the average now absorb a larger portion of the GNP among the developing countries. It should be stressed that major savings will require limitations on conventional as well as nuclear forces.

The special session will be an unwieldy mechanism for negotiating concrete arms control agreements, particularly on such a complex subject as arms transfers, but it can serve an important function in focusing public and governmental attention on disarmament and in formulating an agenda for action. The United States and other concerned countries should make certain that the arms trade is given a higher priority on the international agenda for future negotiations.

If the current upsurge in interest in limiting arms transfers is to be fruitful, comprehensive new approaches must be adopted that take into account the widespread objections to past control efforts. First of all, there is considerable justification for the third world's complaint about the inequity of placing restraints on their only source of armaments without adopting more stringent limitations on the armed forces of the major powers. Greater efforts should be made not only to limit Soviet and American nuclear forces but also more relevantly to control their conventional arsenals and those of their allies.

In particular, attention should be focused on the kinds of conventional forces available for intervention in third world areas outside the spheres of interest of the major powers. As a first step, the USSR and the United States should give a high priority to their incipient discussions on limiting naval deployments and bases in the Indian Ocean. Such an accord would reduce their overall requirements for naval forces and could lay the groundwork for negotiations on limiting the size and capabilities of their naval inventories.

Greater cooperation among the chief arms suppliers is essential but will be difficult to achieve even though the four principal suppliers account for almost 90 percent of the global arms traffic. The basic task is to convince the major suppliers that they have a common interest in cooperating more and competing less for arms sales to the third world. The ultimate objective is not to reduce drastically foreign arms sales, but to reduce the competition among suppliers that leads to "pushing" arms and to qualitative arms races in the third world.

The USSR and the United States should attempt, wherever possible, to extend détente to their relations with the third world. Perhaps informal boundaries or rules of conduct, including limitations on the quality or quantity of arms shipments to particular regions, can be agreed upon to limit their inevitable competition for influence among the nonaligned countries. Traditionally, each supplier has observed certain unilateral constraints on its arms exports and avoided transfers outside of NATO or the Warsaw Pact of nuclear weapons, medium or long-range surface-to-surface missiles, heavy bombers, and nuclear-powered submarines.

The Tripartite Declaration on the Middle East provides a precedent for cooperation within NATO on arms exports to the third world. French and British concerns about the viability of their arms industries and the health of their overall economies could be a significant obstacle. The United States could help solve this problem by purchasing more arms manufactured in Western Europe and thus making NATO procurement more reciprocal. Alternatively, there could be an informal market-sharing arrangment on the basis of geography or the type of weapon involved.

Finally, regional arms control agreements are the key to alleviating the security concerns of local states. While the encouragement and cooperation of the major powers may be essential in the long-term, the initiatives must come from within the regions. It is often pointed out that progress toward arms control depends on the political atmosphere and that the prior resolution of existing political disputes must come first. Yet the two processes are complementary and in many cases can proceed along parallel lines. The achievement of even limited regional arms control understandings can lessen security concerns and build mutual trust, thus laying the groundwork for further progress on both political and arms control issues.

The major powers can do much to support local arms control efforts in addition to dampening their competition for arms sales. The developed countries have largely deemphasized the potential role of military action in resolving their political and economic differences. One way of encouraging the developing nations to do likewise would be for the major powers to refrain from the threat or use of military force in areas that are building regional security arrangements. Arms control measures among local states could provide far greater security and political independence than traditional pacts with outside powers.

The arms trade is so enmeshed in current international relations that many observers question the possibility of developing effective multilateral controls. Clearly, there are no easy or quick palliatives, but a number of incremental approaches are worth further exploration. While President Carter's initiatives may be the vital first steps, further effort must be focused on wider multilateral forums such as the CCD and the Special Session on Disarmament.

Strategic Arms Limitation

BETH BLOOMFIELD

The impact of the United Nations on the nuclear arms race has not been negligible for want of effort. Disarmament resolutions comprise a substantial portion of the annual record of the General Assembly. The thirtieth session of the General Assembly adopted no less than twenty-five resolutions on the subject, and one-sixth of the agenda of the thirty-first session concerned disarmament. Nevertheless, the UN experience in arms limitation has been frustrating.

Although the 1970s were proclaimed a "Disarmament Decade" by the twenty-fourth session of the General Assembly, UN-related arms control achievements have slackened since the 1960s, when agreements were reached on a partial nuclear test ban treaty, the Non-Proliferation Treaty (NPT), an outer space treaty, and the treaty establishing a nuclear-free zone in Latin America.

Concern about the horrifying destructive potential of nuclear weapons emerged in the earliest days of the UN. The founding nations intended the organization to wield some authority over disarmament matters, as Article 11 of the charter indicates. Indeed, the first recommendation adopted by the General Assembly in 1946 was related to disarmament. The General Assembly created the Atomic Energy Commission, defined its terms of reference, and urged their expeditious fulfillment. That same year, the United States proposed the ill-fated Baruch Plan in an ambitious attempt to place virtually all nuclear activity under the aegis of an international authority. The plan would have maintained the United States nuclear monopoly, thereby seriously affecting Soviet military capabilities. The failure of the Baruch Plan illustrates a prime reason for subsequent failures to implement strategic nuclear arms control through multilateral forums such as the UN.

Indeed, the arms control experience is indicative of the central problem that has confronted the UN since its inception. Despite its members' commitment to the concept of an international institution, no nation has been prepared to transfer control over its national security from national to international decision-makers.

The United States and the USSR have jealously guarded their long nuclear lead over the rest of the world while continuing to compete with each other in a spiraling strategic arms race. The only steps toward strategic arms limitation have emerged from bilateral negotiations, rather than from multilateral forums. The UN has been effectively excluded from playing any role in the deliberations and negotiations associated with the Strategic Arms Limitation Talks (SALT), which formally began in 1969.

In May 1972, the United States and the USSR reached a five-year interim agreement limiting offensive strategic weapons, accompanied by a permanent limitation on antiballistic missile (ABM) sites. Continuing efforts to negotiate a follow-on SALT agreement resulted in the Vladivostok accord of November 1974, which set an excessively high ceiling on strategic delivery vehicles and on multiple independently targeted reentry vehicles (MIRVs). Despite bold new proposals by the Carter administration in March and May 1977, the SALT talks have remained deadlocked, with the clear possibility that the interim SALT accord will lapse if no substitute can be agreed on by the fall of 1977. Meanwhile, the pace of technological development is again outstripping the political ability to curb its destabilizing effects, the main subjects of contention being the American cruise missile and the Soviet Backfire bomber. The recent chill in Soviet-American relations further complicates prospects for a new agreement.

In 1978, following years of fruitless UN debate about disarmament, the General Assembly will meet in a Special Session on Disarmament (SSOD). Given the poor prospects for SALT, the SSOD takes on new significance. Disarmament is a universal concern, but the nuclear superpowers bear a special responsibility, and the SSOD could provide a unique opportunity for the international community to move closer toward consensus on disarmament. Although the SSOD faces predictable pitfalls, it holds considerable promise for an expanded and more effective future UN role in SALT and other disarmament issues. To understand why, one must consider the interlocking relationships between strategic arms limitation and other global issues.

Strategic arms limitation is a vital and legitimate concern of all nations, no matter how small or how isolated. The critical world problems for the foreseeable future are fundamentally concerned with resource allocation, including shortages of energy and raw materials, problems of food production, the efficient organization of production and transportation of commodities and industrial goods, the welfare of the world's growing population, and the protection of the global environment. The nuclear arms race, as well as rising military expenditures in the less developed countries, absorbs scarce financial and human resources that could be profitably applied elsewhere. There is also a growing understanding among the world's leaders that real and immediate problems may lie outside the political-military sphere.

Closely related to these changes in world politics is the transformation of national defense into international security. In an era of instant communications and rapid technological advances, security must be redefined in the broadest terms if the concept of the nation-state is not to become extinct. This shift indicates the increased potential of multilateral forums to negotiate and resolve international security problems. Agreements reached in such forums may then influence international political developments and create a climate more amenable to further agreement, followed by a gradual lessening of international tension.

The last several decades have demonstrated the lack of political utility of military power—and especially strategic nuclear power—in a range of international crises and situations. Nuclear primacy did not ensure a successful United States policy in Southeast Asia during the 1960s, nor did the United States's accumulated military might mitigate the severe economic impact of the 1973 Arab oil embargo. Certainly the political and military consequences of being the first to use nuclear weapons are virtually unthinkable today.

Nevertheless, the nations possessing nuclear weapons want to retain the option to us them and to control the development of that option. Accordingly, neither the United States nor the USSR regards SALT as a multilateral issue, and neither power wishes to utilize the UN forum to that end. Both nations are reluctant to surrender political control of the issue and the course of negotiations to a host of lesser powers. Both are anxious not to compromise the principle of national sovereignty in security affairs, and both are suspicious of the political and military objectives of each other and of third powers.

One observer has commented that the identity of interests of the superpowers amounts to collusion at the UN, as evidenced by the striking similarity of their respective voting records on disarmament resolutions, coinciding 76 percent of the time at the thirtieth session of the General Assembly.[1] In addition, when the General Assembly in 1976 considered a resolution expressing its concern about the slow pace and insufficiency of SALT, the Soviet delegate bluntly stated that "the fundamental provision of this resolution is such that it represents an unjustified attempt to intervene in the course of these talks."[2] Both superpowers voted against this resolution.

SALT has not attracted a coalition of countries comparable to the political grouping that forced consideration of the New International Economic Order, and it has therefore not attained a place on the UN agenda. Instead, lack of progress in SALT has been readily used as an excuse for a lack of self-restraint in military programs by the lesser powers. UN success in the economic sphere depends on accommodations between the "haves" and the "have-nots"; in nuclear matters,

---

[1] Homer Jack, "The Disarmament Scoreboard," *Bulletin of the Atomic Scientists* (March 1977), p. 56.

[2] Cited in *Issues Before the 31st General Assembly of the United Nations*, United Nations Association of the United States of America (September 1976), p. 22.

however, where there are so few "haves," arms control proponents have been unable to use enough political muscle.

Another set of obstacles to nuclear arms negotiations at the UN stems from the easily identified problems of a multilateral forum. Its size is unwieldy; it is politically unpredictable, affording an almost irresistible opportunity for political grandstanding; it is unable to guarantee the secrecy of exceedingly delicate international negotiations; and its members lack understanding and technical expertise in strategic arms issues.

These obstacles have severely limited the role of the UN to two basic functions. First, the General Assembly regularly considers and frequently passes a variety of hortatory resolutions, which can have little practical effect except to create minor public relations embarrassments for the offending military giants. Second, the UN can ratify or legitimize arms limitations agreements negotiated elsewhere by passing resolutions of approval or by becoming more deeply involved in their administration. The NPT now provides a good example of this second function; the crucial details were negotiated behind the scenes by the United States and the USSR, but the final product was put forth as a UN sponsored document.

Historically, the United States has taken a rigid attitude toward SALT and the UN. While American delegates make bland and general statements welcoming the concern of other nations about the progress of SALT, the United States has rather pointedly held that the UN cannot direct it with resolutions and that it will seek to keep its nuclear options open at any cost. This attitude may be softening, however, as Washington increasingly recognizes that overly sharp reactions to UN disarmament initiatives may do more political harm than good. When President Carter addressed the UN soon after assuming office, he spoke at length about the nuclear arms race, describing it as "imbedded in the fabric of international affairs" and calling on all UN members to dedicate themselves to "a prolonged and persistent effort" to "maintain peace and reduce the arms race,"[3] among other goals. President Carter's language, coupled with his reputedly deep interest in serious arms control, UN affairs generally, and North-South issues in particular, signaled to some a new American willingness to take a more creative approach to arms control issues in the UN. The appointment of an activist ambassador and a deputy well versed in arms control matters has underscored the possibilities for a new approach.

The American attitude toward the relationship between "horizontal" and "vertical" nuclear proliferation also shows signs of change. The nonnuclear nations have continued to insist that the nuclear powers must live up to the obligation imposed on them by Article VI of the NPT to restrain their own strategic arms race. If new American initiatives to control proliferation are to be successful, the United States may find it politically necessary to concede the legitimacy of their claim. The UN provides an excellent opportunity to do so to

[3] *New York Times*, March 18, 1977.

maximum political effect. In addition, UN involvement in SALT and related matters could bring France and China into an international nuclear arms limitations regime. At least, the appearance of SALT on the UN agenda would argue against their objection that nuclear arms control is a plot by the two superpowers to maintain hegemony in world politics. Although it is argued that China is not yet ready for arms control, China has a more positive voting record on disarmament in the UN than the United States. French reluctance is largely historical and is thought to be fading. The emergence of other nuclear powers also argues for a broader approach to SALT issues and the utility of a multilateral forum.

Indeed, if it is deemed to be in the United States interest to strengthen international institutions and international law in general, then the use of the UN to further strategic arms limitation goals could be doubly valuable. In contrast, the current bilateral SALT process has actually diminished the authority and prestige of the multilateral forums. When Secretary of State Cyrus R. Vance visited Moscow in March 1977, for example, an agreement was reached to set up eight Soviet-American "working groups," including one on a comprehensive test ban, a matter now before the UN's Conference of the Committee on Disarmament (CCD), and one on arms reductions in Europe, which is the topic of the multilateral Mutual Balanced Force Reductions (MBFR) talks. Use of the multilateral arena instead would certainly not preclude bilateral activity; the two might be mutually reinforcing.

Possibilities for a greater UN role in strategic arms limitation fall roughly into four functional categories: educational and informational services, political stimulation, negotiations, and implementation. Most promising, because it is least controversial, is the educational and informational function. The UN could be a "clearinghouse" for SALT-related information, similar to the role fulfilled by such nongovernmental organizations (NGOs) as the Stockholm International Peace Research Institute (SIPRI) and the International Institute for Strategic Studies (IISS). Following precedents set in other areas, the NGOs could have consultative status. Also, existing UN facilities for collecting, compiling, and disseminating information could be upgraded. A prerequisite, however, is complete and systematic joint reporting to the UN by the United States and the USSR on their progress in negotiations, issues in dispute, and obstacles to further progress.

The clearinghouse role could also enhance the future utility of the UN as a SALT forum because member nations would become better and more completely informed on the political and technical issues. Increased UN educational activity could spur development of domestic political organization and of more effective national decision-making for arms control. In addition, the UN could collect and disseminate information on public attitudes (a sort of world public opinion poll) in an indirect effort to pressure national governments to support arms control objectives.

Through the General Assembly, the UN can continue to exert what is best described as "moral suasion" by the passage of resolutions, open debate on the SALT issue, and committee activity. Expressions of morality are not easily translated into political pressure within the UN, but the effective linkage of issues in the General Assembly could generate pressures that even the superpowers could not readily ignore. For example, the repeated passage of resolutions linking disarmament and development—habitually opposed by the United States—has little practical meaning. It might be more productive to focus attention instead on the consequences of unbridled arms competition for the international economic system as a whole.

The UN is unlikely to be directly involved in the SALT negotiating process in the foreseeable future. Nonetheless, the Conference of the Committee on Disarmament (CCD) provides a logical mechanism for promoting UN involvement. Though only loosely associated with the UN, the CCD is regarded by United States officials as one of the best UN related bodies, remarkably free of bloc voting and polemical speechmaking. The problems of publicly or even semipublicly negotiating SALT agreements preclude the use of the CCD or comparable forums for negotiating an agreement. Still, the CCD should be kept informed of progress in SALT. It could be used to greater effect to "ratify" SALT related agreements.

A more promising approach toward a wider UN role in SALT negotiations is the provision of conference services to the negotiating parties. The UN regularly sponsors international conferences on a broad range of subjects and could easily provide the physical facilities and services for formal SALT negotiating sessions, in conjunction with the USSR and the United States. A representative of the UN secretary general might serve as an impartial observer at the SALT negotiations in a symbolic arrangement that would nonetheless remind the superpowers of the global concern with SALT.

Finally, the UN could play an expanded role in the implementation of strategic arms limitation agreements. Various proposals have been made to employ existing UN bodies or to create new ones to verify arms control treaties. The International Atomic Energy Agency (IAEA) provides a precedent for the concept of an international verification organization.

The IAEA evolved out of President Eisenhower's "Atoms for Peace" plan of the early 1950s. It was initially conceived as a means of monitoring the production and movement of nuclear materials in order to prevent their diversion to military purposes. With the successful negotiation of the Non-Proliferation Treaty (NPT), however, the IAEA safeguards system became an integral part of an internationally recognized system of arms control. The adequacy of IAEA safeguards remains a subject of debate; nevertheless, the IAEA illustrates the possibilities of evolution from national sovereignty to an international regime for arms control when the basic political acceptance exists. The agency's statute recognized the relationship between the IAEA and more comprehensive nuclear arms control agreements.[4]

---

[4] Cited in Robert Pendley and Lawrence Scheinman, "International Safeguarding as Institutionalized Collective Behavior," *International Organization* 29 (Summer 1975): 1494.

The credibility of an arms control agreement largely depends on the accuracy and reliability of its verification arrangements. SALT has relied exclusively on "national technical means" of verification, since no agreement on a mutually acceptable system of international inspection has been reached. Without abandoning national verification programs, however, "international technical means" could be instituted, such as a UN related, internationally controlled satellite system. Clearly no nation would be willing to yield enforcement powers to an international authority when national survival is at stake, but an impartial "early warning" function might be acceptable.

The UN could remain a part of the ongoing SALT process by performing certain follow-up functions and services. The Standing Consultative Commission established under the 1972 Interim Agreement to hear complaints of SALT violations is now a bilateral Soviet-American body that could be turned over to a multinational authority. In addition, an international review conference on SALT similar to the NPT Review Conference might be convened under UN auspices and opened to all interested parties. A number of nuclear arms control proposals related to SALT are particularly well suited to discussion in a multilateral forum, and their implementation might enhance the prospects for a SALT agreement. Foremost of these is the comprehensive test ban (CTB), a high-priority item for the CCD and also the subject of annual General Assembly resolutions. Regional arms control agreements, such as nuclear-free zones and regional "zones of peace," are another available option with some historical precedent, and regional agreements may serve as stepping-stones to broader disarmament measures. Certain global concerns—such as weather modification, the prohibition of nuclear weapons in outer space, and development of new weapons of mass destruction—might also form the basis for multilateral agreements. Finally, security guarantees by the nuclear nations for the nonnuclear powers, an issue stemming from language in the NPT, has yet to be resolved.

Can existing UN machinery for arms control be improved to facilitate international agreement? Again, the real impediments to agreement are political, not institutional, and one should not expect too much of bureaucratic reorganization. If strategic arms control objectives remain limited, existing multilateral machinery would probably be adequate; however, if a larger UN role emerges, reform would be desirable. The institutional links between bilateral and multilateral efforts should be strengthened wherever possible.

Reform of the CCD is the subject of much debate, largely between the "ins" (including the joint chairmen, the United States and the USSR) and the "outs." The former favor the status quo, while the latter advocate change. The real problem with the CCD, however, is not its structural defects but the fact that it has not been used to negotiate measures of true importance to the strategic arms race. More universal participation in bodies like the CCD, and the possible inclusion of NGO representatives, may be a desirable goal, but its realization is subject to political considerations.

In 1976, the secretary general's annual report to the General Assembly urged "a basic review of the role of the UN in disarmament."[5] Subsequently, an assistant secretary general for disarmament was added to the Secretariat staff. He will oversee the newly created UN Center for Disarmament, an upgraded version of the old UN Disarmament Division. The center is intended to improve the UN's informational function, direct studies of particular disarmament issues, and oversee preparations for the 1978 SSOD. The SSOD itself will then spur the development of UN institutions, both by improving their organization and by educating UN delegations. Apart from this impact on international institutions, preparations for the SSOD may foster the growth of permanent national arms control bureaucracies, similar to the U.S. Arms Control and Disarmament Agency (ACDA).

As one of the partners in the SALT process, the United States is well placed to guide the UN toward a more meaningful and productive approach to strategic arms control. The national interest clearly dictates that SALT remain predominantly bilateral, and the forum most likely to yield favorable results is a restricted Soviet-American dialogue. Still, there is great latitude in the UN for movement in American policy toward SALT and disarmament in general. A thoughtfully constructed United States policy would further United States objectives both in SALT and in the UN.

The essential element of such a policy would be a changed United States attitude. Strenuous opposition to General Assembly resolutions on SALT, by now a reflexive response, should be quietly dropped. A shift from a "damage limitation" mentality to a more positive approach, both in public and behind the scenes, is a prerequisite for effective United States activity in the future. United States policymakers should explore a range of options for turning UN initiatives on SALT to a positive United States interest, without relinquishing control of SALT. Given the anti-American sentiment characteristic in the UN in recent years, a new United States policy has much to gain at a very small political cost.

The United States should seek to use the UN forum to better advantage in airing its public positions on SALT. This would be in keeping with the Carter administration's pledge for greater openness in international negotiations. Much information is already available to the public on the progress of SALT, and the options for United States SALT negotiating positions. United States spokesmen could use the UN to enunciate SALT policy that ordinarily might be made public elsewhere and thereby stimulate a more receptive attitude toward the United States in the UN, while adding to UN prestige.

The United States should attempt to influence the General Assembly to debate and approve more realistic and limited resolutions on arms control that would be more than polemical. Skillful diplomacy, correctly employed, could produce resolutions that would give the United States a positive incentive to support

[5] Cited in *Issues*, pp. 27–28.

them. United States delegates should also be prepared to do some political bargaining if necessary to influence UN action on SALT.

The United States should take a forceful lead on SALT in the UN by initiating its own resolutions, carefully tailored to win broad political support in the General Assembly yet reflecting a positive United States approach to SALT negotiations. Essentially, United States policy should be designed to wrest control from the USSR of the choicest public postures on disarmament. The United States should be prepared to take the offensive on arms control in the international arena, rather than being relegated to a defensive role in debate and political activity.

Possibilities should be explored for more effective and advantageous linkages between issues in order to develop positive political pressures in the UN for United States arms limitation policy. For example, the United States should be willing to recognize and exploit the link between SALT and the Non-Proliferation Treaty (NPT).

A new American offensive on SALT in the UN would require careful attention not to antagonize disgruntled Soviet negotiators and diplomats. Any action should be discussed with the USSR with an explanation of the limited United States intent to stimulate UN activity and assurances that nothing will be done to slow the progress of SALT in the bilateral negotiations. Whenever possible, the political and diplomatic groundwork should be laid for Soviet-American agreement on SALT in the UN.

The United States should assign a high priority to the 1978 Special Session on Disarmament. The SSOD may provide an opportunity to identify the United States with progressive forces on disarmament issues rather than an exercise in futility, and it offers a chance to reap a diplomatic bonus at relatively little cost. The political benefits from a positive United States approach would be both international and domestic. United States officials profess that since there is going to be a special session the United States is determined to make it productive.

To ensure this, the United States must be willing to invest substantial time and effort both in Washington and at the UN in preparations for the SSOD. Again, tactful diplomacy can be used to help shape the likely agenda and bend it to United States interests when possible. For example, the United States can request the nonaligned countries with the greatest political prestige at stake in the SSOD (Yugoslavia and Sri Lanka, which initiated the proposal in the General Assembly) to restrain the more vocal nonaligned countries such as Nigeria and Cuba.

The need for complete and effective preparation for the SSOD can be turned into an opportunity to rethink American policy on the UN and disarmament in general. Planning is still in the earliest phases, the first policy background papers are only beginning to be drafted, and action officers in the State Department and the U.S. Arms Control and Disarmament Agency (ACDA) have only recently been designated. In all likelihood, SSOD preparations will not come to high level attention until just prior to the meeting itself. Yet what may be needed is greater pressure from policy-level officials to stimulate creative thought in the bureaucracy.

Certainly the SSOD places great pressure on the United States and the USSR to make some real progress in SALT and other arms control negotiations, if only to defend themselves against the inevitable attack by France, China, and the non-nuclear powers. United States policymakers should consider possible initiatives at the SSOD to deflect such criticism. For example, the United States could make positive proposals on subjects likely to receive favorable UN action, such as the status of the Indian Ocean, chemical warfare, military budget reductions, development goals and defense spending in the less developed countries, regional arms control regimes, "zones of peace," and nuclear proliferation. In addition, the United States should seriously consider taking some dramatic SALT related unilateral initiatives prior to or simultaneous with the SSOD. Among such initiatives could be a moratorium on nuclear testing, a limited pledge against the first use of nuclear weapons, a restraint on particular strategic weapons programs, or a negotiating "breakthrough" in SALT.

Finally, improvement in the United States government's policymaking process could contribute to a new outlook on the UN and disarmament. UN disarmament and SALT policymaking should be better integrated, either through formal institutional changes or through informal contacts among the pertinent bureaucracies. SALT policymakers should factor in UN concerns when feasible and be made aware of how the UN could be used to advance United States SALT objectives. The role of the U.S. Arms Control and Disarmament Agency should remain strong in UN disarmament affairs, and effective coordination of the ACDA and the State Department must be encouraged. As in all bureaucracies, opportunities for new opinions must be stimulated so that older, entrenched attitudes can be periodically reexamined. The United States ambassador to the UN can perform an important function in generating new approaches to American policy, and his views and experiences should be heard in Washington.

Congressional action on the UN and SALT might also serve a useful purpose by focusing public opinion and the attention of the executive branch on these issues and could enhance the United States position in the UN as well. Congressional resolutions calling for a positive United States approach in the UN and in the SSOD would lend support to proponents in the bureaucracy of a new and creative policy and would express American concerns to the rest of the world. Congress could hold hearings on SALT and the UN and could request periodic reports from the executive branch on the development of United States disarmament policy in that forum. Congressional action would spur an increase in activity in the executive branch.

The UN, of course, is only one among many tools of international diplomacy for the nations of the world. To be sure, the range of possible and desirable United States policy options for dealing seriously with strategic arms limitation in the UN is tightly circumscribed. The UN cannot and perhaps should not involve itself too deeply in SALT, and clearly, without the requisite political will on the part of the principal actors, only scanty results can reasonably be expected in the UN.

For the most part, those results must consist of symbolic gestures. Politics in the UN is largely conceived and conducted in symbolic terms anyway, but even symbolism can eventually shape a new political reality. The gravity of the issues at stake in SALT argues that all possible and available approaches ought to be explored. Although progress toward a SALT agreement in the UN is likely to be marginal at best, even marginal achievements cannot be forgone lightly.

The Maintenance of Peace

SEYMOUR MAXWELL FINGER

It is clear that a major war threatening the existence of the United States can come only with the USSR. Moreover, the history of the past thirty years and the veto provisions of the United Nations Charter (Article 27) make it equally clear that the UN would be of little or no use to the United States in facing a direct Soviet threat. Consequently, in the foreseeable future, America must rely on its own military forces and NATO for defense against such a threat.

The nuclear arsensals and potentials of the USSR and the United States are so obviously superior to those of any other nation that the "balance of terror" clearly depends on these two countries alone. Therefore, any effort to slow down the nuclear arms race depends on agreements between the USSR and the United States like those under consideration in SALT II, while the equally serious qualitative nuclear race also depends on Soviet-American negotiations. However, the UN is a valuable means of legitimizing Soviet-American arms agreements, and pressure from the General Assembly can serve a useful purpose by prodding the two superpowers. Especially important in this context would be the conclusion of a treaty banning all nuclear tests, including those underground.

International institutions can also play a significant role in deterring nuclear proliferation. The Non-Proliferation Treaty (NPT), negotiated at the UN in 1967, has been useful, even though the unwillingness of certain key countries, such as China, France, India, and Brazil, to ratify it has limited its effectiveness. Nuclear power becomes more important as oil becomes more expensive and the threat of oil reserve depletion looms. Countries with nuclear potential will not forego nuclear development unless assured of nuclear fuels and technology for peaceful uses. Yet the spread of nuclear potential for peaceful uses opens the door to military use and to terrorism; therefore, strict control by the International Atomic Energy Agency (IAEA) is necessary. The inspection provisions included in the NPT are a good beginning, but they must be substantially strengthened to protect the world from the nuclear threat as nuclear energy becomes more widely used. In particular, IAEA inspectors should have unrestricted access to all nonmilitary nuclear installations. Even if the USSR forbids such inspection on their territory, the United States should permit inspection of American nonmilitary nuclear sites as a means of inducing states without nuclear weapons to do the same. Additionally, countries capable of exporting nuclear fuel and processing equipment must agree to include appropriate safeguards in sales agreements.

A particularly complex problem is the proposed sale by France to Pakistan and by the Federal Republic of Germany to Brazil of equipment for reprocessing nuclear fuel. The United States opposes such sales on the grounds that the plutonium resulting from this process can be used for nuclear weapons, while the countries involved argue that the alternative is excessive dependence on uranium exporters like the United States. A recent policy decision against the development, under current conditions, of nuclear processing facilities in this country indicates President Carter's seriousness on this matter. One possible compromise might be the development of regional reprocessing facilities under IAEA supervision, as Henry Kissinger proposed when he was secretary of state.

United Nations Peacekeeping

Even with adequate American defense strength and continued reliance on NATO for deterrence or defense against any direct Soviet threat, conflicts in various parts of the third world remain a substantial problem. If they are not carefully handled, they could draw in the USSR and the United States. To deal with this threat, what Lincoln Bloomfield has called "spheres of abstention" (areas where the United States and the USSR agree, tacitly or formally, to keep out) should be combined with strengthened UN and regional machinery for fact-finding, peacekeeping, and peaceful settlement. The role of the UN in preserving Zaire as a unified, nonaligned country and in helping to stop the fighting in the Middle East is a matter of record. The UN has also helped to deter or prevent at least a dozen other conflicts.

The record of these actions over the past two decades shows that UN peacekeeping, as distinct from enforcement action, has primarily been an auxiliary to political measures, an extension of political action intended to contain conflict and set the stage for peaceful settlement. The purpose has not been to apply military force in the classic sense of coercing the parties to submit to the UN's will, but rather to install a political presence that carries out certain ancillary police duties. The late Adlai Stevenson aptly described this role in "No Mission But Peace; No Enemy But War," an article published by *McCall's* in October 1964.

The essential function of UN peacekeeping is far more political than military, from which follows a number of consequences. First, the mandate of a peacekeeping force must be compatible with the national security interests of the countries concerned, including those contributing troops. In addition, the consent of the host government or governments, on whose soil the force is to be stationed, is necessary for entry of the force. The force itself should resort to violence only when necessary to defend itself and to carry out its primarily political mission. Finally, all principal parties in the conflict must be willing to cooperate with the force. If they are absolutely determined to fight, peacekeeping operations cannot stop them, but when they are willing to observe a cease-fire UN forces or observers can reassure each side that the other is also under observation for honest performance.

The United States, of all the major powers, has most consistently supported UN peacekeeping. This support has usually been crucial, but it is equally true that only the willingness of middle powers—such as Canada, Brazil, Ethiopia, India, Yugoslavia, Ireland, and the Scandinavian states—to provide personnel and financing has made peacekeeping possible.

For more than twenty years the USSR asserted that there was no such thing as voluntary peacekeeping. Its expressed doctrine held that the only legitimate role for UN forces under the charter was the enforcement action governed by Article 42. But in practice, the USSR has been more realistic and has supported or acquiesced in virtually all peacekeeping operations. Their refusal, however, to pay the assessments for the Congo and the United Nations Emergency Force (UNEF) stationed between Israel and Egypt precipitated the Article 19 crisis of 1964–65, and they have insisted, along with France, that voluntary contributions finance the Cyprus operation.

The withdrawal of UNEF, on Egypt's demand in May 1967, followed a few weeks later by the Arab-Israeli war, cast a shadow on the future of UN peacekeeping. Yet six years later UN forces again became an important factor in keeping peace on the Arab-Israeli borders when UNEF II dramatically intervened at the conclusion of the 1973 Yom Kippur war. After calling for a cease-fire in resolutions 338 (October 21) and 339 (October 23), the Security Council in resolution 340, paragraph 3, of October 25, decided "to set up immediately under its authority a United Nations Emergency Force to be composed of personnel drawn from states members of the United Nations except the Permanent Members of the Security Council." UNEF II was established on October 27 when the Security Council approved the report prepared at its request by the secretary-general.[1] This followed a Soviet invitation to the United States jointly to intervene to stop the fighting (and thus save the Egyptian Third Army from annihilation), with a warning that the USSR might intervene unilaterally if the United States refused. This threat impelled President Nixon to order an alert of United States armed forces. Thus the proposal of UNEF II by nonpermanent members of the Security Council was significant not only for helping to keep peace in the Sinai and for establishing a basis for peacekeeping operations on which the USSR and the United States might agree, but might also have prevented a very dangerous Soviet-American confrontation in the Middle East.

[1] United Nations, Security Council, *Report of the Secretary-General on the Implementation of Security Council Resolution 340* (S/11052/Rev. 1), October 27, 1973.

UNEF II is now a force of about 4,300 soldiers stationed along the Sinai disengagement lines negotiated by Henry Kissinger. It includes a Polish contingent, marking the first time troops from a Warsaw Pact country have participated in a UN force. A Soviet desire to include USSR troops required a compromise under which the USSR and the United States each have thirty-six observers with UNEF II.

In addition to its initial value in forestalling a possible Soviet-American confrontation in October 1973, UNEF II renders a continuing service to peace. The disengagement line is quiet now, but in contrast the number of Israelis killed in the three years following the Arab-Israeli war of 1967 roughly equalled the number of casualties of the war itself. (Comparable figures on Egyptian casualties are not available.) Moreover, UNEF II provides some assurance against a surprise attack. Unlike UNEF I, it was established by the Security Council and cannot be removed without the council's consent except at the time of its renewal. The initial six-month mandates have now been replaced by a twelve-month renewal valid until October 1977. True, a force of 4,300 could not stop either the Egyptian or the Israeli forces from attacking if they were determined to go to war, but its mere presence discourages incidents and surprises, while the knowledge of fixed periods during which its presence is guaranteed reduces the need for constant alerts. In addition, following the second disengagement agreement negotiated in September 1975 by Henry Kissinger, 200 American civilian observers were stationed in the Sinai, providing further reassurance to both Egypt and Israel.

UNEF II is an excellent example of both the potential and the limitations of UN peacekeeping. It has the potential to dampen conflicts that might otherwise draw in the USSR and the United States as combatants. On the other hand, Soviet-American collaboration in bringing about a cease-fire and Henry Kissinger's subsequent efforts to bring about two disengagement agreements between Egypt and Israel demonstrate that UN peacekeeping is not a substitute for national efforts. Clearly, the United States cannot avoid responsibility and involvement simply by handing problems to the UN; rather, peacekeeping becomes a sharing of responsibility and involvement, with the bigger powers having a heavier responsibility.

Although numbering only 1,250, the United Nations Disengagement Observer Force (UNDOF) serves a similar function between the Syrian and Israeli forces on the Golan Heights. Established by the Security Council for an initial period of six months beginning May 31, 1974, in order to implement the disengagement agreement negotiated that month between Syria and Israel, UNDOF has been renewed for additional six-month periods, the current one expiring November 30, 1977.

Both UNEF and UNDOF are financed by assessments on the members, determined by the General Assembly each year in accordance with Article 17 (2) of the charter. Costs for 1976–77 are estimated at $76,276,000. In contrast to UNEF I and the Congo operation, the USSR and its allies have agreed to pay their share. China, Albania, Iraq, Libya, and Syria, however, have refused to pay, and Chinese arrears for UNEF II and UNDOF will amount to $22.7 million by November 1977. In addition, the USSR has refused since September 1975 to pay the part of its assessment that it attributes to additional UNEF costs involved in carrying out the disengagement agreement between Egypt and Israel negotiated in that month by Henry Kissinger. The USSR withheld $10.4 million for the year ending October 24, 1976, and $11.8 million for 1977. Since UNEF is now actually smaller than it was in September 1975, it is difficult to see how the USSR could attribute such huge sums to the alleged additional cost. A more probable explanation is a combination of political pique at being left out of the negotiations and the habitual Soviet reluctance to contribute money to operations run by international organizations. In any event, the growing deficit for these two operations, added to large deficits for past operations, is a matter of serious concern.

The United Nations Force in Cyprus (UNFICYP) consists of about 2,900 men, with contingents drawn from the Scandinavian countries, Austria, Canada, and the United Kingdom. Established in 1964, UNFICYP has separated Greek Cypriot from Turkish Cypriot and Turkish forces on the island and has helped to keep peace between the two sides, forestalling a Turkish invasion on at least one occasion. However, it was not the type of force that could fight the Turks when they did decide to invade Cyprus in 1974 and occupy about 36 percent of the island. Even so, courageous action by the UNFICYP commander helped to save the Nicosia airport, and other UN activities mitigated the suffering and helped to end the fighting.

The financing of UNFICYP is entirely voluntary, with about 10 of the 147 member countries providing virtually all the funds. The deficit has been chronic and growing. Costs borne by the UN have totaled about $250 million for the twelve-year period ending December 1976, with cumulative receipts amounting to $187.6 million and anticipated receipts of $17.3 million; the deficit of some $45 million is proportionately much greater than it is for UNDOF or UNEF II. This means there is a serious delay in reimbursing countries that have responded generously to the secretary-general's call for contingents. Moreover, these countries already absorb costs at the rate of about $6 million a year. Thus, these "good peacekeepers" are making a substantial sacrifice on behalf of world peace that benefits all members, while the great majority of member states contribute nothing at all.

The United States pays about one-third of the total UNFICYP costs when direct contributions to the UN fund and costs absorbed by those providing military and police personnel are combined. The USSR, France, and China contribute nothing at all; this is manifestly unfair, but considering the importance to the United States of avoiding conflict between two NATO allies, Greece and Turkey, Americans should not begrudge their contribution of about $9.6 million a year.

The financing of Truce Observer Units, on the other hand, is not a problem because the modest expenses are paid from the regular UN budget. These observer units, unlike the forces, operate individually or in small groups to observe and report truce violations. Such units have been functioning since 1948 in the Middle East (United Nations Truce Supervision Organization in Palestine, current strength 290) and since 1949 in Kashmir (current strength 56).

Prospects for the Future

Given the lack of clear charter provisions for UN peacekeeping and the serious problems, particularly financial, that have arisen with past operations, one may argue that agreement on guidelines for peacekeeping should be vigorously sought, particularly through negotiations with the USSR. I served for many years as the United States representative on the Special Committee on Peacekeeping Operations and was at one time hopeful that agreement could be reached.[2]

The establishment of UNEF II has, to my mind, changed the situation. Its operation is based on a report by the secretary-general that sets out its terms of reference, general considerations, proposed plan of action, estimated costs, and method of financing.[3] According to reliable sources in the UN Secretariat, this document was drafted in the light of proposals and statements made over many years in the Special Committee on Peacekeeping Operations. Remarkably, the secretary-general's document avoids seriously offending any major power, incorporates all elements agreed upon, and draws up a *modus operandi* in which all powers can acquiesce even though they would not specifically endorse some of its features. This technique has been particularly important in the establishment, command, and control of the operations. Consequently, the future of peacekeeping might be better served by using UNEF II as a model or precedent, as in common law, rather than to attempt to codify guidelines.

Specific clauses in the secretary-general's document demonstrate its achievements and advantages as a precedent. First, it states "that the force will be under the command of the United Nations, vested in the Secretary-General, under the authority of the Security Council. The command in the field will be exercised by a Force Commander appointed by the Secretary-General with the consent of the Security Council. The Commander will be responsible to the Secretary-General." This brief paragraph skillfully overcomes some of the main problems encountered in the working group of the committee on peacekeeping by clearly giving the secretary-general a mandate to run UNEF operations on a day-to-day basis and to appoint a force commander, both of which duties were resisted by the USSR in negotiations on general guidelines.

Second, paragraph 3(c) of the secretary-general's document states that "the Force will be composed of a number of contingents to be provided by selected countries, *upon the request of the Secretary-General*." (Emphasis added.) The

[2] Seymour Maxwell Finger, "Breaking the Deadlock on UN Peacekeeping." *Orbis* 18 (Summer 1973): 385.

[3] United Nations, Security Council, *Report of the Secretary-General on the Implementation of Security Council Resolution 340* (S/11052/Rev. 1), October 27, 1973.

Soviets have argued that the Security Council should make the request. The paragraph continues, "The contingents will be selected in consultation with the Security Council and with the parties concerned, bearing in mind the accepted principle of equitable geographic representation." To "bear in mind" equitable geographic representation is less rigid than the preferred Soviet version stating that "it is important to *base it* on the accepted principle of equitable geographic distribution."

Third, this document also indicates in its proposed plan of action that the secretary-general is to appoint the commander of the emergency force as soon as possible, with the consent of the Security Council. The secretary-general had already appointed the chief of staff of UNTSO, Major General Siilasvuo, as interim commander of the force. I can recall months of unsuccessful negotiations with the USSR, during our efforts to develop general guidelines, over this question of what should be done in an emergency before the secretary-general can consult the Security Council about the commander. Here the probelm is resolved in one brief paragraph.

Finally, the closing paragraph of the secretary-general's document stipulates that "the costs of the Force shall be considered as expenses of the Organization to be borne by the Members in accordance with Article 17, paragraph 2, of the Charter." The USSR was long reluctant to agree that the General Assembly could make assessments for peacekeeping under the provisions of this article.

In these important respects the secretary-general's document represents a practical answer to the real problems of running a peacekeeping force. It is apparently easier for the USSR to acquiesce in these provisions in a particular case than to endorse them as general principles or guidelines. That is why a "common law" precedent approach may be better than an attempt at codification. The establishment of UNDOF on the same general criteria as UNEF II reinforces the precedent.

It should be noted, however, that the Soviet viewpoint has also gained some ground in the UNEF II precedent. The operation was authorized by the Security Council, whose overall authority is recognized, and includes a Polish contingent, representing the first time a Warsaw Pact country has provided troops for a UN force. In addition, on Soviet insistence, the USSR as well as the United States has thirty-six observers with UNEF.

Not all of these concessions, however, have been a loss to the United States. By all accounts, the Polish contingent has performed very well. Nor is there any reason in current circumstances for the United States to object to a model in which authorization comes from the Security Council rather than the General Assembly, which is large and relatively unwieldy and has an overwhelming third world majority whose views are often contrary to American policy. In the history of the UN, UNEF is the only major peacekeeping operation ever initiated by the General Assembly. The General Assembly could launch a peacekeeping operation if Security Council action was blocked by a veto, provided the two superpowers and a substantial majority of the General Assembly supported or at least acquiesced in such an operation. But it would be a rare situation in which this degree of support did not result in action by the Security Council itself. It appears, therefore, that neither the USSR nor the United States has sacrificed anything of substance in accepting the secretary-general's proposals for UNEF II. Moreover, their acceptance has given a sounder political and financial basis than the one provided for earlier UN peacekeeping forces.

Coercive enforcement action, however, in which member participation is mandatory, is clearly within the authority of only the Security Council (charter articles 25, 39, 41, and 42). The negative vote of any of the five permanent members of the Security Council can block enforcement action, but this is the clear intent of the charter; it accords with practical realities, and it should assure those who fear that UN action could threaten United States security interests. The UN has taken no military enforcement action in its thirty-two year history, and present strategic and political rivalries among its major members make none likely in the foreseeable future.

Financing

The large and growing UN deficit is the most serious problem jeopardizing the future of UN peacekeeping. Deficits from the two current operations in the Middle East, the accumulation of unutilized nonconvertible currencies, and the $60 million deficit left from earlier operations in the Middle East (1956–67) and the Congo have contributed to the total short-term deficit of well over $100 million. As a result, countries that provided contingents for the Congo and the first Middle East operation have not been reimbursed for the substantial services they provided, and the Working Capital Fund of $40 million has been depleted. The problem remains and is getting worse, despite meetings of various committees and other efforts to negotiate a solution to the financial crisis as well as generous contributions by some member states.

The importance of peacekeeping to the United States and to the world warrants greater efforts to find a solution. Some years ago, a panel of the United Nations Association of the United States of America proposed the establishment of a United Nations Peacekeeping Fund to finance an operation's initial costs when there is a shortage of funds and to make up for withholding, such as China and the USSR practice regarding Middle East operations. The obvious problem with such a fund is that it appears to accept noncontribution by some members and thus might encourage this behavior. Nevertheless, the United States should support the establishment of a substantial fund of this type. The sums now involved in peacekeeping operations are very small compared either to United States defense costs or to total contributions to the UN budget; the United States's total contribution to UN peacekeeping in 1977 will be about $42 million, about a tenth of its contribution to all UN programs and an insignificant fraction of the 1977 defense budget of over $120 billion. For the United States, the most costly UN peacekeeping operation was in the Congo from 1960 to 1964 when it paid about one-half of the total cost of $400 million, but $200 million might have paid for only four or five days of the Vietnam war. While Mobutu's government in Zaire may not be ideal, from the United States viewpoint it is obviously much better than the situation in Vietnam after the loss of tens of thousands of lives and over $150 billion.

If the major powers would agree, a small fraction of national military budgets, perhaps 0.01 percent, could be set aside annually for UN peacekeeping as a supplement to other sources of income. In setting up such a peacekeeping fund, or seeking other solutions to the financial problems of peacekeeping, the United States should negotiate with all substantial contributors to the UN budget, including the USSR. While the United States should make every effort to enlist Soviet cooperation, it should not emulate their penny-pinching attitude toward UN peacekeeping. The United States contributes about forty times as much as the USSR to voluntary programs, including the UN Development Program, which less directly involves the American national interest. Why be penurious only with respect to peacekeeping?

Standby Forces

The availability of earmarked and trained troops is another important problem. Today, only the Scandinavian countries, the Netherlands, Austria, the United Kingdom, Italy, Iran, and New Zealand have taken steps to provide standby forces on call to the United Nations. The Scandinavians have also undertaken practical and helpful training exercises, and the International Peace Academy has undertaken useful seminars for similar purposes. Yet these countries represent only a tiny fraction of UN membership. If there is to be "equitable geographic distribution" in future peacekeeping forces, the UN should have a roster of contingents potentially available from all over the world. Discussion in the UN Peacekeeping Committee revealed no opposition to establishing such a roster; however, the USSR was reluctant to have the General Assembly endorse the concept apart from an agreement on the rest of the guidelines and principles under negotiation.

At various times a permanent force has been suggested, most recently by Colombia. Aside from the major problem of paying for such a permanent force, which Colombia would assign to the great powers, there is some doubt as to its usefulness. Since peacekeeping contingents must be accepted by the host country in which they operate, many such contingents might be unusable in a particular situation.

Peaceful Settlement

As indicated above, peacekeeping represents the interposition of forces in order to end hostilities and enforce cease-fire and truce agreements. They help to save lives and reduce tensions, but continued political instability in the Middle East, Cyprus, and Kashmir underlines the fact that only a political settlement can bring about real peace.

There is no lack of techniques for peaceful settlement. In Article 33, the United Nations Charter refers to "negotiation, inquiry, mediation, conciliation, arbitration, judicial settlement, resort to regional agencies or arrangements or other peaceful means of the parties' own choice." This obviously allows for bilateral, multilateral, or regional efforts, the work of individuals or nongovernmental organizations, or any other method that can bring about a meeting of minds. In most cases the goal is to change the contending parties' perceptions of the nature of the conflict and of the common interest at stake. This may sound simple, but it is extraordinarily difficult. The record of success indicates that great flexibility in the choice of method is the only sensible approach and that many disputes involve fundamental differences that seem to defy solution. Yet stubborn problems do sometimes yield to settlement, as demonstrated by the four-power agreement on Austria after ten years of negotiation. The UN has helped at times by using mediators, fact-finding teams, and commissions of inquiry, but these techniques should be used far more than member states have been willing to accept thus far.

The United States could be most helpful by repealing the Connally amendment under which the United States reserves for itself the right to decide what disputes with other countries fall within its own domestic jurisdiction and thereby decides when to reject the jurisdiction of the International Court of Justice. Unfortunately, the Connally amendment has become a model for many other countries around the world, and as a result the International Court of Justice has little work to do in a world full of disputes. The United States should also work to include in future international conventions a provision recognizing the authority of the International Court of Justice to decide the legal disputes that arise.

A more efficient worldwide communication system, as James Reston suggested in the *New York Times* on May 21, 1975, might also further the maintenance of peace. Reston recalled the failure of communications between Cambodia and the United States during the Mayaguez incident in 1975 and between the belligerents during the Greek-Turkish crisis over Cyprus, and noted that there is no "hot line" network for countries as a whole, though the United States and USSR have deemed it necessary to have their own. Communication by satellite to virtually every nation in the world could be available if the necessary earth stations, costing about $4 million each, were installed—a sound investment in comparison to the cost of conflict through misunderstanding.

The United States's Interest

In order to diminish the prospects of a Soviet-American confrontation, the UN and regional organizations should continue to be used to mitigate if not resolve conflicts among small and medium-sized countries, particularly in Asia, Africa, and Latin America. To this end the United States should give these organizations encouragement and appropriate support, while relying on its own strength and NATO to deter or counter any direct Soviet thrust.

The thinking in this essay is paralleled by certain summary conclusions of the Atlantic Council Working Group on the UN. They state:

We believe there should be a new presumption in U.S. policy that the outcomes of most local conflicts will, in the long run, be more consistent with basic U.S. interests if recourse is made to the Security Council rather than if attempts are made to act unilaterally.

The United States and its allies should sustain to the full the authority and capacity of the United Nations to interpose neutral peacekeeping forces between fighting parties whose actions menace international peace and security.

We strongly urge new commitment by the U.S. government, in concert with a coalition of like-minded states of all persuasions and levels of development, to reactivate the machinery for peaceful settlement of disputes, which today languishes essentially unused.

In our view the most effective U.S. posture would be that of international champion of the principle of nonintervention, except as intervention is used by the United Nations for legitimate peacekeeping or humanitarian reasons.[4]

Perhaps the UN as now constituted can deal with only a fraction of the security problems facing the United States. Yet experience has demonstrated that UN peacekeeping activities are in the United States's interest. Consequently, the United States should use them wherever possible and strengthen the UN's capacity to act effectively.

---

[4] The Atlantic Council of the United States, *The Future of the UN* (Boulder, Colo.: Westview Press, 1977), pp. xxii-xxiii.

United Nations Peacemaking

DAVID P. FORSYTHE

Many things have changed at the United Nations and in its political environment. In the late 1970s the less developed countries dominate the General Assembly, and the People's Republic of China sits in the Security Council, which itself has increased its membership. The Secretariat has lost the dynamism it displayed during the tenure of Dag Hammarskjöld. There is at least considerable talk of reforming the the UN's administrative structure. The organization itself is increasingly oriented away from purely security questions and toward socioeconomic issues. The Vietnam war is over, but the battle for southern Africa is being waged.

Many things, however, remain the same. One is the status and dynamics of UN peacemaking. The need for conflict resolution in the world arena is as great as ever. Werner Levi has noted that "the institutionalization of measures for the non-violent settlement of international conflicts has been called the central problem of international politics and international law."[1] The shortfall between this need and the achievement of peacemaking measures remains immense. Cyrus R. Vance wrote in 1971, "The United Nations, despite twenty-five years of modest achievement, still has little capacity to shape a more orderly world. . . . The political achievements have been sporadic and on the whole unsatisfactory."[2] At the same time a presidential commission wrote about "the disappointing record of the UN in resolving disputes."[3]

This essay will review what might be called the conventional wisdom explaining why a gap remains between the obvious need for and the performance of

[1] Werner Levi, *Law and Politics in the International Society* (Beverly Hills: Sage Publications, 1976), p. 154.

[2] Cyrus R. Vance, *The United Nations in the 1970s* (New York: United Nations Association of the USA, 1971), p. 6.

[3] *Report of the President's Commission for the Observance of the Twenty-Fifth Anniversary of the United Nations* (Washington, D.C.: GPO, 1971), pp. 7-8.

mechanisms at the UN peacefully to settle disputes. It will then examine the implication of this for United States foreign policy.

Conventional Wisdom

Peacemaking can be narrowly defined as the peaceful settlement or resolution of conflict, or broadly defined as peaceful change. In the narrow sense, peacemaking fundamentally manifests itself as the setting of standards, mediation-conciliation, arbitration-adjudication, and enforcement-sanction. States at the UN and UN personnel have of course attempted to institute all these forms, but the member states themselves have jeopardized such attempts by preferring autonomous national decision-making to an institutionalized international order.

UN standards relating to peace and war are not very impressive, although much diplomatic effort has been expended since 1945 in trying to specify the essential obligations contained in Article 2 of the UN Charter. Paragraph three of that article requires that "all Members shall settle their international disputes by peaceful means in such a manner that international peace and security, and justice, are not endangered." Paragraph four stipulates that "all Members shall refrain in their international relations from the threat or use of force against the territorial integrity or political independence of any state." The only clearly permissible use of force under the charter is what Article 51 calls individual or collective self-defense.

There have been two primary efforts at the United Nations to spell out the meaning of these well-known legal principles. One was the attempt in 1974 to define aggression as presumably a use of force against the territorial integrity or political independence of any state and not appropriate to the legal label of self-defense. Much was made of this act and of the new definition, but Julius Stone noted that "that remarkable text rather appears to have codified into itself (and in some respects extended) all the main 'juridical loopholes and pretexts to unlease aggression' available under preexisting international law."[4] Indeed, the wording of the resolution and its legislative history are unclear. Moreover, the Security Council is permitted to make judgments inconsistent with parts of the resolution. For example, the resolution considers the first use of force as *prima facie* evidence of aggression, but the Security Council may find otherwise. It is thus doubtful whether anything very significant has been resolved by this UN resolution.

The second effort to specify basic standards has been the long-standing attempt to define seven principles of friendly relations, based principally on Article 2 of the charter. Agreement was most easily reached on sovereign equality, which buttressed national autonomy. That is not to say that it is really known what sovereign equality and national sovereignty really mean. But it is known that

---

[4] Julius Stone, "Hopes and Loopholes in the 1974 Definition of Aggression," *American Journal of International Law* 71 (April 1977), p. 224.

member states are less readily prepared to come to a precise agreement on the meaning of "force," "intervention," and "noninterference."

The underlying problem in defining aggression as well as principles of friendly relations is that states, especially the so-called great powers, disagree on the legitimacy and values of other states and governments. Is force against Israel or South Korea to be considered aggression? Is it permissible to intervene in behalf of the establishment of Zimbabwe or Namibia? Because states disagree on the legitimacy of extant or projected regimes and their values, they do not wish to agree on a system of international order that precludes national maneuvering in behalf of groups such as the Palestinians, the Kurds, the Eritreans, the Southwest Africa People's Organization, the Zimbabwe African National Union, or whatever.

The Western idea, born of the cold war, that all would be well if the "revolutionary states" would just accept the rules of the game fails to stand up to the evidence. Although the United States supplied arms to the Kurds in their fight with established authorities in Iraq, it did not openly and probably did not privately support Kurdish self-determination. That has to constitute prohibited intervention. In addition, the United States "destabilized" or helped overthrow elected officials in Iran in the 1950s and in Chile in the 1970s. It also directly or indirectly used force to defeat largely indigenous political movements in Guatemala in the 1950s and in the Dominican Republic in the 1960s. In these and no doubt in other places the United States itself acted in a revolutionary fashion, appealing to the "higher law" of anti-Communism to justify behavior in violation of legal norms that prohibited the use of force and intervention. Governments and movements were considered illegitimate because they were either Communist or at least left of center. Illegitimacy took precedence over legality. American foreign policy was Watergate writ large.

The United States did not invent this syndrome of behavior. The USSR "destablished" regimes in Eastern Europe and overtly crushed those in Hungary in 1956 and Czechoslovakia in 1968. The People's Republic of China supported a putsch against the Indonesian government in 1965, and Indonesia itself had challenged the legitimacy of Malaysia. India and Pakistan went to war in 1971 at least ostensibly over the legitimacy of Bangladesh. The legitimacy of Israel is at the heart of the Arab-Israeli conflict.

Violent conflicts also occurred over specific issues where legitimacy did not play a large role, as in the 1969 clash between El Salvador and Honduras over migration and labor standards, but globally disruptive conflicts are over legitimacy. As long as there are competing conceptions of what makes a regime— state or government—legitimate, it will be impossible to get a *working* definition of aggression or a *working* set of principles under the term "friendly relations." First there has to be agreement on legitimacy before one can entertain hope for order in Europe, according to certain standards. While there has been agreement on the two Germanies and while the problem of two Vietnams has been resolved violently, there is not a global agreement clearly evident on regime legitimacy. Does the United States clearly accept Marxist regimes in Latin America or in NATO circles? Does the USSR clearly accept, not just for temporary and tactical reasons, non-Marxist regimes, even when countervailing power is absent? The answers must be ambiguous at this stage in history, and efforts at the UN to set standards for nonviolent interaction necessarily reflect that ambiguity.

If one considers the procedural process of setting standards at the United Nations, criticism about substantive content is tempered somewhat. Inis Claude has correctly noted that one of the important tasks of the organization is that of providing "collective legitimacy."[5] Succinctly stated, agreements fashioned outside the UN are not as stable as those made within it, especially those pertaining to supraregional matters. A collective seal of approval adds a stabilizing component. In legal terms, what H. L. A. Hart terms the "secondary rule of recognition" is at work through collective legitimacy.[6] Norms are obeyed in part because they have been fashioned in procedural due process. The primary rule (the norm) is obeyed partially because of the secondary rule (due process).

Collective endorsement also provides greater legitimacy because the UN, the only all-purpose, global international organization, is composed of ideologically and culturally disparate members. This partially explains why diplomats pay close attention to the wording of UN resolutions.

Thus, the process of standard setting at the UN is a necessary part of organized international society. The only alternatives are less order or fewer efforts to reduce international anarchy. Certainly, regional processes of collective legitimacy do exist. Abram Chayes has demonstrated why the United States preferred one of them, the Organization of American States (OAS), to the UN at the time of the Cuban missile crisis.[7] Louis Henkin has also demonstrated how this choice left the United States on relatively weak legal ground since the OAS has no jurisdiction over the USSR.[8] Supraregional issues cannot be effectively regulated by regional institutions. Global problems require global solutions. This is why the United States, the USSR, Egypt, and Israel involve the UN in the Middle East question, even when one or more of them prefer not to do so. They recognize that the Middle East question is a global problem requiring collective support for a durable solution. For the same reason, UN resolutions on the Arab-Israeli conflict that set standards for self-determination, territory, and refugees are important in diplomacy. Such resolutions usually mirror what will be accepted; the ambiguous portions indicate areas of continuing disagreement are important for that fact.

As for UN standard setting, ambiguity in substance reflects competing conceptions of a legitimate world order and of legitimate regimes. But the process

---

[5] Inis Claude, *The Changing United Nations* (New York: Random House, 1967), chap. 4.
[6] H. L. A. Hart, *The Concept of Law* (London: Oxford University Press, 1961), chap. 5.
[7] Abram Chayes, *The Cuban Missile Crisis* (New York: Oxford, 1974), chaps. 4-5.
[8] Ibid., p. 150.

itself is useful as an indication of disagreement and as a necessary step toward organizing world society. When agreement does exist, as in the opposition to apartheid in the Republic of South Africa, UN resolutions clearly indicate the view of nearly all member states on what is permissible, even though those resolutions do not immediately and necessarily make such situations illegal or eliminate them.

Even if UN standards were set that clearly delineated the permissible uses of force and intervention and clearly specified the procedures for peacemaking, conciliation would occasionally be needed. Since law does not deter all illegal behavior, even the existence of clear norms would not prevent all violations of those rules. One would still need either a noncoercive means of returning to legality or a noncoercive resolution of legally amgibuous conflicts. When the norms themselves are not clear or generally supported, the need for third-party involvement is increased.

The UN has consistently tried to play this conciliatory role in various ways and has increasingly shifted from governmental conciliation to mediation by individuals uninstructed by governments. Regardless of the form and tasks, however, UN efforts at conciliation have met with little success, as noted earlier in the statement by Cyrus R. Vance. Indeed, Stanley J. Michalak has observed that UN conciliation has resulted in only one settlement in accordance with preestablished rules and in very few settlements arranged on an ad hoc basis.[9]

Two phenomena explain much about the paucity of conciliatory successes through the UN. The first is that conciliation is too rational a process for a number of conflicts. To the extent that conciliation has a philosophical underpinning, it is that of classical liberalism. Conciliation assumes that political man is rational. It seeks to interject the voice of reason spoken by a disinterested party, perhaps after a cooling-off period. It seeks a rational meshing of interests, assumed to be possible, which those in the conflict will surely prefer to continued conflict—which is, after all, an aberration from natural harmony.

If UN history in peacemaking demonstrates anything, it is the weakness of classical liberal thought on this subject. The last thing that any number of governments want interjected into a conflict is a disinterested view of what is rational or legal or equitable. Such views compromise policies based on ideology and emotionalism. They also compromise the rational exercise of power, for conflict is viewed as desirable if it produces desired ends. All sorts of UN bodies have been created to provide unbiased facts and impartial ideas, such as the 1949 Panel for Inquiry and Conciliation, the 1949 Panel of Field Observers, and the 1950 Peace Observation Committee. None of these have been used by governments to any significant extent.

To be sure, some UN third parties have been tried. Secretary General Trygve Lie gave his "rational" views on the Korean war, and as a result the USSR refused

---

[9] Stanley J. Michalak, "The United Nations and the League," *The United Nations in International Politics*, ed. Leon Gordenker (Princeton: Princeton University Press, 1971).

to deal with him as secretary general. Secretary General Thant spoke out "rationally" on the Vietnam war, and as a result the United States refused to give him a significant role in helping to end that conflict. Special Representative Gunnar Jarring gave his "rational" views on the Middle East question, and it resulted in his unacceptability to Israel and hence the end of his mission. Groups like the UN Truce Supervisory Organization (UNTSO) have been employed in the Middle East to provide impartial facts, and they have their uses, such as reporting information to the secretary general. But they are used by the conflicting parties primarily as blackboards on which to write accusations of the adversary. This process is also well known in Korea and Cyprus.

Hence it is readily apparent that conciliation is frequently too rational a process of peacemaking in this less than fully rational world. If Menahem Begin believes, on the basis of religious ideology, that Israel should have jurisdiction over the West Bank area, he will not likely accept the judgment of a third party that his view is irrational in the context of Arab opposition. His response will continue to be, as it was during a televised interview on May 20, 1977, that in time the Arabs will accept his view.

Whether he maintains that view depends not on conciliation but on calculations of power. The second factor explaining lack of conciliatory success is fragmentation of coalitions potentially available to support a mediator. The question is whether a party's perspectives on countervailing power will be such that ideological and emotive preferences will be revised for the sake of compromise. John Stoessinger has persuasively argued that a government's perceptions of an adversary's power-capability is the most important variable explaining foreign policy behavior and can offset inflated self-images and deflated images of the opponent.[10] Is there, then, a powerful coalition extant in support of UN conciliation capable of producing a noncoercive settlement through threat of coercion and thus requiring the conflicting party or parties to compromise out of rational fear of something worse?

The answer is generally in the negative, for the same reason that UN standard setting is ambiguous: the lack of general agreement on the legitimacy of actors and order. General and overwhelming potential coalitions are fragmented. The expansion of national power or ideology, or the national pursuit of its version of world order, is preferred over order based on compromise. Both Israel and the Arab states can find support for their positions, in part because of Soviet and American attempts to exercise national influence in the region. The process is not unknown, for example, on the Indian subcontinent, in Cyprus, and in southern Africa.

Some agreement does exist and some strong coalitions can be fashioned. These are more likely to be for peacekeeping rather than peacemaking. The great powers have tended to join forces to stop major violence, but not to join forces to resolve substantive disagreements. Coalitions across the East-West divide have been

---

[10] John Stoessinger, *Nations in Darkness* (New York: Random House, 1975).

formed in support of interposing UN armed forces (borrowed from nations, to be sure) in the Middle East, the Congo, and Cyprus, to name only the major operations. Even successful peacekeeping has not led to successful peacemaking. Indeed, success in the former may impede results in the latter, since once the conflicting parties are free from further violence they have a reduced incentive to make peace.

Moreover, coalitions in support of United Nations peacekeeping have proven fragile. The great powers initial support for the UN Operation in the Congo (ONUC) disintegrated over the process used to create and fund it (majority vote in the General Assembly) and over the non-Communist central government in the Congo that ONUC came to support. France disengaged from the supporting coalition for the first reason and the USSR for both reasons. At issue in this watershed case was the legitimacy of the Congolese central government, as well as the legitimacy of the UN decision-making process and its version of world order. On these issues the coalition fragmented, leaving the United States, the West, the less developed countries, and the UN secretary general opposed to the determined minority of France and the USSR.

The central point to be made in this essay is that large and powerful coalitions in support of UN peacemaking are frequently nonexistent. There are competing conceptions of the legitimacy of actors and of the international order entailed in conflict resolution.

Two further points merit mention. One is that some UN bodies are not in fact for conciliation but for browbeating of the target states into compliance with majority views. General Assembly committees on decolonization and on Israeli practices in the occupied territories do not conciliate but try to pressure the target state via adverse publicity. The second point is that states' calculations of power sometimes cause them to prefer to bypass the UN in favor of national mediators. Henry Kissinger preempted UN mediators in the Arab-Israeli conflict not only because he appeared adept at getting agreements but also because certain Arab states made the judgment that only the United States had the power to make Israel move from its stated positions. UN efforts might be based on good faith, but they would lack power "when push came to shove." Pure rationality would then have to be joined with powerful coalitions.

If states cannot agree on the specific rules of the game of international politics and if they resist suggested compromises, they are not likely to accept imposed solutions. It is, therefore, not surprising that the International Court of Justice (ICJ), officially part of the UN system, has averaged two cases a year during the last thirty years. As John Stoessinger has clearly stated, the basic problem is to get cases to court; once there and a substantive judgment is rendered, states in principle implement the judgment.[11] The exception that proves the rule is the oft-cited Corfu Channel Case, in which the judgment went against Albania for negligence in not giving ample warning about or deactivating a mine field; and

[11] John Stoessinger, *The Might of Nations* (New York: Random House, 1975), chap. 9.

in which Albania refused to compensate the United Kingdom in keeping with the court's judgment.

The basic problem is that states regard most conflicts as too important to trust a third party for binding settlement. National security or prestige is believed to be involved; national efforts—however futile—are preferred, or deemed the only attempts "politically" possible. Even in the time of the League of Nations, when the great powers were in substantial agreement on the nature of international order at least in the 1920s and early 1930s before the USSR was diplomatically active and before Germany rearmed, the Permanent Court of International Justice, the predecessor of the ICJ, rendered only thirty-two judgments. According to Leland Goodrich, "none of these involved serious threats to the peace."[12] In the same period, arbitration treaties fared little better, as George Kennan has often indicated.[13] Many were signed and duly ratified but virtually none were used.

A sense of community, not just a perception of interconnectedness, is a necessary prerequisite for a functioning court, or arbitration arrangement. Courts function effectively in the European Economic Community and within the Council of Europe. Arbitration can function between the United States and Canada, as in the famous Trail Smelter Arbitration case in which the two states created an arbitration panel, which subsequently ruled that a Canadian company had to cease polluting air within the United States. It is not surprising that by contrast this sense of community is lacking on a global scale or even on most regional scales.

The ICJ has of late compounded these inherent difficulties with several judgments producing controversy and criticism rather than respect for the court. In the Southwest Africa Cases (1966), the ICJ refused to give a substantive judgment as to the rightfulness of South Africa's jurisdiction over the territory, after apparently having agreed to do so. The weakness of the court's technical ruling, an obvious effort to evade the substantive issue, angered many less developed countries. Then in the Barcelona Traction Case (1973), the ICJ failed to take the opportunity to increase international law's regulation of multinational corporations, although in the opinion of a number of legal scholars previous case law permitted an expansive and creative ruling.

An essay on UN peacemaking is not the place for an extended analysis of the ICJ, especially since that court tends to function rather independently of the rest of the UN system. The ICJ is clearly not a major actor in the international system, and while various proposals have been floated in the United States Senate, the State Department, and academic circles concerning regional sittings for the court, procedural changes, and more use of the court for minor disputes, there is little evidence to support an increased role for the ICJ in the immediate future.

[12] Leland Goodrich, *The United Nations* (New York: Crowell, 1959), p. 195.
[13] George Kennan, *American Diplomacy 1900-1950* (New York: Mentor, 1952).

Abjudication-arbitration, if it develops, will probably be along the lines of regional or specialized courts and panels. In the UN Conference on the Law of the Sea, the United States has urged the creation of several courts and panels that would have automatic jurisdiction over disputes arising from such activities as deep-sea mining and fishing rights in national economic zones. In the light of past conventional wisdom that the weaker states most need a strengthened system of international law, the less developed countries have been resisting the United States position. It is not yet clear what the outcome of this policy disagreement will be.

Logically there is a need for automatic dispute settlement in proportion to the number of conflicts that arise from increased interconnectedness. Some of these courts or panels could carry a UN label. But a sense of community, based on mutual trust and a prospect for mutual gain, is an elusive prerequisite for obligatory conflict resolution.

Coercive settlements of disputes are essential to noncoercive peacemaking. Leland Goodrich and Anne Simons have pointed out that chapter 6 on United Nations conflict resolution in the UN Charter was envisaged as being read, and acted upon, in conjunction with chapter 7 on enforcement.[14] This attempted linkage of coercive and noncoercive efforts conveyed an accurate understanding of the history of international relations. As the historian F. H. Hinsley put it, "The dilemma confronting all hopes of peaceful international change and settlement is that there can be no change and no settlement, not even peacefully, so long as struggle is avoided. You may count on the fingers of one hand the occasions on which agreements have been made and changes of sovereignty or transfers of territory have occurred in the modern world without the assistance of the possibility of a resort to force, if not force itself."[15] This statement accords with what was said above about the importance of a powerful coalition supporting the efforts of a UN mediator and extends the process of coalition-building in support of an international agreement.

The conventional wisdom on this subject of sanctions was summarized concisely by W. Michael Reisman: "The process of sanctions and enforcement has fared poorly."[16] In the more than thirty years of UN proceedings, the Security Council has made only two decisions. In July 1948, the Security Council reached a decision on the Arab-Israeli conflict and ordered a cease-fire. Sanctions were, in effect, threatened in the event of noncompliance with this resolution but were never invoked.

[14] Leland Goodrich and Anne Simons, *The United Nations and the Maintenance of International Peace and Security* (Washington, D.C.: Brookings Institution, 1955).

[15] F. H. Hinsley, *Power and the Pursuit of Peace* (Cambridge: Cambridge University Press, 1963), p. 318.

[16] W. Michael Riseman, "Sanctions and Enforcement," *The Future of the International Legal Order*, vol. 3: *Conflict and Management*, ed. Cyril E. Black and Richard A. Falk (Princeton: Princeton University Press, 1971), p. 273.

The second decision, entailing mandatory sanctions, occurred in 1968 when the Security Council voted economic sanctions against the Ian Smith regime in Rhodesia. Smith's policies on human rights—his failure to accept majority rule—were deemed to constitute a threat to the peace. An economic embargo was subsequently adopted, which became mandatory under Article 25 of the UN Charter: "The Members of the United Nations agree to accept and carry out the decisions of the Security Council in accordance with the present Charter."

Despite almost universal agreement on that action, the Smith regime still exercised effective power a decade afterwards. This was largely due to the lack of cooperation in the sanctioning effort by the Republic of South Africa (and to a lesser extent by Portugal under Caetano), and to the reluctance of the Western powers to sanction South Africa. The United States itself, subsequent to its affirmative vote in the Security Council, violated UN sanctions by trading with Rhodesia under congressional action making such trade legal under American law while illegal under international law.

The Rhodesian case demonstrates several things about UN sanctions and recalls several lessons to be learned from the attempt through the League of Nations to sanction Mussolini's Italy for invading Ethiopia in the 1930s, the only other attempt to use a global international organization collectively to organize economic sanctions against a state in the twentieth century. One of these lessons is that sanctions cut both ways, which explains part of the reluctance to invoke them and part of the difficulty in maintaining them once invoked. Sanctioning states are hurt, though to varying degrees, as well as the target state. UN sanctions deprived the British economy, one of the economies of the world least able to withstand damage in the 1970s, of imports such as Rhodesian beef, sugar, and tobacco. That economy, and the French, would have been even more damaged by an extension of sanctions to the Republic of South Africa. The same dynamic was at work in League sanctions against Italy.

A second point about UN sanctions is that usually one or more important parties will regard sanctions as less important than something else, thus creating loopholes in the enforcement effort. South Africa and authoritarian Portugal placed white supremacy and what they viewed as anti-Communism above the Zimbabwe version of majority rule, human rights, and self-determination. The United States Congress, with intensive lobbying from Union Carbide, placed "business as usual" above anything else occurring in distant Africa until the Byrd amendment was repealed in the spring of 1977. Likewise in the League's experience with Italy, the United Kingdom and France did not want to embargo oil to Mussolini in an effort to keep him from an alliance with Hitler; neither was the United States, though not a member of the League, in favor of an interruption of normal economic transactions.

A third point is that economic sanctions, as well as military ones should they ever be tried, hurt the masses more and sooner than the elite responsible for the behavior producing the sanctions. This lesson is derived more from logic than facts of the Rhodesian and Italian cases. It seems reasonable to assume that the elite can pass along hardship to the masses, which had little to do with the behavior judged impermissible by the international organization.

Brief mention should be made of the Korean "police action" under the UN banner. That action was not a UN enforcement effort in the true sense since military operations were not authorized by the Security Council but rather recommended by the General Assembly. Moreover, the "United Nations Command" was really a facade for the Pentagon—and still is. From one perspective the Korean war of 1950–53 was alliance warfare, not generally organized sanctions. Some of the dynamics there were the same as in Rhodesia and Ethiopia: a lack of complete agreement, costs to the would-be sanctioners, and suffering by the masses directly involved.

A final point is that sanctions take time to have their effect, and in the meantime other events intrude. The lesson is clearest in the Italian case, where the decision to employ mustard gas produced Ethiopia's capitulation before the economic sanctions—which were in fact playing havoc with the Italian economy—could make their fullest impact. In the Rhodesia case, elapsed time gave Rhodesia a chance to reorient trade patterns, find *sub-rosa* routes, etc.

In sum, economic sanctions entail such difficulties that they have not proven a clearly effective way to rectify impermissible behavior even in the two cases tried. Military sanctions have not been tried through true collective security because of even greater problems—that is, greater costs and greater suffering. Inis Claude has noted a whole series of psychological and material problems impeding effective collective security through the UN.[17] Little on the horizon indicates that these problems will be overcome, and indeed Claude suggests that if they could be overcome a global consensus would support not just collective security but true world government. This insight demonstrates how far the UN is from effective enforcement.

The background thus provides little support for noncoercive settlements through the UN. Conflicting parties are relatively free to continue their conflicts, since they do not have to fear sanctions mandated by the Security Council or effective sanctions applied through alliances or unilaterally. It is well known that Security Council members do not frequently agree on what settlement to advocate benefiting what actors. Even when they do, UN sanctions do not easily control a situation.

The conventional wisdom on UN peacemaking narrowly defined to mean conflict resolution stands up well upon renewed analysis. There is no reason to question the summary statement that "peace requires a permanent structure of change."[18] But, as F. S. Dunn wrote, "It is useless to pile up additional institutions unless they take full account of existing values and attitudes which determine

[17] Inis Claude, *Swords into Plowshares* (New York: Random House, 1971), chap. 12.
[18] Carl Friedrich von Weizsacker, "A Skeptical Contribution," *On the Creation of a Just World Order*, ed. Saul H. Mendlovitz (New York: Free Press, 1975).

basic policies."[19] This essay has focused on precisely that disagreement among the major powers on "values and attitudes which determine basic policies," in conjunction with the powers' determination to use national influence to pursue parochial versions of regional and world order. Given the historical fact of this lack of consensus and ideological homogeneity among the great powers, one is forced to reaffirm that UN peacemaking, narrowly defined, is insufficient for what ails the world. Precise standards on peace and war will not be established, conciliation will not be supported by coalitions capable of persuading emotive and ideological parties to alter policies, sanctions will not be credible or generally effective, and the ICJ will not be consistently used because the issues are seen as too big or the court too small.

As Richard Falk has observed, the nation-state system depends for its viability on "rational" conceptions of balance, equilibrium, and moderation.[20] But the "irrational" state, so defined by a UN body, cannot be effectively regulated or forced to yield to international majority opinion if it is rich or powerful or has powerful friends. There is nothing inherent in the four fundamental forms of UN peacemaking, narrowly defined, to alter that unfortunate fact.

American Policy

In the fact of this somber analysis, can the United States do anything through its foreign policy at the UN in dealing with persistent and dangerous international conflicts? Is there any alternative to resignation and despair?

Even learned writers have suggested that isolationism is a viable strategy. Others, equally learned, have suggested a policy of selective disengagement from the UN. David A. Kay has suggested that the United States should selectively disengage from the General Assembly by working only on important matters when pursuit of cooperation is clearly evidenced.[21] Sidney Weintraub has recommended that the United States should simply disregard UN resolutions based on "one nation, one vote."[22]

As for isolationism, the United States will not find it a viable policy for two fundamental reasons. First, American economic interests will not allow it. Second, as Stanley Hoffmann put it, world order is required for the United States to retrench in safety.[23] The United States must actively build international security before it can safely disengage from some of its present commitments.

[19] Quoted in *United Nations Peacemaking*, ed. David P. Forsythe (Baltimore: Johns Hopkins University Press, 1972), p. 12.

[20] Richard Falk, *A Study of Future Worlds* (New York: Free Press, 1975), p. 64.

[21] David Kay, "On the Reform of International Institutions," *International Organization* 30 (Summer 1976), pp. 533-38.

[22] Sidney Weintraub, "What Do We Want From the United Nations?" *International Organization* 30 (Autumn 1976): 687-95.

[23] Stanley Hoffmann, "No Choice, No Illusions," *Foreign Policy* (Winter 1976-77), pp. 97-104.

Selective disengagement would be undermined by mutual parochialism. Who is to determine what is cooperation, seriousness, or good faith, and when are they present in UN proceedings? If the United States disengages from the General Assembly when Cuba discusses Puerto Rico, then may the USSR disengage when the United States discusses civil and political rights in Eastern Europe? May Tanzania disengage when the United States defends the rights of private property? The United States's selective disengagement from debates and efforts it opposes would only encourage rampant parochialism by any state that found some international opinion running against some of its cherished values. That is not to say the United States should consider Zionism a form of racism because a certain number of states said so in the General Assembly. Nor should the United States support UN committees more interested in *machtpolitik* than truth. But it should stay engaged at the UN to exercise what influence it can, to defeat or oppose what it considers unwise efforts.

Engagement achieves the minimum objective of impeding pernicious symbolism through UN channels. Inflammatory words and concepts that are destabilizing can be opposed and thereby reduced in importance as international symbols. That, however, is not to endorse the "Moynihan style" of attacking all opposing opinion loudly and abrasively.

Another requirement of United States policy at the UN is the more difficult task of restructuring voting. Voting is needed in any heterogenous international organization that wishes to accomplish anything. Consensus resolutions do emerge from time to time from such organizations; but these resolutions contain contradictory wording or lead to contradictory interpretations of vague wording, as in the case of the Consensus Definition on Aggression or Security Council Resolution 242 on the Middle East concerning "territories" occupied (some territory? all the territories?). Since voting is needed, the objective should be to work for improved voting.

Two approaches are available. One is for the United States to propose weighted voting in the General Assembly. Several versions have been suggested by scholars. The State Department could formally submit a preferred position on the question and encourage other states seriously to consider the matter. A second approach is for the United States to resurrect the idea of coalitions for peaceful settlement and indicate that it is American policy to consider as binding certain UN resolutions backed by specified coalitions. In one version of this policy, resolutions on peaceful settlement affirmatively supported by two-thirds of those voting and including the veto-possessing powers would be considered as binding. Whatever the formula or version of a policy statement, the goal is to make UN voting more serious and significant, as long as minority rights are protected.

It could be objected that the numerous less developed countries would object, especially since some of them seem to feel entitled to vote for provocative resolutions because of their impotence outside the UN and because they regard provocative resolutions as an effective way to draw the attention of the West to LDC concerns. This view can be countered by noting that weighted voting and qualified majorities would bring more Western support than otherwise for matters of economic development and that the third world still has a numerical advantage in advancing its values.

Voting is at present a problem at the UN, but neither total nor selective disengagement will aid peacemaking in places like southern Africa and the Middle East, necessarily entailing UN votes on resolutions, creation of subsidiary organs, or adoption of mediators' reports. A new voting structure that encourages cosmopolitanism and moderation is clearly needed.

The United States could promote peacemaking narrowly defined by encouraging and supporting activities by individuals uninstructed by governments. It is striking that an essay by the current assistant secretary of state for international organizations considers the UN totally as a passive framework for debate, not at all as a relatively independent actor in world politics.[24] Of course, one does not rise to high office in the United States by recommending that power be given to others, and the security managers in Washington have long been noted for their emphasis on unilateral exercise of power.[25] Realism, however, increasingly dictates the use of instructed intermediaries untainted by national power struggles. Such intermediaries would not be a substitute for national policy. The objective would be to mesh national and international perspectives via the secretary general or his representatives or via nonterritorial actors such as the International Committee of the Red Cross. The end desired is a settlement of conflicts entailing not just reflections of a current distribution of national power but power blended with considerations of equity. The interjection of uninstructed individuals, though not a sufficient condition for successful peacemaking, would be helpful in many situations.

In a broader perspective, the United States can promote UN peacemaking narrowly defined only by promoting it more broadly defined. Consistently successful conflict resolution will only occur in a context of successful peaceful change. There must be some movement on the big issues that divide nations before they will be inclined to resolve specific conflicts peaceably. Nations have to believe that order in general is beneficial to them before they will be willing to give up or moderate objectives for the sake of maintaining general order. They have to believe that the general order is good for them most of the time in order for them to agree to lose something some of the time.

This dynamic was recognized by Secretary of State Kissinger in his policies toward the USSR and China. He sought to make his "revolutionary" states conservative by giving them an interest in maintaining the status quo—hence accelerated East-West trade under the label of détente. This dynamic has been more broadly recognized by Assistant Secretary Charles William Maynes, who has

[24] Charles William Maynes, "UN Policy for the Next Administration," *Foreign Affairs* 54 (July 1976): 804-19.

[25] Lincoln Bloomfield, *In Search of American Foreign Policy* (New York: Oxford, 1974), chap. 3.

taken a position encouraging the participation of LDCs in international decision-making and encouraging a positive United States response to "legitimate" LDC demands.

The United States, by responding to the needs of other countries, will do what it can to promote mutual trust among nations and a vested interest by all in world order. There will be no overnight successes. The Marxist states as well as the LDCs must also exercise restraint, moderation, and understanding. The process of co-operation will not be automatic. Nor will there be an automatic dynamic of ever-expanding cooperation. It has been amply demonstrated that cooperation can be contained to one issue area without more general effect.[26] But only with the pursuit of that mutual responsiveness and trust among nations will the process of peaceful settlement be adhered to even when some specific value is lost.

Peaceful change is required to reach a situation in which peaceful settlement can work. Peacemaking broadly defined must precede consistently successful peacemaking narrowly defined. The United States should be responsive to demands for social-economic change, leading to a more equitable distribution of wealth and justice, and should encourage changes that lead to security for states (which means relative security built on compromise and moderation, since absolute security for one protagonist means absolute insecurity for another).

It is only realistic to recognize that "world order politics is obviously in."[27] The United Nations can contribute to both peaceful settlement and peaceful change, not just as a debating society used as a facade for serious bilateral diplomacy but as a forum for exchange of views and necessary voting according to new rules and also as a source of uninstructed individuals. The UN does indeed have a role to play in restraining virulent nationalism and, as David Kay has noted, in blending national autonomy into the needs of interdependence. As Professors Nye and Keohane have persuasively argued,[28] situations of complex interdependence require collective leadership from the United States directed toward using international organizations—including the UN—to fashion the transnational coalitions needed to manage peacefully international conflicts.

---

[26] Ernst Haas, *Tangle of Hopes* (Englewood Cliffs, N.J.: Prentice Hall, 1969).
[27] Hoffmann, p. 139.
[28] Joseph Nye and Robert Keohane, *Power and Interdependence* (Boston: Little, Brown, 1977).

Index

Proceedings of
The Academy of
Political Science

1975-77
Volume 32

The volume is not indexed. See table of contents of each issue.

The Academy of Political Science
2852 Broadway
New York, New York 10025